ADMISSIONS
BY
DESIGN

Stop the Madness and Find
the Best College for You

LISA FISHER
M.A.T, M.A.

For permission requests, please address Elevate Publishing

Editorial Content: AnnaMarie McHargue

Cover Design: Brad Foltz

Graphics: Camille Myhre

Layout: Aaron Snethen

This book may be purchased in bulk for educational, business, organizational or promotional use.

For more information, please email info@elevatepub.com.

Published by Elevate, a division of Elevate Publishing, Boise, ID

ISBN-13: 9781943425082

Ebook ISBN: 9781943425556

In Memoriam

Ellen Rudnick Fisher (1945-1988)

To my mother, Ellen, whose bright light has guided
me and helped me to cross many thresholds.

TABLE OF CONTENTS

PRAISE FOR *ADMISSIONS BY DESIGN*

"Students are hungry for the message contained within the pages of *Admissions By Design*. Fisher compassionately challenges college bound students to begin the admissions process from a new starting line: the self."

Teresa Poppen
Executive Director and
Ultimate Difference Maker, One Stone

"Lisa Fisher's *Admissions By Design* is a wise, deeply insightful response to what is wrong with our 'winner take all' society, the forces that undermine good parenting, and the college admissions monolith. The genius of the book is placing the locus of control with the young men and women whose futures are at stake. Fisher brings together the best research and thinking on how to navigate the college process and the future in a healthy, happy and successful way. Her approach is innovative and long overdue."

David Holmes, Ph.D.
Executive Director of Strategic Initiatives and
Head of School Emeritus,
Community School, Sun Valley, Idaho
Author and speaker on college admissions reform
Former Vice President, College for Every Student

"*Admissions By Design* is a call to assure that the college admission and selection process has heart and soul. With Lisa Fisher's book students are invited to bring their whole self to the college decision process. Therein lies the design."

Ed Taylor, Ph.D.
Dean and Vice Provost
Undergraduate Academic Affairs
University of Washington

"As the former Head of School and Director of College Counseling at four International Baccalaureate World Schools, I wish I had *Admissions By Design* as a resource a long time ago. Fisher's book mitigates the madness that has defined the college admissions process for decades and offers an innovative and empowering approach for students (and their parents) as they embark on their journey to college."

Joe Kennedy
Head of School, Saint George's School (IB World School),
Spokane, WA

"Bringing design thinking into the traditional college admissions process has the potential to be transformative for many young people and their families. Lisa Fisher's book deftly cracks open the topic and helps the reader question assumptions in important ways."

Susie Wise, Ph.D.
Director, K12 Lab Network
Hasso Plattner Institute of Design, Stanford University

Dedication

To Sydney, who, in unapologetically being herself and in boldly chasing her dreams, has inspired her mother to do the same.

May you always spread your wings wide and fly, Sweet Bird.

I love you.

THE
U MAP

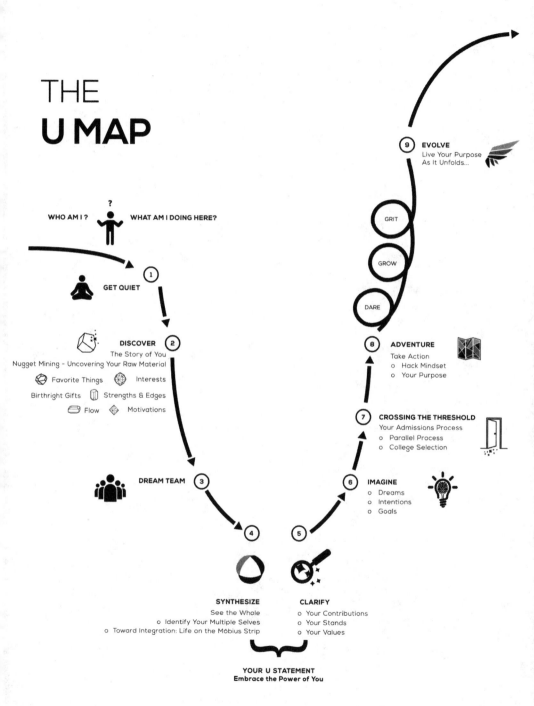

WHO AM I?   **?**   WHAT AM I DOING HERE?

1 GET QUIET

2 DISCOVER
The Story of You
Nugget Mining - Uncovering Your Raw Material
Favorite Things   Interests
Birthright Gifts   Strengths & Edges
Flow   Motivations

3 DREAM TEAM

4

SYNTHESIZE
See the Whole
o Identify Your Multiple Selves
o Toward Integration: Life on the Möbius Strip

5

CLARIFY
o Your Contributions
o Your Stands
o Your Values

YOUR U STATEMENT
Embrace the Power of You

6 IMAGINE
o Dreams
o Intentions
o Goals

7 CROSSING THE THRESHOLD
Your Admissions Process
o Parallel Process
o College Selection

8 ADVENTURE
Take Action
o Hack Mindset
o Your Purpose

DARE

GROW

GRIT

9 EVOLVE
Live Your Purpose
As It Unfolds...

Gratitude

It is nearly Thanksgiving as I complete this acknowledgment of the many people who have supported my efforts to write this book, and that I write these final words during this American season of gratitude is not lost on me. While it is impossible to thank the many people who have so generously and meaningfully given their time and energy to me and to my work over the years, I'd like to take this opportunity to recognize some of those who have been most directly involved with this particular project.

To my inspiring students and clients, past and present, who, through having the courage to find and express their passions and gifts, have gone on to serve the world in wondrous and meaningful ways. Each of you has left your handprint on my soul. The world is a better place with you in it.

To my editor, Anna McHargue, for your belief in and unending advocacy for this book and for being a true partner to me in this effort. Your incredible encouragement, professionalism, generosity, and patience allowed me the creative space I needed to complete this project; simply put, it could not and would not have happened without you. You have been an unbelievable cheerleader, coach, supporter— and, most of all, friend. I am so very grateful to you. And to the other members of the team at Elevate—Mark and Laurie Russell, Bobby Kuber, Todd Carman, Anita Stephens, and Aaron Snethen—who took a brave leap with a first-time author. It was important to me not only to be supported in my effort to complete this book, but also to do so with a publisher that actively practices the values I hold most dear to my heart. I found all of that and much more in working with you. Thank you.

To Catherine Fishman and Camille Myhre, former students turned dreamy research assistant and talented designer respectively, who worked diligently and tirelessly with me on this book. I can't thank you enough for your dedication, support, and indefatigable work.

To David Cates and Rosalie Sheehy Cates for your willingness to step in with incredible support and encouragement under very tight deadlines—and for pushing me to be more precise in my thinking and writing, to use my authentic voice, and to "stop throwing chairs." Thank you.

To Dr. Stephen Luber, dear friend and the world's best pediatrician, for review of sections of this book. I can always count on you.

To Lisa Persky for many years of soulful friendship and support, for rich conversations based in a mutual love of reading and writing, for steadfast belief in me and my ideas, and for encouragement to "never settle."

To Gary Lachman, Dr. Carey Newman, Aaron Hurst, Ryan Honeyman, and Scott Marchant for the deep-dive learning you provided about the proposal and publishing process, and to Dr. Paul Hill for early counsel and connections to others to support the launch of the project.

I have been fortunate to work in places that that have allowed me both to express my creativity and to innovate. Thank you to Riverstone International School, where my first ideas for this book were formed; to the J.A. and Kathryn Albertson Foundation for allowing me the room to work with large-scale college access efforts in new and creative ways; to Jefferson Street Counseling and Consulting for embracing me in their community of practice and helping me to hone my skills as a counselor; and to The Giving Practice/Philanthropy Northwest and Pinchot University for providing tremendous support and encouragement as I completed the project. Thank you specifically to Joe Kennedy, Jamie MacMillan, Blossom Johnston, Jennie Sue Welter, Melissa Merritt, Jo Buglione, Audrey Haberman, Jeff Clarke, Carol Lewis, and Ted Lord and an extra special thanks to Mark Sedway, Rosalie Sheehy Cates (again), and Marsha Willard who served as active thought partners during my writing process, leaving their marks of support on particular sections of this book.

To Lisa Johnson, who helped me find my voice and start anew. I am forever indebted to you.

To Jamie Mitchell, who provided the safe space for me to return to self and who instilled in me an understanding of the power and beauty of yoga.

To Sue Furness, who has been a remarkable and inspiring mentor and guide. I hope someday to be a fraction of the amazing woman you are.

To "mother" Mary D'Agostino for reminding me of my true callings and for being my faithful soul guide for so many years. Your voice is ever alive in my heart and mind. Without your support of my choices toward a more soulful and integrated path, the manifestations of the amazing life I've been gifted never would have been possible. You are a tremendous gift from beyond (and a superhero goddess of the highest order).

To my LIOS family and to the LIOS/Saybrook faculty, thank you for helping me to find and become the truest version of myself and for showing me the true meaning of "beloved community."

To my amazing tribe of women: my LIOS wives—Rachel Butler, Yasmin Mudah, Larke Brost, Catrina Cuevas, and Erica Olsen—and to our dearest Afifa Ahmed Shafi, whose own dream of writing and faithful encouragement was with me every page I wrote; and to Jessica Rolph, Christine Hall, Tara Russell, Lisa Persky (again), and Courtney Robinson Feider—your individual and collective creativity, risk taking, and enterprising spirit continually inspire me to be a braver and more authentic me.

To Susie Wise at the Hasso Plattner Institute of Design at Stanford for friendship, support, and instilling in me an even deeper love for design thinking and its many applications. And to the wonderful folks at IDEO, including Sandy Speicher, Kate Lydon, Kim Cullen, Annette Diefenthaler, and Emily Boren; to Juliette LaMontagne at Breaker; and to Teresa and Joel Poppen at One Stone for showing me the beauty of design thinking in action.

To the inspiring faculty and participants at Mind and Life Institute's inaugural Academy of Contemplative and Ethical Leadership (ACEL), including instructors Dr. Arthur Zajonc, Dr. Diana Chapman Walsh, Dr. Dan Siegel, Dr. C. Otto Scharmer, Dr. Peter Senge, Dr. Daniel Goleman, Dr. Edward Taylor, Dr. Sharon Daloz Parks,

Mirabai Bush, Arawana Hayashi, Aaron Stern, and Thomas Jaggers, who provided teachings, counsel, and encouragement that influenced this book, and to participants Kelly Camak, Laura Schwartz, Lisa Napora, and Mi'Jan Celie Tho-Biaz, who encouraged me forward by insisting this message was an important one.

To Sam Brakebill at PCC Natural Markets - Columbia City, who supported me with his smile and humor and unfailingly checked in with me about my progress on this book during the many times I wandered the grocery aisles on my "brain breaks."

To my family members—my remarkable father, Chip Fisher, and his loving wife, Sandra Fisher; my wonderful sisters, Suzanne Long and Sarah Grinnell, and their thoughtful and kind spouses, Matt and Scott; and my nephews, Andrew and Alex Long, and nieces, Denna and Kaylin Grinnell—for the powerful journey of family that has shaped me, supported my growth, and informed my way of being in this world.

To my grandparents, Milton and Edna Rudnick, who, when they were alive, traveled back and forth across the country by car many times and for many years to visit me. And who, even now—after their passing—still regularly come to me when I need them most.

To my mother-in-law, Susan G. Seelye, for your friendship and loving support. I'm so honored to be a member of your family.

To my wonderful step-daughter, Indigo Williams, for your ongoing patience, care, love, and encouragement throughout this process—and for sharing your dad with me. How very fortunate I am to have you in my life.

To my faithful and magical husband, Rand Harper, who not only cooked and cleaned for the better part of two years, but also got up early and stayed up late; worked through countless ideas, paragraphs, and chapters; slayed dragons of fear; coached me back into the "arena"; and laughed and cried with me as I transitioned to birthing this dream. Thank you for making and holding space for my "castles in the air" and putting the foundations under them, and for gently and powerfully encouraging me forward with your predictable and powerful mantra "when you finish your book." It was your unending faith in me, which I borrowed unabashedly and often when my own well had run dry, that allowed this dream to come to fruition. To have found you and to have the opportunity to walk through life with you will never cease to astound me. You are living proof that impossible dreams do, indeed, come true.

To my beautiful, brave, and strong daughter Sydney Davis—I conceived of this book cradling your tiny body in my arms, dreaming of your future with the deep and powerful hope that you'd always listen to the callings of your heart and follow your dreams. Watching you grow, I've witnessed you do just that every day. And thank you for your powerful encouragement of and support for me to do the same. Words will never do justice in expressing just how proud and honored I am to be your mother. You are my greatest treasure.

To my mother, Ellen Rudnick Fisher, both a gifted educator and a perpetual student, who instilled in me a deep love of teaching, learning, social justice, and the written word. And who, when she could no longer travel with me through life in physical form, took to accompanying me in spiritual form—and has remained by my side every step of the way.

And, finally, to my own still, small voice, who, for years, quietly, lovingly, and patiently encouraged me to write this book—until I was finally brave enough to do it. Thank you for your graceful persistence. It is because of you that my life has unfolded with unpredictable magic.

Lisa Fisher
Seattle, WA
November 2015

Introduction

This is not your typical college admissions book. In it, I do not provide the advice and checklists that you can find in any number of books on the market. I do not tell you which extracurricular activity holds more weight; if your family's long-lost friend, who is an alumnus of the school you want to attend, should call the admissions office on your behalf; or how many Ivy League schools you should apply to in order to get accepted to even one. There are plenty of books that address these topics, and, in having read most of them and worked in this field for nearly two decades, there aren't a lot of new things to say. Respectfully, many of the books on the market provide much of the same information with a different-colored bow.

The aim of this book is something entirely different. *Admissions by Design* is a new paradigm in thinking about the college admission process. In this book, I challenge what has become the norm in our discussions about college admissions and highlight the negative impact the process is having on students and families. I also introduce you to compelling research that supports a healthier way to approach college admissions. But most importantly, my aim is to help you take the critical first step of knowing yourself.

Books that offer standardized approaches to college admissions are often missing the most important conversation of all: the development of you. With their lists of dos and don'ts, and checklists and things that are musts and things to avoid, they provide a bevy of information, but none of this will help drive you closer to your heart, soul, and purpose – or toward the path that is best for you. Following such rules might bring relief from anxiety and doubt in the short term, but doing so misses the point of what this journey really should be about: the discovery of the person you are meant to become.

To design an authentic path forward, there needs to be a new set of standards. So what are these new standards? And, more importantly, if everyone is adhering to the "old standards" how will the "new standards" get you into college? In walking the *Admissions by Design* path, you'll uncover a new way—one that is unique to you. You also will learn more about you, and in the process, develop genuine and lasting self-confidence and resilience. This book will help you create the foundation from which you will launch into the "real world" to pursue your dreams and become the person you are meant to become.

The journey to adulthood, a ritual not often marked in today's Western society, is an important milestone not just for you as you leave high school and head toward college, but also for your family. Historically, the purpose of rites of passage is to acknowledge and give meaning to a person's transition from one phase of life to another. In the case of college admissions, this is a shift both from child to adult and also from dependency toward autonomy. While this transition point marks a time of enormous promise and opportunity, it also brings with it the stress and uncertainty of change and challenge. The contents of this book offer and promote a more human-centered approach to this important juncture. My desire is to instill in you the notion that college is but one step on a larger journey of life. As such, what is uncovered about life will undoubtedly evolve and change over time as you change and evolve.

"If everyone is adhering to the 'old standards' how will the 'new standards' get you into college?"

To engage you in this new paradigm of searching first for one's own soul, a new way of thinking is required. As Dr. Michael L. Cohen writes in *Great Transitions: Preparing Adolescents for a New Century*:

> Ensuring the healthy growth and development of adolescents requires the combined commitment of all the institutions that have a profound impact on youth. No single entity can be responsible for a young person's successful transition from adolescence into adulthood – not today and certainly not in the next century. Families, the schools, health care organizations, community organizations, and the media must work singly and in concert to launch all young people onto a successful life course.[1]

Admissions by Design, then, while addressed to you, the student, is written for more than just students. It also is for all those supporting your efforts: your parents, mentors, coaches, counselors, admissions officers, and so on. It is my belief that this important ritual in its highest form rests in a shared journey, and it is my intention to provide support to all of those who engage in the process. For you, the student, my hope is that this book will offer you a new way to think about the college admissions journey in the context of your larger journey to adulthood. If you are a parent, a counselor, or a coach reading this book, it is my hope that I am able to provide relevant information as to how you might reconsider the ways you are providing support to students on the road to college and beyond.

The book is set up in the following way: The first chapter explores why design should be applied to the college admissions process. Chapters two, three, and four examine the frenzied college atmosphere that exists today, some disturbing trends, and the truth about the devastating impact our current system has on youth. These sections of the book are dense with research, so I have provided summaries at the end to help you track the most important "take-aways" from these chapters and to serve as a quick reference to their contents. In chapter five, I help you to uncover your mental models and beliefs about the process, and in chapter six I reveal the truth related to some of the prevailing myths we carry about the process. Beginning in chapter seven, I introduce a tool—the U Map—to assist you to hone your emerging sense of identity and to become clearer on who you are and what you want. In chapter 14, I specifically address the process of applying to college. I want to be clear: I do not offer a step-by-step guide to the nitty-gritty of the actual application process (you can find books that help with that in the Selected Resources section). What I do provide are new ways to think about and approach the process. And because I do not see college acceptance as an "end point," chapters 15 and 16—which guide you through the final two steps of the U Map—provide ways for you to adventure and evolve beyond high school and to become more clear about who you are and what is important to you. In journeying through the U Map, you will actively engage in self awareness and in the creation of your own path, not only to college, but also to your next stage of life and beyond.

The framework I offer allows you and the adults lending their energies to your success to engage in the college admissions process more authentically and effectively. Most importantly, the framework will create a healthy and balanced approach to helping you move toward your best future and find the pathway to your best self.

Finally, my intention has been to write this book in a voice you, the student, can digest. Too many college books on the market are overly serious, tired, and boring. They leave very little room for the excitement, joy, and thrill the college admissions process can contain. (Really! This process doesn't have to be crazy making!) Having spent much of my career teaching and coaching teenagers, I know firsthand that laughter and zest are part of the experience. My hope is that this book will offer a rewarding and inspirational way to approach what traditionally has been a stressful, all-consuming process.

In the pages ahead, I'll paint for you the full picture of what college admissions is today and what it can be in the future. I hope to help you understand how the current crazed system of college admissions works and the negative impact we all are experiencing as a result. Equipped with this new understanding of the system, it is my hope that you will see another, far better way to approach the college admissions process.

It is time to reimagine this process and take charge of its very design. The way forward I'm proposing will be one of self-discovery and self-actualization. With this book as a guide, you will take a lead role in designing not only your path to college, but your path to life. With your heart as your compass, you will be equipped to discover and employ your unique talents and powerful dreams in service of yourself and the world.

Chapter One:
Admissions By Design

"Everything is design. Everything!" — *Paul Rand*

"Miserable," "scary," and "overwhelming" are just some of the words that students and their parents use to describe the college admissions process. And they're right. I know this because over the past 17 years, I've worked with hundreds of students, supporting them on their journey to college. And though I hate to admit it now, I spent the bulk of my early career being a college counselor known for helping students apply and get accepted to the "best" colleges. For years, stressed out, exhausted students would attend meetings with me, barely able to keep their eyes open, running from one extra curricular activity to the next, and then to the math tutor before completing five to six hours of homework, getting too little sleep, and waking up the next day to do it all over again. And because these students were gaining admission to the best colleges in the country, I, like many others, took pride in the fact that both the students and I were going about this the "right" way.

But I was wrong.

My recognition of this and the seeds of revelation came at a meeting with one of my students one late fall afternoon. A high performer, she'd set up an appointment with me to discuss her college essay for the only 30-minute window she had that week, jammed between the end of the school day and a chemistry tutoring session. Racing into my office, she spoke quickly, wondering what I thought of the essay draft she had submitted.

By this time, I was trying something new with students—encouraging them to bring their authentic selves to the process. Unfortunately, this message rarely carried the day, often drowned out by the siren call of the "elite" school. Before getting into the details of my specific feedback, I thought this student might best be served by thinking more about *why* she was applying to the college in the context of *who* she was and who she wanted to become—a focus I'd begun to integrate into my work with students. So I posed the following question:

"What do you want the admissions officers to know about you as a person?" She stared blankly at me. After a couple of minutes, I tried again, this time with a slightly different question: "What is meaningful for you to have admissions officers know about the growth you have experienced these last few years of high school?" This again was met with a blank stare, but this time with a head shake and a shrug. "I don't really have time to think about that," she said, finally interrupting the silence. "What do you think I should say?" she asked. "I mean, what will the admissions officers want to hear?" The lack of connection to oneself coupled with the desire to say and do the "right" thing to get into college was never more clear to me than in this moment. Worse, as I gently pressed her during the remainder of our time together, she couldn't offer anything. She wasn't being defiant; she honestly didn't know. And then she ran off to her chemistry tutoring session.

All college counselors have stories like this one, but this particular incident haunted me, and, as a result, I became even more intentional in posing these types of questions to students. But in more actively asking students questions related to knowing themselves, I found that very few were able to answer them. More often than not, they wanted to know the "right" answer rather than the answer that came from their own hearts. Though these same students were rich in activities, they were not rich in self-awareness or even the knowledge of how these things would translate to a future they wanted. And worse, I knew this was not their fault. This had everything to do with the prevailing culture surrounding admissions and how we have taught students that there is only one "right" way to be to gain acceptance to college. I had built a reputation for success in helping students to gain admissions to the country's best universities—something for which most college counselors are very proud—but with this new awareness, day after day, I returned home from working with these incredibly "successful" students with a pit in my stomach.

The conflict I felt only worsened. During my morning runs, I became consumed with thoughts related to my ambivalence: If these students did not gain admission, were they designated "failures"? Were their parents failures? Was I a failure? By not getting in, did it mean they would no longer go on to lead successful lives? Did it mean that the sum total of their high school experience was nothing? Wasn't it just as important, if not much more important, for these students to know themselves and what they wanted as it was to be accepted to an elite school? I was faced with the reality of my increasing reticence to support a system that ran counter to my values about happiness and well-being. I imagined my own daughter, just a year old at this time, in the chair across from me as a junior or senior in high school, and I felt sick, realizing that I was responsible for actively contributing to a system I knew was flawed.

Later in my career, the need for a new approach became even more evident. I started to make the connection between the students in my college counseling practice and adult clients in my private coaching and therapy practice who were miserably unhappy in their careers. The career trajectories of my adult clients, which had begun at an early age, unfolded without support for finding and pursuing a path of the heart. In session, I encouraged and worked with these clients to take steps—both to live and to make a living—in the direction of their dreams. At the same time, I was working with middle and high school students who were receiving little to no guidance as it related to a future that best supported their soul development—the important learning of who you are and what you are called to do.

"Later in my career, the need for a new approach became even more evident. I started to make the connection between the students in my college counseling practice and adult clients in my private coaching and therapy practice who were miserably unhappy in their careers."

Through this, I came to two conclusions and a revelation. First, I concluded the prevailing approach to college admissions is all wrong. Call it what you will—stress-inducing, hair raising, or angst-evoking—the fact is that we must acknowledge the flaws in a system that set students on their journey to adulthood through a harrowing and riddled process, one that spends more time and money on test preparation and pursuit of the "right" activities than on helping them to know themselves.

Second, I concluded there could and should be another way. I began to reflect on what might serve to improve the way we approach college admissions. I explored and revisited educational and humanistic theory and became immersed in the new research in neuroscience, all of which serve as the evidence and underpinnings of the need for the development of a different approach to college admissions. Through these conclusions and my subsequent research came the revelation, my "aha" moment: The prevailing approach to college admissions is missing an important first step; that is, **students should**

begin this process by looking inward rather than outward for the answers. More often than not, when students dig inside themselves, they have the answers they seek as to how to set a true course for their lives.

I began to experiment with a new approach to college admissions. By applying my knowledge and developing a unique human-centered process—one that was focused on students designing their experience and one that was purpose driven—I saw how profoundly transformational this different way could be, both for me as a college admissions professional, for other counselors, and, most importantly, for students and their families. By turning inward, the steps of the path become illuminated. You then are able to design your way forward.

"The prevailing approach to college admissions is all wrong."

Think of it this way: When you are a child, you eat what is put in front of you. But as you grow older, you begin to develop tastes and preferences and ask for particular things. Fast forward to life today, if you were in charge of making a meal for yourself, how would you go about it? You might ask yourself questions like these:

What am I hungry for?
What am I craving?
What would be satisfying to me?
What do I need to feel sustained?

It would be crazy to eat smoked trout if you want an apple (though it happens). To not step back and ask these same kind of questions when it comes to a decision like where you go to college is nuts! (Pun intended, of course.)

As a result, I've created and implemented a new method for making the college admissions process much more than just the checklist activity that it often is. Yes, it is true that my methods are unconventional. It's also true that they do not fit into what traditionally may be deemed the "right" way to approach the process. But as I have implemented them, I have seen life breathed back into students and parents in the face of what otherwise is a difficult and confusing process and one that hardly acknowledges the humans at its center.

Why Design?

A long time ago in a far away place—in my 20s and living over-seas—I started my career in the for-profit world as a design assistant to a men's fashion designer. It was in this job that I first learned how the designer generated the ideas for his clothing line from the world around him, with a special emphasis on taking inspiration from in-trospection, from his life experience, and from nature. I have often thought of how deliberate and thoughtful he was in his choices. I also recall how he'd sometimes make a choice and then later re-make that same choice based on his evolution of thought about how he wanted his design to manifest. His selection of everything, from the lining, to the buttons, to the font

"My hope in incorporating the definition of design is to begin to seed the awareness of the need for purposeful planning..."

on the tags, was representative of his choices, and of his instincts and intuition. Seeing the many thoughtful decisions that went into the cre-ation of just one article of clothing, I learned the truth of what Charles Eames said about design: "The details are not the details. They make the design."

As I noted earlier, it's become clear to me that the college admis-sions process was lacking any system for students to really come to know themselves and to think of their internal world as the starting point in their college application decisions. It wasn't until after I'd spent many years thinking about the process and what it lacked that I remembered what I'd learned many years before about design.

In using the word "design," I am not meaning to evoke the images that sometimes come with that word, or even the associations with "design" I myself have long held; that is, it is not my intention to elicit images of fancy designers, runways, or products on Fifth Avenue. Quite the contrary. I am referring to design as a way of thinking and as a creative act.

Let's start with the standard definitions of "design":

A) A particular purpose held in view by an individual or group

B) Deliberative purposive planning

Most folks think that the "purpose" of applying to college is to "get in." But really, the college application experience in its highest form can and should be much more than that. Unfortunately, not nearly enough students have any "particular purpose" beyond seeking admission when they complete their applications. Even worse, rare is the student who is supported in the "deliberative, purposive planning" that is required for the process of college admissions if you want it to be the starting point for a journey into adulthood. Consider the noun version of the definition: "The purpose, planning, or intention that exists or is thought to exist behind an action, fact, or material object." This definition serves to emphasize that which is missing in the process of college admissions—the woeful lack of "purpose, planning, and intention" before the act of engaging in the admissions process. Of course, without this purpose, planning, and intention, the action cannot have the result or outcome that is most meaningful.

But, most of all, I want to focus on the verb form of the definition:

1) To plan and make decisions about (something that is being built or created); to create the plans, drawing, etc. that show how (something) will be made

2) To plan and make (something) for a specific use or purpose

3) To think of (something, such as a plan); to plan (something) in your mind

I like the verb form best because it represents the task ahead of you—to design and develop a life—which is the focus of the book. The first step is to look within to your inner compass before you know what choices will make sense in the external world.

You deserve a process that is about much more than just you getting in to a particular school. My hope in incorporating the definition of design is to begin to seed the awareness of the need for purposeful planning—beyond the planning that is taking place in the current system. Such planning should include the desire to find out what will make you happy in the long run instead of just at this moment (though this is important, too.) I am not talking about the list of colleges, the due dates, and the checklists of things to get done. I am talking about the deep reflection that you need to do to really think about how your gifts and desires will be supported to catalyze you in next step of your journey to adulthood.

The following list of synonyms for "design" underscores just how tied the meaning of the word is to what the process can and should become—a process that best manifests the hopes and dreams students and parents have for their future.

Purpose	**Target**
Plan	**Hope**
Intent	**Dream**
Objective	**Wish**
Object	**Aspiration**
Goal	**Ambition**
End	

Design is at the heart of the college admissions process because inherent in all these forms of the word is a sense of flexibility about the outcomes. In designing or drawing something, you are exploring a path forward. Not the *only* path forward, but *a* path forward. Often students and parents become married to just one pathway, to one outcome in the admissions process. Instead we should liken the experience to the drafting of a paper. At the outset of a process, you may have an idea of what you want to have happen, but along the road, things change. The design is alive. You must make adjustments, modifications. People give you feedback. You have epiphanies. You make connections, revisit your original thoughts, and make changes accordingly.

Similarly, the journey toward adulthood is a process of *becoming*. Just as is the case with anything that requires design, there are early sketches and prototypes. Life is a series of steps toward refining our purpose. We refine and refine until we get things closer to how we'd like them to be. With design, things change.

Why *Admissions by Design*?

All great products first begin with design: Houses. Cars. Electronics. So, really, why shouldn't this same idea be applied to the development of you and your process of college admissions?

What do great designers do? They search deeply into the user's needs. The process of developing design requires one to really immerse him or herself in the experience of the user, to take on his or her perspective. It also involves searching deeply into the user's desires and experiences, trying to uncover any unstated and unexpressed needs.

After nearly two decades of working in and studying the field of education, I have noticed too little time is spent on the process of design, especially in designing and developing your life. Nowhere is this more evident than in the case of college admissions.

Having helped hundreds of students apply to college, I have seen first hand that it is not very often that students' hopes, dreams, wishes, and aspirations are at the core of the process. Much more than designing their lives for themselves, often the students are designing for others, whether that be for parents, or even worse, only that which will ensure the promise of college acceptance.

As Steve Jobs said, "Design is not just what it looks and feels like. Design is how it works." In college admissions, there is plenty of thought about the external "look and function" of getting into a certain type of college (like the Ivies), but too little time spent on having students reflect on how their internal world, or the process of applying to college from the vantage point of the heart and soul. Moreover, when students create a map of the direction they hope to head based upon their gifts and callings—one of the exercises in this book—it changes the way they step into the next stage of life and impacts the trajectory of their lives moving forward.

Admissions by Plan vs. Admissions by Design

I want to make an important distinction between what I call "Admissions by Plan" and "Admissions by Design."

You know the folks who are on the Admissions by Plan path— mostly because from a very young age, these students have a checklist with everything planned out perfectly to the tiniest detail. If you are one of these people, you know the school you will attend and where you will live. You know the exact partner, job, and car (down to the make and model) you will have. Often you are lockstep in a previously carved path: the one society has dictated as the path to success. And this all sails along fine until suddenly it doesn't. Right? Like when you don't get into the perfect school, or don't get the dream job, or the person you are bananas about, well, thinks you are a toad.

In my experience, these plans seem to be developed to quell the anxiety you (and likely your parents) feel about the sometimes unspoken reality that, in fact, we actually only have partial say in what happens to us in our lives. There are unpredictable events we cannot control. Worse, while these plans can sometimes provide comfort in knowing exactly what direction you are heading, they also can keep you imprisoned in an identity that is not yours.

A student shared with me that she keeps telling people she is going to be a doctor because that is what everyone now expects (since she has been saying that since she was a young child). She feels like she would only disappoint everyone by

> **"It is for this purpose that I evoke the definition and principles of design: to challenge the system by offering another path."**

sharing that she's not interested in being a doctor now—and so she follows her true passion, writing, solely in isolation, not sharing it with anyone. Even worse, if you do not have one of these plans, you may feel like a total slacker. I recently talked with a student attending an Ivy League school who said that she felt like a fish out of water because it seemed to her that everyone had a five- or 10-year plan, and she did not. When I asked her what she decided to do, she said she just made one up because she felt so stupid not having one. Now she tells people she is on a path that she has no real desire to be on (but it sounds good and calms fears). Lately, she's been considering this fake plan more seriously (even though she has no heart for it) because she doesn't really know what else to do.

Listen, there is nothing wrong with having a plan, but let's face it, life does not always unfold according to plan. Moreover, it also doesn't leave much room for inspiration or the evolution of your thinking about what might be best for you and your future happiness. This is where *Admissions by Design* comes in.

The phrase "Admissions by Design" doesn't mean you are without a plan or that you don't have a sense of the direction in which you are going, but it does mean you are conscious of the need to actively design something that allows for a natural and authentic unfolding of events in your life. It also means that while you may have a sense of what you are excited about, you remain open and aware to new things and acknowledge the differing priorities you will likely have at different stages of your life. In taking an approach of design, you, like a designer, are co-creating with the internal and external elements of your life. You acknowledge the various twists and turns your life and the lives of those around you will take, and you work these into what you are creating (rather than fighting against them). You acknowledge what makes your heart sing and what makes you feel like you are sinking in quicksand (even if people really applaud your treading and drowning there). For these reasons, *Admissions by Design* is not lockstep or linear; it is about reclaiming yourself and your power. It's about identifying what is important to you and setting intentions and beginning on a path that is true to your callings with room for the natural course of life to unfold.

But listen. Design is hard. It is much easier to follow an equation about the "right" actions to take at the "right" times. Again, this is why design is a differentiator. Think about it: The reason design is so important is that while you make a plan for getting into college, you don't often spend much time considering your intentions behind those plans. Design will help you to answer the questions, "Why am I doing this?" and "What's this all for?" It is for this purpose that I evoke the definition and principles of design: to challenge the system by offering another path. Through the incorporation of design into the college admissions process, it is my hope to put the power back into the hands of the students — where it belongs — and to reframe and enhance the process of applying to college as a way for students to come to really know themselves and to embrace the designing of their own life. The purpose of taking the *Admissions by Design* approach is for you, the student, to do some soul searching, to dig into the soil of your dreams, and to actively craft your own powerfully unique, purposeful, and rewarding path.

Heart, Soul, and Purpose in College Admissions?

As a long-time educator and college counselor, I realize, of course, the topic of design and the topics of one's heart, soul, and purpose have not been at the forefront of the admissions conversation, and, as such, it may seem strange as the foundation for an approach to college admissions. But it's not. Why? Consider the following:

- At this time more students are depressed and on medication than at any time in our country's history.

- Given the ways jobs and careers are changing, students will need their intuition, resourcefulness, and creativity every bit as much (if not more) as they will need particular job skills.

- By not including students' inner lives as part of the process, we run the risk of skipping over the greatest gifts today's students have to offer tomorrow's future.

Having already defined what I mean by design, it is important to take a moment here to define what I mean by "heart," "soul," and "purpose" because I use these terms often throughout this book.

When I refer to heart, I'm not referring to the organ that pumps blood throughout your body, of course (though that is very cool, too). My definition of "heart" encompasses several things. First, I define it as "the central or innermost part of something." The use of "heart" in this book, then, refers to the central or innermost part of you.

This definition of heart comes from the Latin root of the word "cor." Think of the core of something as its essential center, like in the case of an apple core or the Earth's core or the core of a problem. This Latin root was morphed in the French language to "cour" (or "coeur," the French word for heart), and where words like "courage," "encourage," and "discourage" come from. Think about it like this: courage is the heart to do something, to encourage is to support someone's heart to do something, and to discourage is to separate heart from something or to dishearten. If we are talking about you designing your future, you can see how things like your core and courage are essential. In English, the Latin root "cor" and "cordis" (with the same meaning of "heart") gives us "cord." Some examples of words from this root are concordant (agreeing, harmonious), accord (to be in agreement or harmony or to make agree or correspond), and cordiality (warmth of feeling; heartiness). I offer these details because I know how essential it is to find and follow your path from the center of you, but to also do so with courage and in agreement with passions and gifts you have been given.

Second, the heart is sometimes referred to as the "locus of feeling of intuition." In referring to your heart, I am asking you to incorporate your feelings and instinctive knowing. I talk about ways of knowing later in this book, but it is critical to spend a bit of time on this here. Your feelings and your intuition—or your "felt sense" of your life today and of your future—are as important as your logical, cognitive thoughts about this process. So when I refer to heart, this is what I mean: To claim the richness of your life, you must embody more than the use of your mind. You must also engage the heart, which includes your emotions and intuition as well as the courage and agreement to live your own unique life.

Here is how I distinguish your heart from your soul: The soul is the housing of your spirit. I don't mean spirit in a religious sense here, but in the sense of a "being-ness." The soul is the complete being that you are. It is the presence and consciousness of you.

"

If **you** would **rather do fashion** school than **medical school** and your parents are **only** going to **pay** for **medical school,** know that if you go to **fashion school,** you **will be happy** because there is **meaning in it** for you. **But** if you go to **medical school,** you **will not be good** at it because your **heart isn't in it.**

STUDENT VOICE

And finally, there is purpose. Purpose is considered a lofty and aspirational term. I use it unabashedly throughout the book because, as you already know, I think of college in the larger context of your life—and, from my experience, a life of meaning is rooted in the notion of purpose. Purpose is much more than just a declaration of things important to you; it is a weaving of life experience and a discovery of what matters to you and where you want to place your energy. There will be more discussion of purpose later in the book, but for now, I want you to understand it as what brings meaning to your life. It is also something more than just what you tell life you want from it; it's also what life tells and brings to you.

At the outset of writing this book, I was encouraged not to use the words "heart," "soul," and "purpose." I was told such a discussion was passé and meaningless, especially to students your age, who don't yet know yourself well enough to know your heart and your soul, let alone your purpose. I wonder what you think of this? Because I wholeheartedly disagree.

It is my experience that you want to make thoughtful decisions about your life, and that you have plenty to say about what it is you want for yourself and your future. In having worked with many students, I see that many do, in fact, know their hearts and souls. Or, perhaps, and equally legitimately, you may not have any clue or have just a slight inkling of what nourishes your heart and soul. Realize, of course, that both of these are perfectly fine. The discovery of oneself is like the blooming of flowers: In nature, flowers bloom when they are ready and not on some artificial timeline. Even if you were to stand in front of flowers and shout at or beg for them to bloom, they would not. We understand that flowers need time, cultivation, and the right conditions to unfold into their full glory. This is true for you, too.

It is my belief that if we were to talk about heart, soul, and purpose with you earlier in life, affording you plenty of room to grow, learn, and experience while giving you encouragement to trust yourself and the callings of your truest path along the way, you may, in fact, by this time in your life, be close friends with your heart and soul. And this is essential to a life of purpose because ultimately only you can determine what a life of meaning is to you. As a friend in his 60s recently told me when I described my intentions of this book to him: "I have had my ups, and I have had my downs. There have been so many decisions I made and forks in the road I didn't expect. But I have had a fulfilling life, and I regret nothing, because I always saw it as a journey of adventure and made my decisions from my heart."

Your Unique Life

In considering the future of your life, I want to echo the wisdom of Viktor E. Frankl in *Man's Search for Meaning* in which he makes the important point that the tasks and circumstances of one's life, and thus the very meaning of life itself, differ both from one individual to the next and from moment to moment. He writes:

> "Life" does not mean something vague, but something very real and concrete, just as life's tasks are very real and concrete. They form man's destiny, which is different and unique for each individual. No man and no destiny can be compared with another man or any other destiny. No situation repeats itself, and each situation calls for a different response.[1]

It is for this reason that the best advice you could receive for college admissions is the same advice for life—that your life experience is your own. No book telling you the equation for getting admitted to a particular school in a particular way is going to help you more than becoming friends with your own life, callings, and purpose. Life is much bigger than college. This is why there is a different and healthier way to approach the process.

The Design of Your Future is Yours to Claim

At no other time has there been as much choice or as many options in how to engage in education. The time is ripe for you to grab the steering wheel and drive in the direction of the future you want to create. This is at the heart of my desire to write this book: to help you understand the power you have to design your future in a way to make it representative of the things that are important to you.

There are several factors—adults, the system itself—often encouraging you to engage in a process that requires you to plan your lives by old-fashioned standards that are quickly becoming relics of the past. We can and should let go of these outdated metrics.

Despite the pressures you might feel to do what others want you to do, you actually get to choose some things, including how to think about college and how to approach what it has to offer. Using introspection, inspiration, trial and error, and life experience, you can reframe the admissions process to become one that is focused on design and purpose and one that is you-centered. In doing so, you cast away many of the elements that create a process so fraught with anxiety. You may then blossom with the joy of self-discovery that comes from engaging in a soul-filled design process.

To offer your greatest gifts to the world, you must decide to become the designer of your life. Once learned, this road of self-discovery will serve you well beyond college. It will set the stage for your constant evolving toward full expression of the person you were meant to become. It is not stagnant; it grows with you. Best of all, this process of self-discovery will become something that you will use throughout your life.

But before we get to the details of how to do this, let's spend some time examining the current state of affairs and why a new paradigm in thinking about college admissions is not only necessary but critical.

Chapter Two:
A Culture of Crazy

"A sort of mania has taken hold, and its grip seems to grow tighter and tighter."
— *Frank Bruni*

Without question, today's frenzied state of college admissions has become a Culture of Crazy. From Tiger Mothers to headlines like "Kids of Helicopter Parents are Sputtering Out" and "Ruining our Children: The Scourge of College Admissions" to stories of families paying upwards of $50,000 annually to hire private college consultants, the college application process has become nothing short of an arms race. How did it all come to this? Allow me to create some context by offering up some of the reasons all of this insanity exists.

The Issue of Supply and Demand

One of the main reasons that college admissions is seemingly so competitive is often attributed to a simple issue of supply and demand. According to National Association for College Admissions Counseling's (NACAC) 2014 State of College Admission report, in 2011–2012, a population wave fueled a record number of high school graduates, which peaked, after two decades of steady growth, at 3.45 million. Enrollment at public four-year and private, non-profit, four-year institutions during the same time period also increased, and application growth has continued for most colleges; for example, for 10 of the past 15 years, more than 70 percent of colleges reported year-to-year application increases. The U.S. Department of Education projects a gradual increase in the number of college students from 2013 through 2023 to 23.8 million.[1]

Despite this steady rise in graduates and in applications, the number of available "seats" in some of the nation's most competitive colleges has largely remained the same; that is, while the college-going population has increased, most of the elite schools have not increased their enrollment at the same pace. According to NACAC's 2014 State of College Admissions Report, over the last decade college acceptance rates have declined by nearly six percentage points.[2]

In a recent *New York Times* article, Pamela Paul writes, "An applicant from the Harvard class of 1985 would have faced an admission rate of 16 percent, compared with 6 percent for the class of 2015."[3] Other elite schools have experienced the same trend.

In short, with the number of applicants and applications having increased significantly and growing all the time, competition at some schools is much, much tougher than it was when the adults in your lives were applying to school. Couple this with the desire of many students to attend a "name" school, and "Houston, we have a problem." This is what all the media hype is built upon, and the core of what may be keeping you (and your parents) up at night. There is, in fact, more to it than first meets the eye (check out Myth #1 later in the book for more information), but the Culture of Crazy is, in part, built on the assumptions related to issues of supply and demand.

The Rise of the Common Application

There are a few factors as to why the demand for seats at what are considered the top universities has so steadily increased. One major contributing factor to this is the rise of the Common Application. Whereas several years ago, to apply to college one had to submit all applications by paper—a different application for each school— students nowadays use the Common Application, or what is referred to as the "Common App," a single application accepted by a wide range of colleges. This, as you already know, makes applying to many schools less difficult than it used to be. Online applications are now the norm; according to NACAC's 2014 State of College report, four-year colleges and universities received an average of 92 percent of their applications online during the fall 2013 admissions cycle.[4]

Some background: The Common App has been around since 1975 when it began as a pilot program with 15 member institutions, most of which were selective liberal arts colleges. In 1980, it had more than 100 members. By 2013, the organization passed 500 member organizations and retired the paper version of the application all together.[5]

While it took several decades for students and colleges to use the Common App, now it's humming right along. Today, applicants can use it to apply to any of the more than 500 member schools in 47 states and the District of Columbia—and, drum roll please—in the U.K., France, Germany, Austria, Switzerland, and Italy. To understand the growth, in 2001, 861,877 Common Applications were submitted, and in 2012, that grew to 3,283,886. As Frank Bruni notes in his book *Where You Go Isn't Who You'll Be*, in 2008-2009, about 417,000 students used the Common Application. By 2013-2014—just five years later—that number had nearly doubled to 809,000 students.[6] Not only does the Common App save students time, but it also fosters a jump in the number of applications to schools because students can apply to many more schools much more easily. Generally, in accepting the Common App, colleges and universities can expect an increase in applications of anywhere between 10 to 20 percent. Some argue that its use has led to greater diversity in the in the applicant pool, and many more elite colleges, having once looked down on the Common App, now use it as part of their competitive admissions strategy.[7]

While the widespread use of the Common App has been positive in terms of the way it has fostered the ability for more students to apply to more colleges, it also has contributed to important pieces of the competitive environment puzzle.

Increase in International Applicants

Another contributing factor to the perception of admissions craziness is the rise of the international applicant pool. According to a 2015 *Wall Street Journal* article entitled, "International Students Stream into U.S. Colleges," there are now 1.13 million foreign students in the U.S., and the vast majority of these students are in college degree programs. This number is a 14 percent increase over 2014, almost 50 percent more than in 2010, and 85 percent more than in 2005.[8] According to the article, colleges and universities are recruiting more international students than ever before due to a wide range of factors including economic reasons to a desire for increased international diversity on campuses.

Given these statistics, you are likely beginning to catch my drift here: With more students applying to more colleges, and many of them focused on entry to "elite" or "name" schools—and with the seats at many of those schools not having increased significantly—there is a natural shrinking percentage of students accepted relative to the size of the overall applicant pool.

STUDYING ABROAD[9]

Most foreign students in the U.S. come from Asia, and most of those students come from India and China.

Foreign students in the U.S., on student visas, all grade levels and programs, as of February 2015.

by region of origin

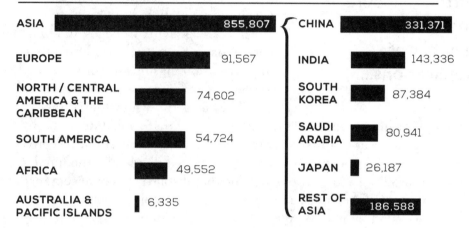

ASIA	855,807
EUROPE	91,567
NORTH / CENTRAL AMERICA & THE CARIBBEAN	74,602
SOUTH AMERICA	54,724
AFRICA	49,552
AUSTRALIA & PACIFIC ISLANDS	6,335

CHINA	331,371
INDIA	143,336
SOUTH KOREA	87,384
SAUDI ARABIA	80,941
JAPAN	26,187
REST OF ASIA	186,588

by school of study

U OF SOUTHERN CALIFORNIA	12,480
PURDUE UNIVERSITY	10,516
COLUMBIA UNIVERSITY	10,436
U OF ILLINOIS URBANA-CHAMPAIGN	10,352
NEW YORK UNIVERSITY	10,334

Source: *The Wall Street Journal*

Selectivity: Great News for Colleges, Not So Great News for You

Though this increase in the number of applications is part of what is driving the culture of applying to college to become more and more crazy, it's good news for colleges, and something very important to them because selectivity means improved rankings. Let's take *the U.S. News & World Report* college rankings, for example, which first provided its education rankings in 1983 and which uses a number of different factors, including graduation rates, alumni giving, and academic reputation, but also heavily considers selectivity. Colleges and universities are smart, and they know that improved rankings mean more qualified applicants and increased alumni giving. They also know how long it takes (years!) to improve some of the other factors that contribute to their rankings, such as graduation rates and academic reputation. Selectivity is the number of students who are accepted divided by the number who apply. Take a look at the graphic that displays recent acceptance rates at some of America's most competitive schools.[10]

"Institutions of higher education further encourage the increase in number of applications..."

The easiest and fastest way for a school to improve its rankings is to bolster the number of students who apply, which decreases a school's acceptance rate. Simply put, if the number of applicants increases, but the number of students a school accepts remains the same, the school's selectivity increases.

And because this is a business, institutions of higher education further encourage the increase in number of applications through practices like easy apps, or pre-populating applications with admissions data, or by emailing students that they have the opportunity to apply with an abbreviated application or a reduced or no fee application. All of this encourages more students to apply.

Yield

Another layer of this discussion is something called "yield." Yield is the number of students who have been accepted to a college who decide to enroll. Say you have been offered admission to three different schools. The school that you decide to attend has the benefit of having their yield rate increase—that is, they offered you admission,

ACCEPTANCE RATES FALL 2014

school (state)		percentage accepted
STANFORD UNIVERSITY	(CA)	5.1 %
HARVARD UNIVERSITY	(MA)	6 %
YALE UNIVERSITY	(CT)	6.3 %
COLUMBIA UNIVERSITY	(NY)	7 %
ALICE LLOYD COLLEGE	(KY)	7.1 %
PRINCETON UNIVERSITY	(NJ)	7.4 %
MASSACHUSETTS INSTITUTE OF TECHNOLOGY	(MA)	7.9 %
UNITED STATES NAVAL ACADEMY	(MD)	7.9 %
COLLEGE OF THE OZARKS	(MO)	8.3 %
BROWN UNIVERSITY	(RI)	8.7 %

Source: *U.S. News & World Report* (2015, November 3)

and you accepted the offer. Yield rates only reflect first-year, first-time, degree-seeking students. Just as you stress about getting into college, colleges stress about how to demonstrate their selectivity and about how many of the accepted students will decide to attend.

Yield rates can be impacted by a number of things. One of the most positive ways colleges and universities can positively impact their yield rates is through their Early Decision (ED) policies. If you apply to a school Early Decision, you are stating that if offered admission, you will attend the school. Naturally, this helps a school's yield rate because they can count on students that apply ED to attend the school. Some schools fill their incoming freshman classes with a significant number of ED students, obtaining the students they need to fill their classes while ensuring positive yield rates. Of course, when a sizable group of acceptances come from an ED pool, colleges get a two-punch benefit: 1) they can accept fewer students overall, increasing their selectivity, and 2) they are still ensured a high yield rate.

Yield rates were an important factor in college admissions rankings until just a few years ago when, because of the controversy around it, *U.S. News & World Report* stopped including it as part of its rankings. And lately, yield rates have been wildly fluctuating. With more students applying to more schools, it becomes more difficult for schools to predict who will enroll, thus leaving colleges and universities in a bit of a pickle. They are as uncertain about who will accept their offers of admissions as you are about who will extend those offers to you.[12] This has led to some colleges and universities placing more students on their waitlists simply to increase their yield rates.[13]

According to Tanya Abrams in her *New York Times* article, "Colleges Report 2013 Admissions Yields and Wait-List Offers," colleges and universities employ many strategies to "make their yields, and themselves, look good." She writes:

> Just as institutions can make themselves look more desirable by broadcasting low acceptance rates, they can also defer students who they believe are likely to enroll elsewhere. By not accepting those students, the institution is able to appear more selective, report a higher yield, and, perhaps, increase its rankings in some publications and its aura of prestige among prospective students.[14]

EARLY DECISION[11]

VS

EARLY ACTION

PROS AND CONS

Early Decision is a binding process, which means that once accepted, one must attend the college or university.

Early Action plans are non-binding. Students receive an early response to their application but do not have to commit to the college until the normal reply date of May 1.

EARLY DECISION (ED)

A student who is accepted in ED must attend that college.

Get advice from your school counselor before applying Early Decision. While it may seem appealing to get the process over with early, it might be too soon to know that you've made the right college choice.

Apply early to 1st choice college

Receive admission by December

Agree to attend college if accepted

Apply to only one college ED

Withdraw all other applications if accepted

Send non-refundable check before May 1st

If financial aid is needed, ED might not be a good idea

Only 400 colleges offer an ED plan or EA plan

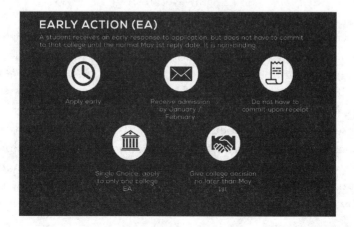

EARLY ACTION (EA)

A student receives an early response to application, but does not have to commit to that college until the normal May 1st reply date. It is non-binding.

Apply early

Receive admission by January / February

Do not have to commit upon receipt

Single Choice: apply to only one college EA

Give college decision no later than May 1st

YIELD RATES

CLASS OF 2016	ACCEPTED	ENROLLED	YIELD	TOTAL INVITED TO WAIT LIST
BOSTON UNIVERSITY (MA)	19,903	4,140	20.8%	57
CARNEGIE MELLON UNIVERSITY (PA)	4,807	1,524	31.7%	100
CLAREMONT MCKENNA COLLEGE (CA)	688	291	42.3%	54
COLLEGE OF WILLIAM & MARY (VA)	4,259	1,363	32%	141
COOPER UNION FOR THE ADVANCEMENT OF SCIENCE AND ART (NY)	251	191	76.1%	15
EMORY UNIVERSITY (GA)	17,493	1,354	7.74%	37
GEORGIA INSTITUTE OF TECHNOLOGY	8,038	3,158	39.29%	51
HARVARD (MA)	2,076	1,665	80.2%	46
JOHNS HOPKINS UNIVERSITY (MD)	3,626	1,397	38.53%	1
KENYON COLLEGE (OH)	1,408	463	32.88%	7
LAFAYETTE COLLEGE (PA)	2,286	649	28.39%	8
MIDDLEBURY COLLEGE (VT)	1,728	699	40.45%	26
PRINCETON UNIVERSITY (NJ)	2,093	1,360	64.98%	0
ST. LAWRENCE UNIVERSITY (NY)	1,962	644	32.82%	20
STANFORD UNIVERSITY (CA)	2,423	1,765	72.84%	0
UNIVERSITY OF MARYLAND AT COLLEGE PARK	11,849	4,030	34.01%	0
UNIVERSITY OF MICHIGAN AT ANN ARBOR	15,551	6,735	43.31%	74
UNIVERSITY OF SOUTHERN CALIFORNIA	8,380	2,566	30.62%	N/A
UNIVERSITY OF WISCONSIN AT MADISON	15,829	6,535	41.28%	0

Adapted from *The New York Times* (2013, May 13)

Self-Reporting

It is worth noting that all this admissions data is self reported. Yep, that's right. There is no outside body that verifies the admissions data that colleges and universities submit. While *U.S. News & World Report's* Robert Morse has commented, "There is no reason to believe the misreporting is widespread," colleges and universities have been caught in misrepresenting their numbers. In 2012-2013, for example, five colleges—Claremont McKenna, Emory, Bucknell, George Washington University, and Tulane University's Business School—admitted to an inflation of their admissions statistics.[15] Moreover, in a survey conducted by *Inside Higher Ed* in the fall of 2012, 91 percent of respondents stated they believe there is more misreporting than has been exposed, suggesting that even admissions directors—and a lot of them— are wary of the numbers being reported.[16]

What I hope you are catching on to now is that college—like many things—is a lot about being a business. Universities are invested in sharing things like their high number of applications, their lower and lower acceptance rates, and their high test scores to make

> **"There is no outside body that verifies the admissions data that colleges and universities submit."**

them more attractive to the consumer—you. Don't forget: This gives them a competitive advantage. This is why it is so critical that you not only focus on what school will accept you, but also take a balcony view and a consumer's mindset and become aware of the many ways that schools can inflate their own statistics in order to influence how they are perceived.

Test Prep

All this competitiveness has given rise to other industries. Just one example of this is the booming 840 million dollar test preparation industry. In the hopes of increasing scores (even marginally), more and more students are enlisting the services of expensive testing prep centers or test prep coaches. This is based on the prevailing belief that when it comes to test preparation, students being coached will perform significantly better than if they had not been coached. Most forms of test preparation cost a fee—and many times a hefty fee—for services. According to Liz Weston in her *Reuters* article (2014) "Resist the Fear to Go Overboard on College Test Prep," it is not unusual for families to spend $3,000-$5,000 on test preparation and related costs.[17]

Over the years, schools have shown more interest than ever in the SAT scores of the incoming class because it is one of the criteria by which they are evaluated in the *U.S. News and World Report* annual rankings. So, really, it is not without reason that the industry has exploded. To get a sense of the meteoric growth, the number of test preparation centers doubled from 1998 to 2012, the last year of which this census data is available.[18] The tutoring business has grown fastest in Georgia, where the number of establishments quintupled over that 14-year period.

TEST CENTERS[19]
Where Tutoring Businesses Thrive

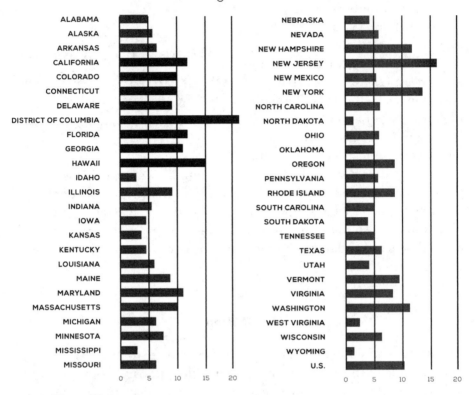

Source: U.S. Census

Per 100,000 residents 23 or younger

Does all of this test prep frenzy lead to an increase in scores? Despite all of the growth and the different forms of classes offered, SAT scores over the same period of time declined slightly, leaving us to question how much impact all of this test preparation has. In fact, a 2009 paper from the National Association for College Admission Counseling suggests that while test prep courses help students improve their scores, it is only marginally.[20]

Shortage of School Counselors

According to U.S. Department of Education data, in 2011-2012 public school counselors had responsibility for 475 students.[21] Ahem. Let me repeat: The average caseload is 1 to 475 students. And this situation is getting worse all the time. In California, for example, the ratio for all grades has increased from 1-to-810 before the 2008 economic downturn to 1-to-1,016 today. That's for all grades. In high schools, where counselors are often the primary source of information about college, each one is responsible for a nationwide average of 266 students, according to recent NACAC survey data. In California, it's 1-to-500, and in Georgia, according to a Georgia School Counselors Association survey, it's 1-to-512.[22] In Timothy Pratt's 2013 *Time* Magazine article "The High School Counselor Shortage," he shares the result of this "overtaxed system": "many students either never go to college, go to institutions that are the wrong for them, or never learn about financial aid for which they may qualify."[23]

Ready for more bad news? These same counselors are responsible for much more than college counseling alone. They are also the ones who proctor exams and who provide social and emotional support for students. In short, their plates are very, very full—often too full to offer more than nominal help to any individual student. Moreover, there is a significant gap in the world of counseling between those who serve at private schools or at more highly funded public schools, and those who serve at underfunded schools. According to NACAC, on average, public school counselors spent 24 percent of their time on post secondary counseling in 2013. Private school counterparts, on the other hand, spent 52 percent of their time on college counseling. Moreover, in 2013, 32 percent of public schools reported employing at least one full- or part-time counselor devoted exclusively to provide college counseling. At private schools, however, this number was 71 percent.[24]

Add to that the notion that many counselors don't receive adequate training to help with college applications. According to the 2012 National Survey of School Counselors, though counselors are among the most highly trained professionals in the education system (83 percent hold master's degrees), more than half (56 percent) report they felt only "somewhat prepared" for their job, and roughly a third (28 percent) said their training did not prepare them well.[25] What's more, most training for school counselors does not include coursework on college admissions, from the details of the admissions process to the ins and outs of financial aid. What's worse is there are a great number of counselors who are unable to attend professional development opportunities aimed at college access because of budgetary constraints or budget cuts. This woeful lack of training means that, in many cases, counselors find themselves in a blind-leading-the-blind scenario.

Mark Sklarow, Director of the Independent Educational Consultants Association, in a recent article stated, "The current economy has meant that school districts are increasing caseloads for school-based counselors." He went on to state, "We've heard from so many families

"

The **SAT** was **also stressful** because **my parents hired** a **company** to **help me study,** which made me **feel inadequate** from the **get-go.**

STUDENT VOICE

"

who say the school counselor not only doesn't know their child but there's just not enough time for them to help."[26] An understanding of the experience of college counselors is perhaps best expressed by Ms. Claire Nold Glaser, a former school counselor turned independent college counselor, who was quoted in a 2005 NPR story, as saying:

> I felt like I was kind of turning into almost a counseling machine, where students would come in and I would ask them some key questions: What they were interested in, what they were passionate about. And then I would ask them to just be quiet and I would generate a list of colleges for them and kind of shove it at them and tell them if they needed a letter of recommendation, to feel free to come back.[27]

Sadly, Ms. Glaser's words reflect what the state of college counseling has become in most schools.

A Systems View

As you can see, the culture of college admissions is, indeed, crazy. This is a system with numerous pieces and parts, all of which are interconnected and feed into a larger whole. In this section, we have covered some of the elements and components of this complicated and often anxiety-laden system. The purpose of this section is to provide some context and to invite you to stand back and see a broader perspective that may help you to better understand how college admissions has become so wildly insane. This is evident in everything from the activities of the colleges and universities themselves to things students and parents do to achieve a competitive edge. By seeing these various pieces and parts as a complete system, you are empowered to understand the system differently and your role in it. From there, you can make decisions and act based on the design you create for your future.

Chapter Summary

- The culture of college admissions is indeed crazy, and the absurdity of the system isn't wonly imagined but supported by significant research.

- Universities are invested in sharing things like their high number of applications, their lower and lower acceptance rates, and their high test scores to make them more attractive to the consumer—you.

- It's important to take a consumer mindset and become aware of the many ways that schools can inflate their own statistics in order to influence how they are perceived.

- Though access to college information and counseling is important to the college admissions process, for many students college counseling is limited at best, especially in public schools. Counselors have large caseloads, are few in number, and are limited in the amount of time they can devote to college admissions and in training they receive.

Chapter Three:
The Ten Disturbing Trends of the Culture of Crazy

"It's so much easier to write a résumé than to craft a spirit."
— Anna Quindlen

In taking a systems perspective to the process of college admissions, and understanding the system has indeed become crazy, it isn't shocking to discover that this insanity has surfaced some pretty upsetting consequences. The following trends indicate where we have gone so very wrong in service of you, the student, and, even worse, at the very moment you are launching your adult life.

Disturbing Trend One:
Achievement as the Goal of Child Raising

Looking across the landscape of the Culture of Crazy, it is easy to witness an abundance of examples of parents treating children like performance machines or placing their child's academic achievement above other values. One example is parents pressing children to take courses and participate in extracurricular activities in which they have no interest. "Achievement as the Goal of Child Raising" might also look like parents constantly arranging achievement-boosting activities in which their kids have little authentic interest. Young adults caught in the turmoil of this trend often wind up unnecessarily stressed and feeling like their actual personal qualities are not valued by others.

Disturbing Trend Two:
"Super People"—Excellence as the New Average

If you have been groomed to make your family proud through high academic achievement, then nothing short of getting straight "A's" is acceptable. Actual learning takes a backseat to things like GPAs and test scores, and only perfection will do. Simply put, "good" is no longer good enough. Former Yale professor William Deresiewicz describes such students as "super people": They are "the stereotypical ultra-high-achieving elite college students of today. A double major, a sport, a musical instrument, a couple of foreign languages, service work in distant corners of the globe, a few hobbies thrown in for good measure."[1] To be considered the best of the best, students feel the need to create an image of perfection, which breeds a whole host of polarities — from obnoxious confidence levels and extreme competitiveness to disappointment with oneself, feelings of unworthiness, and a constant sense of never quite being good enough.

Disturbing Trend Three:
Activity Overload

As noted above, the pursuit of perfection involves far more than academic performance. These "super people," along with their schoolwork, also juggle SAT test prep, school tutoring and college admissions activities, and a whole slew of extracurricular activities, which are often added to an already overloaded plate. Too often the motivation is rooted not in genuine interest, but in the misguided belief that their heavy dose of extracurricular activities will make them shine as they do their best to keep up with their peers.

A recent graduate of Sarah Lawrence College told me no one in particular pressured her to take on more than she could handle in high school, "It was more so the atmosphere of my peers I felt pressured by. The comparison of myself to another individual is usually what led me to overload myself with activities."[2]

Students are missing opportunities to discover and participate in activities that spark their imaginations and fuel their passions. A former student who attended Columbia University and now attends medical school at Vanderbilt University says:

> I made empty commitments to a lot of different activities. I never felt passionate about my extracurriculars. I liked them and so I used them to pass the time and load my CV. I don't look back on this with a lot of pride. I often feel I missed an opportunity to focus on things that I really liked, rather than shallowly engage in a lot of things I moderately liked.[3]

The current college admissions system cultivates a culture of competitiveness and constant comparison of oneself to other students. Everything from SAT test scores, school grades, even personality comes under fire. As if that weren't enough to worry about, students then have the added pressure of making themselves the perfect candidate through piling their plates high with multiple extracurricular activities. The pressure to be "perfect" and to get into college "is producing the most anxious, stressed, sleep-deprived generation ever."[4] The impact of this kind of stress "has escalated to the point of becoming a public health problem.[5]

Disturbing Trend Four:
Imposter Syndrome

Imposter Syndrome is described as "an internal experience of intellectual phoniness." This term was first coined by Pauline Clance and Suzanne Imes in 1978 in their article, "The Imposter Phenomenon in High Achieving Women: Dynamics and Therapeutic Intervention." According to Clance and Imes, "Despite outstanding academic and professional achievements…women who experience the imposter phenomenon persist in believing that they are really not bright and have fooled anyone who thinks otherwise."[6] It is clear today that it is not just women who experience this; indeed, the syndrome cuts across gender lines.

John Belcher, who has taught physics at MIT for 44 years, said in a recent article, "I think impostor syndrome is a real effect here at MIT." He goes on to say, "The students come in and they're surrounded by very bright students; they tend to think that they're the dumbest student here and everybody else is brighter."[7] A recent graduate of Columbia University felt this effect. He told me, "My first semester of college, I felt like a fraud. I did not feel that I deserved to be where I was, and so I compensated by studying a lot."[8]

Disturbing Trend Five:
Afraid to Fail

Naturally, with excellence as the new average and the belief that you have to maintain a certain facade, failure is not an option. If you and everybody around you are already perfect, then, to maintain your position in this culture of competiveness, there can be no missteps. These relentless environments are causing a whole generation of students who are afraid to fail. Even receiving a "B" can cause some students to fall apart. Meeta Kumar, a counselor at University of Pennsylvania, says instead of seeing a "B" as "what you and I would call disappointments in life, to them feel like big failures." And these failures become internalized. Rather than acknowledging an event or an experience as a failure, they begin to believe they themselves are failures.[9] This pressure can have serious consequences: "Children who grow up in an environment that relentlessly expects and values perfection do not grow into flexible, resilient young adults. Like over-hammered steel, they become work-hardened and brittle. When demands get too great, these kids don't bend, they break."[10]

Disturbing Trend Six:
Escalating Contagion of Achievement and Perfection

Pressure to achieve and to be perfect is an escalating contagion. In pursuit of perfection, students, parents, and schools often wind up competing with and feeding off of one another. A parent of an eighth grade student told me she hired for her son a math tutor for the SAT because her friend had done this, and she didn't want her child to fall behind.[11] As another parent said, "It's incredibly competitive out there, and I don't want my child left in the dust."[12]

And, the bar seems to continually be raised higher and higher. In a 2015 *New York Times* article, Julie Scelfo describes a high-achieving student who attended University of Pennsylvania: "But having gained admittance off the wait list and surrounded by people with seemingly greater drive and ability, she had her first taste of self doubt." The student herself reported, "One friend was a world-class figure skater. Another was a winner of the Intel science competition. Everyone around me was so spectacular and so amazing and I wanted to be just as amazing as they are."[13]

Even more disturbing is that these competitive environments seem only to breed more anxiety and stress. Rather than seeing their peers as friends and ones with whom they can develop authentic relationships, students view them as competitors or threats—or even view them as examples of how they themselves are not doing enough. Not only do students then have a diminished sense of themselves, but they also have a diminished sense of the ability to be in relationships with others. As one counselor noted, "Some of my students who have gone to schools such as Harvard or Princeton found their college experiences overly demanding and extremely stressful. Several at Ivy League

"

I felt **pressured** by my **peers** **because** I went to an **extremely** competitive school and **a lot** of them were **applying** to **Ivy Leagues.** So there was **a lot** of **pressure** to keep up **academically** and **achieve** the **same** status.

STUDENT VOICE

"

schools had to switch out of their pre-med major because the competition was so fierce."[14]

Disturbing Trend Seven:
"All or Nothing" Thinking

I have seen a marked increase in attitudes of "all or nothing" thinking over the years. It's either Ivy League or bust. Perfect SAT scores or nothing. This thinking can sometimes be traced back to a lack of a thorough working knowledge of the vast number of institutions there are outside of the familiar big names. Students already feel pressured to apply to college; they then have the added pressure to apply to the "best" colleges. Students are seldom asked to explore their options, such as taking a year off before going straight from high school to college or looking into different ways to design their higher education experience. Says one student, "There wasn't any outside influence encouraging me to take a gap year or look at a trade school or any other option at all—it was all Ivy League school or nothing."[15]

Disturbing Trend Eight:
Begone the Days of the Moral Compass?

With escalating contagion, some parents and students will do anything—and I mean anything—to get into a prestigious college. In "The Overpressured Student," Richard Weissbourd tells the story of giving a talk on moral development at a school and having a parent state, "I agree with you that it's important for kids to be good people, but, realistically, that won't help my child get into a place like Harvard." Another parent chimed in with, "Can you change Harvard so that being a good person counts in the application?" Weissbourd also reported that in a study his research team conducted at an independent school, more than one-third of the 40 juniors surveyed identified "getting into a good college" as more important than "being a good person," and nearly one-half of students said that it was more important to their parents that they get into a good college than that they be good people.[16] Further, some argue that the "do anything to get in" culture perpetuates privilege and inequality and separates students from the society they want and need to serve.

Disturbing Trend Nine:
Commoditization of Education

More and more, people are talking about the "return on investment" a college education provides. These days, I get the "return on investment" question more than any other. This notion of "return on investment," or what some are now calling the commoditization of education, is facing serious criticism. The issue, in part, is no one seems to be clear on what the "return" should be. Is it development of character? A job with significant earning potential? More knowledge of a certain field? Exploration? Happiness? Even more challenging is the fact that many of the stated purposes of education are hard to quantify and measure.

There are many ways to view the value of a college education. I personally like the way David Brooks describes the three potential purposes of college: the commercial (preparing to begin your career), the cognitive (learning and learning how to think), and the moral (determining your own independent beliefs and building an "integrated self."[17] Of course, there is a big difference between attending college for a commercial purpose versus a moral purpose. And pursuing college for just one of these purposes does not prevent you from pursuing it for the other reasons, too.

To me, college is a powerfully unique opportunity. As Deresiewicz writes, "College is an opportunity to stand outside the world for a few years, between the orthodoxy of your family and the exigencies of career, and contemplate things from a distance."[18] College is a time to question and determine what you truly think and believe.

In only focusing on college as a return on investment, you risk what Deresiewicz cites as a potential pitfall of this approach: students looking "right past their college careers, focusing instead on an idealized starting salary post graduation."[19]

Just one piece of evidence of this is the ever-growing lists ranking colleges and majors by average starting salary. Moreover, the pressure of the commoditization of education has led to pressure on students to know early what their career plans are. Rather than using college as a time to explore, learn, and grow, students have to hit college campuses with five- and 10-year plans all mapped out and ready to go.

Disturbing Trend Ten:
Asking the Wrong Questions

Being so caught up in the busyness and competitiveness of the system keeps students from asking important questions like "Who am I?," "Am I happy?," and "Where do I thrive?" Instead, in the current system, students seem to be asking themselves questions like: "Am I winning or succeeding?" and "What does it take to get in?" Not only are questions like this fueled by the fear of failure and pursuit of perfection, but it also assumes one cookie cutter mold of achievement. As one student told me: "Overloading yourself with AP classes and extracurriculars is something you just do. You don't ask why."[20] Another chimed in with: "Everyone is just focused on the future—like college and your career. No one has time to ask 'Am I happy?' or 'Does any of this matter?'"[21] Instead, if students ask questions that drive more at knowledge of themselves and what conditions are required for them to thrive, they acknowledge their individuality, as well as the importance of their state of well-being. As one student recently put it: "Is it really worth it to be winning if it's at a game you don't even like playing? I mean, does it matter if the answer to a question is 'right' if you are asking the wrong question?"[22]

Making Meaning of the Disturbing Trends

Given these disturbing trends, it is clear there is much work to be done to address and eventually improve the experience of applying to college. My aim is not to make it sound like being around intelligent, driven people is only destructive. Of course, this is not the case. Different people thrive in different environments based on a wide variety of factors.

My goal, instead, is to the change the conversation to ensure students are on a path not only toward success, but also toward happiness. As it stands now, especially in the dog-eat-dog world of college admissions, all we really end up with is a lot of half-eaten dogs. And, personally, I like dogs.

In the current system, these Disturbing Trends indicate the places we have fallen down. And to me, thinking about the future of our world and the future of you, this is a sign of failure. In the next chapter, we will address how the Culture of Crazy and these Disturbing Trends are taking quite a toll.

Chapter Four:
The Culture of Crazy Takes a Physical and Mental Toll

"The price of anything is the amount of life you exchange for it."
—Henry David Thoreau

As the crazed frenzy to gain admissions marches through our hallways, resulting in the trends I have just described, both the physical and mental health of students have been negatively impacted at an astounding rate. The highly-competitive nature of admissions today is creating an entire generation of over-pressured students and taking an extreme physical and mental toll.

The Physical Toll

To help you become aware of the ramifications of our current state of college admissions, let's begin with a discussion of the many ways it may be physically impacting you.

Your Brain

We are very fortunate that we live during a time when, more than ever before in human history, we have information about the brain. This new information is being applied everywhere, including in classrooms. Brain research has helped us to understand the way we operate better, and it has equipped us with making more informed decisions about everything from education to parenting. Despite this, the excellent brain research has yet to make its way into informing our thinking about how best to tackle college admissions, which is why I've included this information in this book. While I will be discussing some of the science related to the brain and its functioning, it is the brain's place in the larger context of self in which I believe we should take special interest (we tackle that later).

Now, admittedly, I am a geek, and I love this brain stuff. So, in light of all this great research, it's my belief that we should be educating students about their brains. After sitting through hours of training and sifting through countless tomes on brain research, here is something I've noticed: There are a lot of adults talking about this, but I am not sure how readily it is making it directly to you. I don't think it is fair to make the case for including all this cool brain research stuff in how we think about college admissions without you having a sense of why this is important. And, since the brain is responsible for so much in our lives, let's give it the honor it deserves, shall we?

How the Brain Works

To understand why the information about the brain needs to make its way into the conversation about college admission, we need to start with the fundamentals of how the brain works. From there, we can tie it to why it can—and should—have implications for the way you think about your future. Now this is pretty heady stuff (get it?), and it will help to make the case for why we need a different approach to college admissions. I am going to do my best to break this down into regular person language, which is what I had to do to understand it myself. In describing this, I am using the work of the brilliant Dr. Daniel Siegel, M.D. and Clinical Professor of Psychiatry at UCLA's School of Medicine.

The Parts of the Brain

Basically, there are three main parts of your brain—the brainstem, the limbic area, and the cortex. These three regions comprise what is called the "triune" brain, and they developed in layers over the course of evolution.

The Handy Model of the Brain

The best way to understand how these different parts of your brain work together is to create what Dr. Siegel calls the "hand" or "handy" model of the brain. I like to use "handy" model because with Dr. Siegel's model, you can just use your hand as a way to understand how your brain works. Dr. Siegel's handy model of the brain works like this: In looking at an open hand, the base of your palm represents the reptilian brain, your thumb represents the limbic system, and your palm represents your emotional or mammalian brain.[1] Confused yet? Good. Maybe you'll be inspired to read on.

You Reptile, You

The brainstem, what we will also refer to as your "reptile brain," is in charge of all of the functions of your body that are required to stay alive: you know, little things like circulating blood, maintaining your blood pressure, digesting your food, and breathing air. The brain stem connects the rest of your brain to the spinal cord. It is often referred to as your "reptile" brain because it is similar to brains in reptiles in form and function.

Using Dr. Siegel's handy model, if you hold your hand out with your palm open, your brainstem sits right in the middle of your palm. The brainstem also is the center point of your fight, flight, and freeze response. This fight, flight, and freeze response is totally normal, by the way, and part of being a human being on this earth. You can't always predict what is going to set you off, but you can count on it happening. It is often the brainstem at work when something feels like it just takes you over.

The Emotional Side of You

Next is your limbic system. The limbic system is the center point of your emotions and your relationships. In the handy model of the brain, the limbic system is represented by your thumb. To understand the positioning of limbic system, with that palm open, cross your thumb over the face of your palm. The limbic system rests on top of your brainstem, so you can appreciate how these two things are really tied. The brainstem and limbic center work together to regulate your emotions and arousal. And your emotions and how worked up you get matters when it comes to college admissions, which is why you need to know about this part of your brain.

The Neocortex

Up next is the neocortex. "Neo" means new. This part of your brain is considered "new" because it isn't as old evolutionarily as the other parts of your brain (like the brainstem and the limbic system). This is the part of your brain that is often seen in pictures, or horror movies, or biology class: It's the corky and intestine looking stuff that looks a lot like the shape of your fist. If you fold your remaining four fingers over your palm and thumb, the fingers represent the neocortex. You can see how your fist now looks a little like the pictures of the brain that you often see.

There are some important reasons to care about this part of the brain. First and foremost, it is important to understand that this is the part of your brain that distinguishes us as mammals. Animals like reptiles and birds can do a lot of things that we can because we have the same older brain structures, like the brainstem and the limbic system. This new brain, the neocortex, is what allows mammals more advanced behavior (though, I admit, sometimes with our social and environmental practices, it certainly doesn't always seem this way). Such behavior includes mostly social-type behavior, things like our ability to speak, to make and apply tools, to exercise our creativity, and to have a higher-level of consciousness.

Get this: The neocortex is so large that it covers up most of the other parts of the brain. It is also separated into four main parts (or "lobes"): the frontal lobes, the parietal lobes, the temporal lobes, and the occipital lobe. For our purposes, I am going to focus only on the frontal lobes for now.

The Frontal Lobes

The frontal lobes of your brain are in charge of executing behavior. Let's say you want to get off of the couch to get that bag of chips that is sitting in the cupboard. This first begins with your idea and planning to get off the couch (which can be a feat in and of itself) all the way to exercising the control of your muscles to get you there. See what I mean? Important stuff. But you do most of this without even a consideration for how all of these things happen from a physiological standpoint.

The Prefrontal Cortex

The prefrontal cortex is what comprises most of the frontal lobes in humans. This is what is responsible for nearly everything you do that requires the planning and execution of an idea. This is why the prefrontal cortex is larger in human beings than in other primates and why they argue that human beings are more sophisticated in their interactions and planning than other primates. The prefrontal cortex is what is behind something called "executive functioning," which includes things like working toward goals and determining right from wrong. Most of our problem solving, goal setting and achieving, and processing complex emotions and abstract thoughts happens in this part of the brain. And guess what? It is still developing right up to about age 25. In the handy brain model, the prefrontal cortex is the space from your middle two fingernails down.

What is so cool about this particular time in your life—your teen and early adult years—is what Dr. Siegel calls the "reconstruction of the cortex," or what physiologically allows for "out of the box thinking to occur."[2] What does this mean? From a physiological point of view, you are in a better position at the age you are right now to be dreaming and scheming of amazing things for yourself and this world. But, sadly, this is being overshadowed by the fact that you are running around all stressed out about getting into college, so you are living in the reptile zone of your brain rather than making the best use of this time of reconstruction.

Stress and Your Brain

Stress is a natural part of life, and something we all handle differently. But how the brain is wired sometimes makes stressful situations feel even worse. Rick Hanson, psychologist, Senior Fellow of the Greater Good Science Center at UC Berkeley, and *New York Times* best-selling author, suggests that the brain is constantly working to help us achieve safety, satisfaction, and connection.[3] If these needs are not being met, the brain kicks into a different mode of operating.

According to Hanson, the brain developed two primary ways to meet these basic needs. He says that if your need for safety, satisfaction, and connection are generally met, the brain can return to a state of equilibrium or resting when the brain can repair and recover from these bouts of stress. When the brain feels this way, it is filled with peace, representative of feeling safe; contentment, an indication of feeling satisfied; and love, which represents connection. All of this is what Hanson calls the "Green Zone" or the brain's default mode when needs are met, allowing the brain to be in a calm state. The Green Zone is what makes you feel grounded, centered, peaceful, and like everything is all right. When you trigger your Green Zone, you can lower your sense of stress and lift your mood, in part because living in the Green Zone reduces blood pressure and strengthens your immune system.

There is also another setting in the brain when one of our needs—those of safety, satisfaction, and connection—is not met. The body either goes into fight or flight, or it goes into a deeply intense freeze mode, where the body systems shut down. This is the reptilian brain in action (from Dr. Siegel's handy model of the brain above), and what Hanson terms the "Red Zone."

The Red Zone is meant to be visited infrequently; that is, physiologically, our bodies are meant to only experience the Red Zone in brief bursts. This is because the Red Zone is your body's alarm or "go" mode. The Red Zone is not meant to be a place where we hang out and eat ice cream or look at flowers. This is because in the Red Zone, body systems are significantly interrupted and disturbed, and the body uses resources faster than it takes them in. Too much Red Zone living leads to problems like anxiety, panic attacks, hypervigilance, hypertension, problems with digestion, and poor sleep. Things essential to your body functioning—like your body strengthening its immune system—are put on hold. Even worse, the more you spend time in the Red Zone, the more your amygdala—an almond-shaped limbic system structure in your brain, which is the integrative center for emotions and responsible for detecting fear and preparing for emergency events—will be reactive to what it perceives as a threat. And guess what? With more activation, the amygdala just becomes more and more sensitive.[4] Yikes.

We need both the Green Zone and the Red Zone; that is, both the relaxing, calming elements of the Green Zone and the energizing elements of the Red Zone are critical to our existence as human beings. The essential piece to high level functioning is the balance of these systems. If these are out of balance, that is when we get into trouble. If you are in the Red Zone all the time, you turn into a crazy, hair-on-fire human being (you know the kind I am talking about). If you were only in the Green Zone, you might not have those bursts of energy necessary in the final push of an athletic event or a project or to run quickly from a burning building. Yep, you need both.

Your goal is what Dr. Rick Hanson and Dr. Rick Mendius call "aliveness and centeredness," which is the basis of peak performance.[5] For a balanced and rich life, and for peak performance, you want a foundation of Green Zone activity with some Red Zone sprinkled in for excitement.

Allostatic Load

Our bodies can handle hanging out in the Red Zone for a stretch, but if we hang out too long there, having Red Zone experiences over a prolonged period of time (AP classes anyone?), these experiences start adding up and begin doing significant damage to our bodies both physically and mentally. Allostatic load is the physiological consequences, or the "wear and tear" on the body, which grows the more you are exposed to repeated and chronic stress. "Oh," you might think, "I am not stressed *all the time*," or "I can handle the stress." But can you?

In the 19th century, a series of science experiments resulted in the suggestion that if a frog is placed in boiling water, it will jump out. Alternatively, if it is placed in cold water that is slowly heated to boiling, it will not perceive the small but fatal changes to its environment and slowly will be cooked to death. While today there is some question about the validity of such experiments, this still offers a useful metaphor because it illustrates the manner in which damaging changes can slowly creep up on you. In the case of allostatic load, or being too far in the Red Zone for too long, it is the same thing. Pretty soon you have no idea how far you are into the Red Zone, and you are a boiled frog.

Why All This Weird Brain Stuff Matters

It is the middle prefrontal cortex that gives us that internal knowing through the wisdom of the body. This might strike some as a little freaky, but, in fact, this deep wisdom or knowing, or what we often refer to as a "gut feeling," is really important in seeking your future path. It is a different form of knowing than the purely logical one we often come to value and rely upon. Reasoning is not just logical; it also is (and should be) heart felt.

The trouble is that when we burn hot in the limbic areas of our brains, we shut down our access to this internal knowing. We also have a hard time accessing any ability to be reflective. Dr. Siegel talks about this ability to be reflective in the context of what he calls "three legs of a tripod": openness, observation, and objectivity.[6] I call these Vulnerability, Vision, and View. Consider how each of these relates to the process of college admission.

Vulnerability

When our brains are hijacked, it is very challenging to allow the unfolding of the college admissions process. What happens is that students and parents become married to a particular outcome, or a way things "should go" or "should be." If you are in a calm emotional state, you can more readily release your preconceived notions of who you are and who you should (or must) be in the college admissions process and instead allow the process to unfold as it will. In accessing vulnerability, parents and students can connect in a heart-centered way about their independent and collective dreams for the future. Also, in vulnerability, students write better essays and are more comfortable with being themselves.

Vision

Vision in the context of college admissions, is about allowing for the larger context of the narrative you are in to help inform your process and your thoughts about college admissions. Rather than the idea that you will have somehow "arrived" in gaining admission to a school, the idea is more that you are supporting yourself toward your dreams and vision of your future. It goes without saying that you also cannot be a reflective observer of your experience if you have been hijacked by the process itself.

View

Finally, with the brain hijacked, it is absolutely impossible for students and their families to have the type of perspective that is needed for college admissions to be a healthy process. In discussing "view," I am referring to the 10,000-foot view. This allows room for students to gain perspective on the process in which they are engaged, to understand how the process itself will assist them in becoming more fully themselves with clarity about what it is that they want.

If you want to really geek out, check out the Selected Resources section of this book, which provides links to Dr. Siegel's work. Basically, that guy is a brainy superhero. If that's a thing. Well, let's make it a thing. Boom. Done.

Why This Matters to Your Future Process

You may have guessed already where I am headed with this. When I see all this cool stuff that is informing our thinking about people in their optimal states, and then I think about the college admissions process, there is a serious disconnect. If you are always in the panic state—the fight or flight response—it is very difficult for you to access all parts of your brain as you are thinking about your future, let alone apply any self expression or creativity. Layer on top of this the panic that parents are feeling—including their own reptilian brain responses—and, well, you have a recipe for a prehistoric meltdown.

This is why all this doom and gloom talk, while certainly feeding the industry, really isn't productive for you in thinking about your future. Even worse, it is creating a reptilian, fear-based culture. I am not sure about you, but the future seems a lot less fun when thinking about your future from your reptilian brain. Though the reptilian part of our brain is certainly useful when we are being chased by a wild animal, the truth is that you really want access to all parts of your brain, and celebrate your out-of-the-box thinking, when you are thinking about applying to college and your future in general. This is what allows for forward momentum and a positive outlook on you and your gifts and the many things you have to offer the world.

Sleep

All this Red Zone living also negatively impacts your ability to get the rest you require. Teens need a *minimum* of 8 1/2 hours of sleep a night, but only 15 percent of teenagers report sleeping this much.[7] The National Sleep Foundation found that late nights not only impact academic performance but also emotional well-being. So all of those extra hours spent late at night studying Mandarin or practicing your cello are having a very negative effect on your body.

Though studies show adults and teens in industrialized nations are becoming more sleep deprived, the problem is most acute among teens. A 2006 National Sleep Foundation poll, the organization's most recent survey of teen sleep, indicates more than 87 percent of U.S. high school students get far less than the recommended eight to 10 hours.[8] Worse, the amount of time teens sleep is decreasing, posing a serious threat to their academic performance, health, and safety.[9]

We need sleep because of its restorative impact on our bodies. Without it, you can become irritable and tense. More importantly, not sleeping wreaks havoc on your body systems, throwing off your circadian rhythms and sleep patterns. Then you over compensate with substances like caffeine. Pretty soon, a lack of sleep has triggered a vicious cycle with a compounding snowball effect.

According to the UCLA Sleep Disorders Center, the sleep problems teens face can begin long before they turn 13. The sleep habits and changing bodies of 10 to 12 year olds are closely linked to sleep in the teen years.[10] Something else to note: The sleep patterns of teens also are firmly set in their lives, making it very difficult for teens to change. For this reason, any sleep problems that take hold in the teen years are often carried into adulthood.

And what about these goals you have for your future? Sleep impacts those, too. Good sleep helps support your willpower and follow through. Author Frank Ryan argues that not getting enough sleep can impact your willpower in two ways:

1) It negatively impacts your mental concentration and short-term memory

2) It makes you more emotionally sensitive and reactive, especially to negative events[11]

Obviously being able to sustain, attend to, and remember things is important to creating the life you want. And the ability to balance your emotional reactivity to set backs is also of critical importance.

In her article "Among Teens, Sleep Deprivation is an Epidemic," Ruthann Richter writes, "Sleep deprivation increases the likelihood teens will suffer myriad negative consequences, including an inability to concentrate, poor grades, drowsy-driving incidents, anxiety, depression, thoughts of suicide and even suicide attempts. It's a problem that knows no economic boundaries." Research shows that sleep problems among adolescents are a major risk factor for suicidal thoughts and death by suicide. According to some studies, the link between sleep

"

I lost about **30 pounds** my **senior year** of **high school** and **averaged** about **six hours** of sleep a night. It **wasn't** that **big** of a **deal** at the time because I was young and **all** of **my peers** were **experiencing** the **same** level of **stress**, so I found it to be **normal.**

STUDENT VOICE

"

and suicidal thoughts is strong, regardless of whether a teen is depressed or has abused drugs or alcohol.[12] Simply put, a lack of sleep makes it difficult to make good decisions, makes it impossible to feel well, and makes everything seem worse than it is.

High Levels of Cortisol=Depression?

All this Red Zone living and lack of sleep impacts one's cortisol levels. Cortisol is the body's stress hormone and is secreted at higher levels during your body's "fight or flight" response. These high levels of cortisol, which are brought on by stress, are also linked to depression. The study involved 96 adolescents with no previous history of depression or other psychiatric disorders. The sleep cycles and cortisol levels of participants were recorded and then monitored for five years. At the conclusion of the study, researchers found that "adolescents with higher cortisol levels were more likely than others to become depressed."[13]

Having explored some of the ways this system is having a negative impact on your physical health, it is now time to explore how the Culture of Crazy is impacting your mental health.

The Mental Toll

In a 2014 article in the *San Jose Mercury News*, Cristy Dawson, an assistant principal of Los Altos High, said the following about students in the ultra-competitive college-going culture: "They're not expected to be great; they're expected to be stupendous."[14] Because of this competitive environment and the existing perception about what admission to college requires, you, eager to gain admission, fall in line with what you believe is expected of you, working yourself relentlessly, often to the point of exhaustion. Elite college cultures have built their reputations on the seemingly effortlessness act of working oneself to the bone while appearing flawless. At Stanford, it's called the Duck Syndrome—or the appearance of gliding effortlessly and calmly across the water while paddling like crazy below the surface. At University of Pennsylvania, it's the Penn Face—the effort to act happy and confident even when one is depressed or stressed. In fact, the Penn Face is so pervasive that it shows up in skits performed at first-year orientation.[15]

The result of all of this exhaustive activity? We are producing an entire generation of students facing a mental health crisis. According to the American College Health Association (2013), 32 percent of students say they have felt so depressed "that it was difficult to function."[16] Another 10 percent of students reported they "frequently felt depressed," up from 6.1 percent in 2009, and the highest percentage of students reporting feeling that level of depression since 1988. In 2014, the American Freshman Survey, an annual report published by the Cooperative Institutional Research Program at the Higher Education Research Institute at UCLA, now entering its 50th year, reported the lowest rate in emotional health of college students since the survey began in 1985. The responses came from approximately 153,000 full-time, first-year students at 227 four-year public and private institutions. Rating their emotional health in relation to other people their age, only 50.7 percent of the students reported that their emotional health was "in the highest 10 percent" of people or "above average."[17]

Some believe this is a trend that is only impacting youth of wealthy and educated families, or those tenacious and driven students who plan to attend top schools; in fact, though, the trend cuts across in-

MENTAL HEALTH CONCERNS AMONG COLLEGE STUDENTS

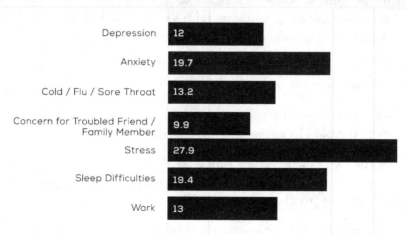

The Percentage of Students Reporting the Following Factors are Impacting Their Academic Success

Depression	12
Anxiety	19.7
Cold / Flu / Sore Throat	13.2
Concern for Troubled Friend / Family Member	9.9
Stress	27.9
Sleep Difficulties	19.4
Work	13

ACCORDING TO THE FALL 2013 AMERICAN COLLEGE HEALTH ASSOCIATION NATIONAL COLLEGE HEALTH ASSESSMENT SURVEY

come level. It also cuts across social class, race and ethnicity, and even academic ability. Educators and psychologists are reporting earlier and earlier incidents of negatively-impacted mental health. In her article, "Teen Health: Depression, Anxiety and Social Phobias Rising in Kids, Educators Say," Sharon Noguchi (2014) writes, "Educators are seeing more and more students suffering from depression, anxiety and social phobia. The acuity of mental illness among students has sharpened, they say, and it's striking even younger children, though many quietly bear the stress for years before snapping."[18]

In short, this is a problem that stands to threaten and engulf an entire generation of our best and brightest. Anxiety disorders have increased. Depression has increased. As students have worked themselves to the bone, both they and we have witnessed their mental health escape like sand through their fingers. Says one Los Altos student, "I was raised on how to sell myself, which buttons to press, which phrases to drop," she added, until one day "everything just shattered."[19]

Failing to recognize that we have a systemic problem on our hands, and remaining silent because of the social stigma, students and families often struggle with this alone, believing it is only an issue in their specific household rather than a symptom of the prevailing culture and trends that require our attention.

But, as a 2014 survey reveals, families are not alone. Consider these disturbing trends in mental health as offered by the National Survey on College Counseling Centers:

- 94 percent of directors reported that recent trends toward a greater number of students with severe psychological problems continue to be true on their campuses.

- 89 percent of directors noted an increase in anxiety disorders in the past five years.

- 58 percent of directors noted an increase in clinical depression over the past five years.

- 86 percent of directors reported that there has been a steady increase in the number of students arriving on campus that are already on psychiatric medication.[20]

High performing schools notably absent from the list of respondents include Stanford, MIT, and Harvard, to name just a few.[21]

When parents and students come to me facing some of these challenges, I share these statistics, not to frighten families, but to help encourage families to consider a more sane way of engaging in the college admissions process, the same one I am offering to you in this book.

Mental Health Counseling

These trends in diminished mental health are showing up at earlier and earlier ages and are carrying straight through elementary, middle, and high schools and on to college campuses. Colleges are reporting that mental health counseling on campuses is at an all time high. In a 2014 *USA Today* article, "Students Flood College Counseling Offices," Kip Alishio, Director of Student Counseling at Miami University, said, "The mental health common cold for this generation of students is anxiety disorder, whereas for previous generations it was depression."[22] Numerous statistics serve to underscore this point: As just one example, in 2014, Tulane's Counseling and Psychological Services Center saw 40 percent more students in the fall semester than in 2013.[23] Just one example to illustrate the importance of availability and quality of counseling on a college campus is the tragic story of Madison Holleran, a University of Pennsylvania freshman track star, who committed suicide in January 2014. The excessive wait time at Penn's counseling center is sometimes referred to as the reason for her death. According to Nina Golgowski in a recent *New York Daily News* article, the controversy surrounding Holleran's death is that although she sought care before she took her own life, she was given an intern and told she had to wait two weeks for a counselor.[24] In the aftermath of Holleran's death, Holleran's former teacher, Edward Modica, argued this is unacceptable. Modica is now working to pass a law to make it a requirement for colleges to list the number of suicides and suicide attempts on campuses annually and to provide certified suicide prevention personnel.

Holleran's story is not the exception. Tragically, Holleran was the third of six University of Pennsylvania students to commit suicide over a 13-month period. According to *The Stanford Daily*, 23 percent of students considered suicide in 2014.[25] At the time I am writing this, six MIT students have committed suicide in the past 14 months, leaving MIT's suicide rate to surpass the national average both last year and this year. This past year, Tulane lost four students. Appalachian State lost three. In 2014, George Washington University had four. The College of William and Mary had four, and a total of eight since 2010.[26]

According to the national student organization, Active Minds, nearly 50 percent of college students say they have felt so depressed in

"

Mental health facilities **were available**, but **most** of **my friends** who were **seeing a therapist** through the **college discouraged** any of **our other friends** to go because of how **terrible** the **staff handled most** situations. I **never went to see** a **therapist** through my **college** because of **that.**

STUDENT VOICE

"

the last 12 months that is was difficult to function, and 66 percent of students who need assistance don't get any.[27] And lest you believe this is a relatively new phenomenon, it isn't. In 2009–2010, Cornell had six suicides. Yale and Bard lost students to suicide that same year, and five students from elite Palo Alto high schools took their own lives. A 2003 article in the *Harvard Crimson* reported that "nearly half of the Harvard College student body felt depressed during the last academic year, and almost 10 percent of undergraduates reported that they had considered suicide," citing the results of a survey released by Harvard University Health Services.[28]

Professionals suggest that it isn't right to connect these suicides to over-pressured kids. According to Victor Schwartz, medical director of the Jed Foundation, which assists colleges to address mental health and improve their suicide prevention programming, "There's actually no empirical evidence at this point that schools that are more competitive or more pressured actually have higher rates of suicide deaths than other colleges." He states, "With undergraduates, the information we have suggests more that suicidal behavior is more often associated with relationship or family problems."[29] According to an April 2015 *Washington Post* article, Kelly Crace, the Associate Vice President for Health and Wellness at the College of William & Mary, cautioned "that it is easy to over-connect academic stress and the risk of suicide" when, in fact, "it is actually a low predictor of suicidal feelings." He says the best predictor is a long history of mental health issues.[30]

While the arguments of Schwartz and Crace are ones often heard, there is no question that increased stress and pressure are exactly that: increased stress and pressure. Given the extreme rise in both depression and anxiety, we have to recognize that *something* is happening. And, of course, any additional stress has an impact on students who may already be in a vulnerable state.

Consider the words of a 2013 graduate of the College of William & Mary. In an email to the *Washington Post* on the suicides at her alma mater, and reported on in an April 2015 *Washington Post* article, she wrote, "I don't know— I cannot presume to know—why these students chose to take their own lives." She continued, "But maybe, just maybe, it had to do with a feeling of worthlessness, of suffocation, of loneliness. This is what I felt, to a lesser extent, during my time on campus. I felt the need to constantly prove myself—the need to show that I belonged to this renowned college and was worthy of both its academics and its people. I know what its like to have to keep up— and to feel like a failure when I don't."[31] Another alum had a similar response in an Open Letter to the College of William & Mary on April 16, 2015:

> Now, as an alumna, I readily admit that each individual student helps to foster a stressful, stress-feeding environment. We feed off the stress from each other, and use the pressure put forth by our professors to drive our work. Everyone's had the conversation around exam time that escalates into a competition of "who's more stressed?" It gets to a point where you can't even mention your worry without hearing the busier agenda of each person around you. And as much as we hate it, we continue to do so to validate not only our own self-pity, but to have others validate our hard work.[32]

College Magazine recently provided their rankings of the Top 10 Most Stressful Colleges.[33] No real suprises here. Some of the country's elite colleges top the charts as the most stressful environments.

College Magazine's
TOP 10 MOST STRESSFUL COLLEGES

10. University of Pennsylvania

9. Northwestern University

8. Washington University in St. Louis

7. Cornell

6. NYU

5. Wake Forest

4. MIT

3. Tulane

2. Stanford

1. Harvard

Not Just Elite Campuses

Much attention is paid to suicide at elite colleges. Dr. Ali Benazir's 2010 article, "How to prevent your Ivy League Child from Becoming Suicidal" serves to underscore this fact, but the problem is widespread and indeed prevalent on all types of campuses.[34] While suicide at elite, highly competitive colleges is certainly a concern, this tragic scenario plays itself out in colleges of all kinds.

According to the Center for Disease Control and Prevention, youth suicide results in approximately 4,600 deaths each year, and suicide is the third leading cause of death for youth ages 10–24. But these numbers only account for part of the problem and do not include the thousands of children who attempt suicide but are unsuccessful. An often undiscussed and little known fact is the actual number of those who try to commit suicide. Each year, approximately 157,000 youth between the ages of 10 and 24 receive medical care for self-inflicted injuries, sometimes resulting in severe and debilitating consequences, in the attempt to end their lives.[35]

A 2011 nationwide survey of youth in grades 9–12 in public and private schools in the United States (U.S.) found that 16 percent of students reported seriously considering suicide, 13 percent reported creating a plan, and 8 percent reported having made an attempt to take their own lives in the 12-months prior to the survey.[36] And the numbers in recent years have only worsened.

Not surprisingly, these disturbing statistics have led to increased attempts to address the issue. The 2013 National Survey of College Counseling Centers reported an increase in the percentage of campuses that provide services thought to be essential for addressing suicidal behavior. This included 82 percent of campuses providing programs for faculty, coaches, advisers, and resident assistants (up from 8 percent the previous year), and 78 percent reported the use of stress reduction programs (up 9 percent from the previous year).[37]

The Most Disturbing Fact of All

Despite these harrowing statistics, according to a survey conducted by The Jed Foundation, more than half of all parents say that a school's mental health services had little or no influence on their family's college selection process.[38] In other words, if students ran into trouble, they would be uninformed as to whether or not there were onsite services to help. Knowing this information is critical.

According to the 2014 National Survey on College Counseling Centers, 30 percent of centers report that (with some exceptions) they limit the number of counseling sessions students are allowed. Forty three percent do not have a specified limit on sessions but promote their center as a short-term counseling service, and 28 percent tend to see students as long as it takes to resolve the student's presenting issues but will make external referrals when deemed clinically advisable.[39] Holleran's experience provides a cautionary tale.

In addition to the services that are provided through the counseling center, it has become enough of a crisis that schools and organizations have finally started to address the issue.

The Stigma of Mental Health

Though there is no question that these disturbing trends exist and continue their meteoric rise, they often go unacknowledged. Many students do not want to be identified as depressed because of the stigma of mental illness. "I've had parents refuse to sign permission for counseling for one boy," said Helen Hsu, a supervisor at the city of Fremont's Youth and Family Services, which provides therapists to several area schools. Also according to Hsu, "They were afraid it would negatively affect his college application."[40] This stigma leads to a culture of keeping these issues private and to addressing them as "one-off" incidents, rather than recognizing them as the symptoms of the systemic problem they are.

Increasingly, efforts are being made to break down the stigma of mental illness and to help students understand that asking for help is OK. The resource section at the end of this book highlights a few of the efforts underway, including those supported by Active Minds, the Jed Foundation, Project Lets, Inc., and Project Semicolon, to name only a few.

That any of these efforts exist, let alone all of them, is a monumental step in the right direction. And with the efforts increasing to address the sometimes tragic results of struggling with mental health issues, we also must seek to address the issue at its core. We can no longer ignore the evidence of the public health crisis we face. With anxiety disorders and depression on the rise, we have an obligation to recognize the consequences of the system we have created.

Why This State of Mental Health Impacts the
Future of Students

Not surprisingly, a lack of sleep, stress, depression, anxiety, and any other negative impact on one's mental health inhibits students from fully engaging in the future that awaits them. If you are already struggling to get up in the morning or to complete the pile of homework that you have, making decisions about your future adds another layer of complexity and stress, often leading students to feel even more overwhelmed – especially if you already struggle with depression or anxiety. Says Laura Gumbiner, a therapist who specializes in treating teen depression and anxiety, "I have met with adolescents who already struggle to find the motivation to get up every morning to attend school, complete school assignments, and engage socially. Most of these students are not in a place to make long-term decisions about college or their career path; it will only make them feel more overwhelmed."[41]

These challenges carry from college admissions to college campuses right on to students' careers. Consider Vernon Zunker who has argued that issues of mental health may interfere with career problem-solving and decision making.[42] This makes sense, doesn't it? If students are always walking around in the Red Zone, they are not making decisions from their healthiest state. In another related study, Jerry Walker and Gary Peterson studied 158 college students enrolled in a career development course. The results indicated that "career thoughts and occupational indecision were related to depression symptoms, with decision-making confusion being the best predictor."[43] This epidemic of depression—the same depression that many of these students are carrying from elementary, middle, and high schools into college—is resulting in career confusion. This is an alarming trend. We simply cannot have our "best and brightest" confused when it comes to what gifts they have to offer the world.

Of course, clients seeking college or career counseling come with widely varying degrees of distress related to their challenges. And, as I have shown in presenting the statistics on the increase in anxiety and depression, these challenges are very much a part of the current environment. According to researchers Janet Lenz, Gary Peterson, Robert Reardon, and Denise Saunders, the presence of mental health issues can contribute significantly to career seeking and career decision-making challenges.[44] Clients who experience career decision-making difficulty, for example, often exhibit behaviors that suggest possible mental health issues such as depression or anxiety.[45] Moreover, individuals with depression often report difficulty in such areas as memory, attention, and decision making.[46] Because of this, career counseling not only should offer high degrees of value in these particular areas, but also should provide a more holistic approach to mental health services and referrals.[47]

Because mental health issues often interfere with the progress of one's schooling and career, it is critical that mental health issues be addressed, not only as part of an individual's college and career counseling, but also in the structure of the larger system – and as soon and as young as possible. It has become critical for parents, students, and school personnel to take mental health into consideration as they work to obtain a more comprehensive and holistic range of services that translate to meaningful college and career guidance.

Is This the Platform on Which to Launch Our Young Adults?

We have now established that operating from a state of anxiety or of depression can have a negative impact on you physically as well as on your mood, memory, and ability to make decisions. You recognize the process of applying to college as one steeped in competition and rooted in fear and anxiety, sometimes to devastating and deadly ends. And, if you tie this back to the previous chapters, you see that all of this is the result of an absurd system!

In examining the highly competitive experience of applying to college or of attending a college where competition and stress is the cultural norm, the problems with the existing approach and structures become evident. When you are engaged in competition, the reptilian parts of the brain are activated—yes, that same fight or flight response you might have if you were being chased down the street by a pterodactyl is what is happening in your brain. You are living in the Red Zone. The problem with competition is that it is driven by fear. Fear and stress can lead to depression and anxiety, and, as you have seen, this can lead to devastating and sometimes deadly results. And this is really the last place you want to live when you are thinking about college admissions or your future.

Summary

- The "Red Zone"—where the body either goes into fight or flight; or it goes into a deeply intense freeze mode, where the body systems shut down—is meant to be visited infrequently.

- Red Zone living also impacts one's cortisol levels. These high levels of cortisol, which are brought on by stress, are also linked to depression.

- Hanging out in the Red Zone negatively impacts one's sleep. Good sleep helps support your willpower and follow through. Not getting enough sleep can impact your willpower in two ways: 1) It negatively impacts your mental concentration and short-term memory and 2) It makes you more emotionally sensitive and reactive, especially to negative events.

- Eighty-seven percent of U.S. high school students get far less than the recommended eight to 10 hours of sleep. A lack of sleep can lead to numerous negative consequences, including an in ability to concentrate, poor grades, drowsy-driving incidents, anxiety, depression, thoughts of suicide and even suicide attempts.

- Elite college cultures have built their reputations on the seemingly effortlessness act of working one self to the bone while appearing flawless. This is creating a world in which many students lose their way.

- Trends in diminished mental health are showing up at earlier and earlier ages and are carrying straight through elementary, middle, and high schools and on to college campuses.

- Anxiety and depression on campuses are at an all time high. Eighty-nine percent of university counseling directors noted an increase in anxiety disorders in the past five years and 58 per cent noted an increase in clinical depression over the past five years.

- Suicide rates on college campuses are disturbingly high.

- University counseling centers often cannot handle the high demand for services, leaving students without help or with limited support and in a state of vulnerability.

- Despite the rise in anxiety and depression on college campuses, according to a survey conducted by The Jed Foundation, more than half of all parents say that a school's mental health services had little or no influence on their family's college selection process.

Chapter Five:
Questioning Our Assumptions

"The key to wisdom is this—constant and frequent questions, for by doubting we are led to question and by questioning we arrive at the truth."
— Peter Abelard

Earlier in the book I stated how important it was to take a balcony view of our approach to college admissions. In the same way it can be hard to see the interconnections of the parts and pieces of a system, identifying the function or purpose of a system also can be challenging. This is because, in the words of Donella Meadows, "A system's function or purpose is not necessarily spoken, written, or expressed explicitly, except through the operation of the system."[1] Even in the cases where a system has a stated function or purpose (like a university's Mission Statement or Values Statement), you cannot be certain that is the actual function or purpose; that is, though this may be the communicated function or purpose, the reality may be much different. Because of this, often the best way to identify a system's purpose is to observe it and watch the way it behaves.

That is what we are doing by taking a look at the current system of college admissions. By examining it and thinking about it, we are acknowledging there is a certain way this system behaves, and a certain way those within the system act. In part, this is built on our beliefs that this is the way the system *must* behave and on the assumptions and mental models we have for how to engage with the system. In the case of college admissions, we are caught up in a system that promotes a culture of fear and competition. Our assumptions are that without taking part in the Culture of Crazy, we are somehow not doing enough to see our students into the best path for their futures.

But, often it is our assumptions that get us into trouble. These assumptions (also known as mental models) are very powerful forces in the decisions we make. Similarly, values and beliefs near and dear to our heart also can lead us down the wrong path. I know this probably sounds a little strange (aren't we supposed to have values and beliefs, after all?), but sometimes we run these unconsciously, and they influence our actions. By not examining the values and beliefs that drive our actions, we may be causing ourselves more heartburn than is necessary.

To stop contributing to our own problems, and to expose the game of smoke and mirrors in college admissions for what it is, you need look no further than your nearest and dearest iceberg to gain a little understanding.

The Iceberg

Imagine an iceberg. Everything above the waterline is clearly visible, but you have no idea of the contours and magnitude that lie below the surface.

Consider the case of the Titanic. It sank not because of what the captain could see, but because of what could not be seen. This is a good metaphor since systems sometimes sink based on what is below the waterline.

One of the best ways to understand systems thinking is through the following image, adapted from the work of Peter Senge, a professor at MIT and one of my heroes.[2] The image serves to underscore the point that so many of the actions we take and the events we experience are rooted in patterns of behavior, systemic structures, and mental models.

Everything above the waterline is what we observe as events or activities, presumably moving toward specific goals. Everything below the waterline is everything we cannot see, and everything at play that is driving the events and activities above the waterline. No matter how much we try to change the events above the water, we really cannot change them if they are deeply rooted in patterns of behavior, systemic structures, and mental models.

Mental Models

Mental models are our ideas about how some part of the world works. This can include things that really have nothing to do with you directly (like how the universe works or how a car engine runs) or things that you are involved in (like your ideas about how to best earn money or what success is). These can be really helpful, like in the case where you are making more sense of the world, or they can be very destructive and nasty little fellers, like when they keep you stuck in

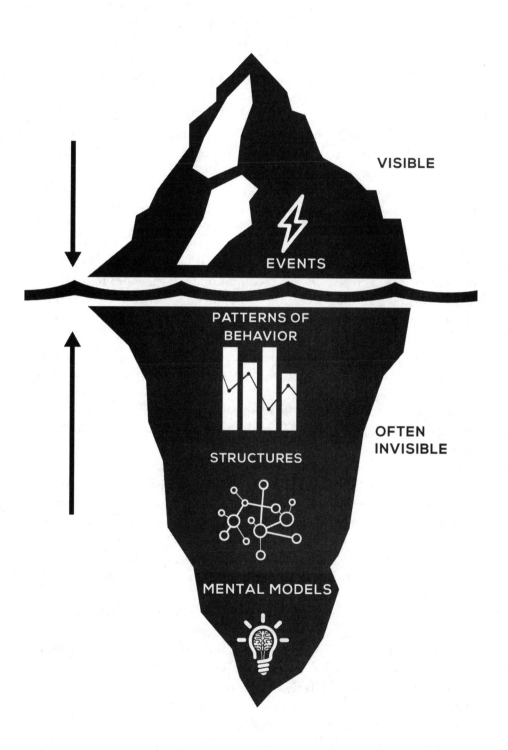

ways of thinking and being that do not serve you (or even run counter to what you hope for yourself). To complicate things further, not only do we create mental models on our own all the time (it's how we make sense of the world), but then we share them with others. This is probably why Einstein once said, "To break a mental model is harder than splitting an atom."

Some suggest that the cognitive psychologist Kenneth Craik first came up with the more contemporary idea of mental models in the 1940s when he proposed that people turn external events into internal models and then use these models as the basis for their reasoning and beliefs in particular situations. It is these models, then, that guide people's actions. Peter Senge, the MIT professor I mentioned earlier, popularized this idea in 1990 with the publishing of his book, *The Fifth Discipline*, in which he describes mental models as "deeply held internal images of how the world works, images that limit us to familiar ways of thinking and acting." In a subsequent book, Senge and his colleagues also wrote, "Very often, we are not consciously aware of our mental models or the effects they have on our behavior."[3] So the point of this chapter and the exercises contained herein is for you to become more aware of the mental models you hold and how they impact your behavior. Then you can decide if instead you'd like to explore alternatives.

Do you remember teachers telling you that in 1492 people believed that the world was flat until Columbus arrived in America, which helped prove that the world was, in fact, round? Well, even though this is a myth (if you think I am kidding, look it up), this story still helps to illustrate mental models. If you had believed the Earth was flat and then later came to learn that the Earth was round, it would upend a mental model. Similarly, if you think that you cannot get an "A" in math, but then you get an "A" in math, it changes your story about how the world works. For these reasons, mental models can sometimes get you into trouble. This is why you have to become conscious of them.

It is important to become aware of and reflect upon these mental models as oftentimes, we have no idea as to how they influence our decisions and behaviors. By clarifying and choosing the way we make meaning of our internal world, we shape our interactions in the external world. This is particularly true in the case of college admissions. As Senge et al. suggest, "We look for solutions that will 'fix' problems, as if they are external and can be fixed without 'fixing' that which is within us that led to their creation."[3] More simply, your ideas about

CHARACTERISTICS OF MENTAL MODELS

- Mental models reflect what a person thinks is true, but in many cases not what is actually true.

- Mental models impact what we see and what we hear.

- Mental models are often more simple than the thing or concept they represent.

- Mental models of others are easier to see than mental models of our own.

- Mental models are incomplete and constantly evolving.

how this works—you underlying values and beliefs—must first be examined before you will see or do something different.

Before you can fully realize the role you play in this larger system of college admissions, you must first recognize your role as an individual and the fact that you are having your own intrapersonal experience. Your own understanding of the mental model you hold about the experience becomes the starting point for future action.

The Ladder of Inference

To better understand the idea of mental models, let's dive even more deeply into them using the Ladder of Inference. First introduced in the 1970s by Harvard Professor Chris Argyris, the Ladder of Inference is a really helpful tool to understand how we draw conclusions about the world we live in. The Ladder of Inference helps describe how you move from a piece of data (a comment made to you, something that you have observed or experienced, etc.) through a series of mental processes to a conclusion.[4]

This is how it works: Starting at the bottom of the ladder, you have "observable data and experiences." From there, we:

1) Select data based on our beliefs and prior experience

2) Interpret what they mean through our own personal and cultural lens

3) Apply existing assumptions, often without much thought about them

4) Draw conclusions based on our interpretation of facts and our assumptions

5) Develop beliefs based on these conclusions

6) Take actions on what seems "right" because the actions are based on what we believe

In other words, you start by selecting from the data, translate it into your own terms, make meaning of it, and then draw conclusions. This can be somewhat dangerous, because it all happens extremely quickly in your head, and you are likely unaware that you are only selecting some of the data. Nobody else sees your thought processes, or knows what stages you have gone through to reach your conclusions. All that they see is the action you take as a result.[5]

The Snowball Effect

Your beliefs tend to reinforce the data that you select and how you interpret it. This, then, becomes something called a positive feedback loop. But, in this case, "positive" does not necessarily mean "good." It means the data you select and how you interpret it becomes the feedback that drives the process forward. Think of a giant snowball, rolling down a hill and building on itself. This "snowball effect" serves to confirm what you already believe. Our beliefs have a big effect on how we select data and can lead us to ignore the facts altogether. Soon we are jumping to conclusions – by missing facts and skipping steps in the reasoning process. This can create either a really positive or very vicious cycle.

Understanding Relationships in the System

Let's dive more deeply into this by taking a look at how the parts and pieces impact one another in the current system of college admissions. To do so, I like to map them through the use of plus (+) and minus (-) signs to show increases and decreases (not positive and

I take **ACTIONS** based on my beliefs

I adopt **BELIEFS** about the world

I draw **CONCLUSIONS**

I make **ASSUMPTIONS** based on the meanings I added

I add **MEANINGS** (cultural and personal)

I select **"DATA"** from what I observe

OBSERVABLE "DATA" & EXPERIENCES (a videotape recorder might capture it)

The **REFLEXIVE LOOP** (our beliefs affect what data we select)

negatives). I also like to use an equation-like sentence to show relationships between factors and to uncover patterns. Here is an example of a sentence:

> As college admissions become more competitive **(+)**,
>
> the admissions process becomes more crazy **(+)**.

This example illustrates how the competition fuels the frenzy, and reciprocally, how the frenzy fuels the competition. Now let's add another factor.

If getting into a certain caliber of school is somehow a badge of honor in the world of parent or student success, this fuels the competition, thereby fueling the Culture of Crazy. Or, you can think of it the opposite way: The more crazy the culture, the more competitive getting in is perceived to be, the more it is considered a badge of honor to be accepted. Here is how those factors would look:

> As college admissions become more competitive **(+)**,
>
> the admissions process becomes more crazy **(+)**,
>
> and it becomes a (perceived) greater "badge of honor"
>
> to gain acceptance to an elite school **(+)**.

We can switch this one around, too.

> The more it is a perceived "badge of honor" to gain acceptance to an elite school **(+)**,
>
> the more crazy the college admissions process becomes **(+)**,
>
> and the more competitive entrance to such schools becomes **(+)**.

Let's do one more, but we will mix up the **(+)** and **(-)** a bit this time:

> The busier you are **(+)**,
>
> the less you have time for reflection **(-)**,
>
> the less you know yourself **(-)**,
>
> the less apt you are to be "on path" **(-)**.

Now you try some. What factors can you think of? Write them here.

_____

_____

_____

_____

_____

Now step back for a moment and reflect. What do your discoveries about the system and the way you may be engaging with it mean to you?

If, Then Exercise

Often mental models can be boiled down to "If, Then" thinking. The very best way to unearth them, then, is through exploring your "If, Then" thoughts.

Here are some examples:

- If I get good grades and do a gazillion activities, then I will get into a good college.

- If I get into a good college, then I will be successful.

Now it is your turn to create a few:

_____

_____

_____

_____

_____

_____

What insights do you have as a result of your "If, Then" thinking? What mental models do the statements reveal?

The What, How, Why Exercise

Another one of my favorite ways to unearth mental models is to back into them using the "What, How, Why" exercise.[6] Using the chart below, let's explore mental models by stepping into a place of deeper observation.

Think of someone involved in the process of college admissions, and apply this exercise to your observations.

WHAT?

These are your concrete observations. What is taking place? Do your best to only capture the details and refrain from making any assumptions. Write down only what you observe.

HOW?

With this question, you are attempting to observe how the person is doing what he or she is doing. Does it seem like a positive experience or a negative one? Use as many descriptive words as you can to describe the "how."

WHY?

Next, you are going to take a guess at why the person you are observing is doing what he or she is doing. In asking "why," you get to project your own interpretation and meaning onto what is happening. Take a guess as to what might be motivating the person you are observing and what emotions he or she might be having.

What? (What are they doing?)	**How?** (How are they doing it?)	**Why?** (Why are they doing it this way?)

From here, you can create statements that unearth some of the mental models you might hold; for example, the "What, How, Why" exercise might translate to your understanding through the creation of statements, like this one:

I observe someone
[INSERT WHAT]

by **[INSERT HOW]**

in order to
[INSERT WHY].

Create some of these statements based on your observations.

_____

_____

_____

_____

_____

What is helpful about creating these statements is that they often reveal the underlying assumptions you (and others) may hold.

In order to engage in the college admissions process in a more holistic way, you must have a systems view to understand all the various forces at play. In doing so, you must first identify the values and beliefs fueling the system and then you must decide if they are really yours, or if you have unconsciously been operating from the values and beliefs and the mental models you've inherited.

Systems: You Are What You Eat

My grandmother used to tell me "you are what you eat." Never has this been truer than in the case of college admissions. Let me explain.

Think of the current Culture of Crazy as a digestive system. As I have described in the first chapters of this book, more competition, more pressure, and more frenzied activity are the factors we "eat" (or the inputs to the system). All of this is not well digested, especially given the shortage of support for students as exacerbated by the shortage of counselors and lack of training they receive to support the admissions process. And what comes out the other side? What are the outputs of the system? Decreased physical and mental health. To understand this, refer to the graphic on the opposite page.

In other words, "garbage in, garbage out," as my grandmother liked to say.

A Different Approach

Isn't it high time we realize the impact of this destructive system on you, our youth, the greatest resource of our future? What if instead of placing the power in the hands of the colleges and the industries that have been created around this fear-based approach, you set about the process in a student-centered way? What if the power was placed back in the hands of placed back in the hands of you, the student, to own your next steps into your promising future? What if, in fact, a different approach to tackling this process is the solution we have been waiting for?

I've addressed how a systems approach is necessary to understand the mental models with which we are operating. You have unearthed some of those mental models you hold for yourself, and we are going

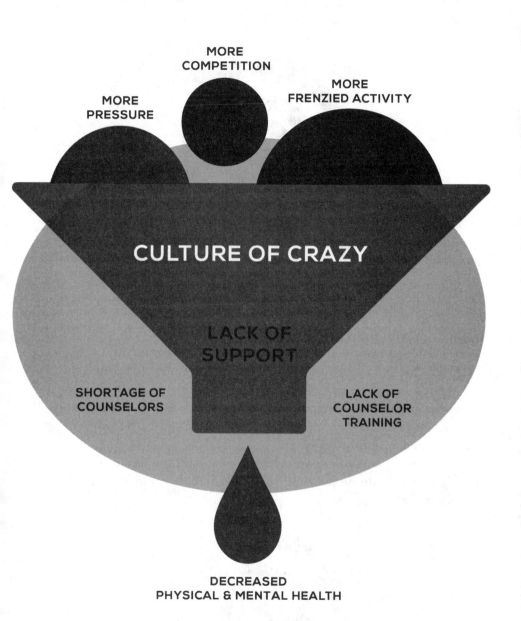

MORE
COMPETITION

MORE
PRESSURE

MORE
FRENZIED ACTIVITY

CULTURE OF CRAZY

LACK OF
SUPPORT

SHORTAGE OF
COUNSELORS

LACK OF
COUNSELOR
TRAINING

DECREASED
PHYSICAL & MENTAL HEALTH

to do more of that collectively here by looking at how one little tweak in how we have developed our mental models can change everything.

For a long time, we have been operating with select schools or a particular school at the center of students' efforts in the college admissions process, which looks like this:

By placing the school at the center of our universe and process, we build the system around it. With the school at the center, all activities relate to the effort for that school to be the driving force behind the actions we take—everything from how often we take the SAT or the manner in which it is prepared for, the activities in which we engage, the summer camps we sign up for, and so on. You get the picture. With this mental model, everything becomes organized around the school and the effort to be accepted. And let me now throw this in for thought: With there being a high level of criticism that the system itself is flawed, it is even more disturbing to think that we are organizing ourselves around this disordered process.

Now what happens if, instead, we place the student at the center of this effort. In doing this, college admissions starts to look much different. Let's take a look.

With the student at the center of the effort, the activities and efforts toward college admissions are not the singular focus, the student is. This, then drives a different way of engaging in the process; for example, with the student at the center and actually taking the student into account, we may factor the number of times a student takes the SAT based on much more than what it will take to get into a school. We see the student as a whole, capable being regardless of the school he or she attends; it becomes just one factor in his or her future – not the only factor. That becomes just one part of the larger ecosystem of the student.

So why not consider the radical notion of stopping the madness by placing the student—not the school— at the center of this effort?

Based on what I have experienced in my own life and what I have seen over the years in my students and clients, growth is a long-term prospect and a long-term commitment. It's much more than the school you select to attend or if you make a six-figure salary upon graduation. By putting you, the student, at the center of the target (rather than a particular school or set of schools), new things come to light—especially how we view and engage with the process itself. In making this shift, power is placed back in the hands of students and families. We then begin to reframe the way we think of this process, recognizing the starting point for the process, the very foundation on which it is built, must be revisited.

Chapter Six:
Revealing the Myths

"I'm a big fan of the misunderstood, the vilified, the underdog,
the breaking of myths."
—*Dominic Monaghan*

It has come time for all of us to challenge some of the prevailing beliefs about college admissions and recognize the ways in which there is room for more than one mental model in how we engage in the process. Much of the dialogue we hear about college admissions is based in fear and competitiveness. Indeed, there are statistics and movements that suggest another way of approaching college admissions is possible and is in progress, so it is time to widen the lens of what is available to you. Let's examine some of today's prevailing myths. My hope is that these will provide ample evidence for us to begin to question the "how it's always been done" and begin to see the alternatives to how we have (or have not) been serving students.

Myth #1: Getting into College is Harder Than Ever

To address the first of these prevailing myths—that getting into college has gotten harder—let's begin with a recent article by John Katzman. Katzman is the founder and CEO of Noodle, a website that provides advice on education. He is also the previous founder of The Princeton Review and 2U. In his September 11, 2014 *Washington Post* article entitled, "Relax. Getting into College has Actually Gotten Easier," he outlines the ways in which the competitive environment we promote is actually a bit of smoke and mirrors. Yes, Katzman acknowledges that in the case of the top 100 colleges, things have become increasingly competitive in the last 30 or so years—to the tune of a 22 percent decrease, from 54 percent in 1984 to 32 percent in 2012. And, yes, the acceptance rates at some of the elite institutions can make your fingers turn to rubber: 5 percent at Stanford, 6 percent at Harvard and Yale, and 7 percent at Columbia. You get the picture.

STUDENT ACCEPTANCE

Adapted from J.S. Katzman & Noodle (2014, November 23)

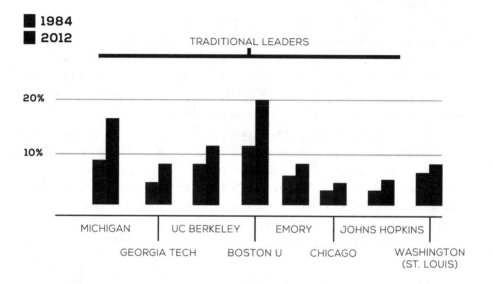

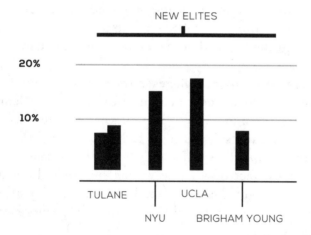

There are approximately **9%** more American students but **55%** more seats for them.

According to Katzman, two factors—early decision and the rise of electronic applications—means that, all else being equal, if a college accepted 30 percent of applicants 25 years ago, it would accept just 8 percent of applicants today.[1]

But even as this growth in applications to college has continued, even as nutty as it has become at some institutions and as the majority of colleges have reported an increase in the volume of applications, this trend has been offset by another fact: several top colleges, many of whom are considered selective (Berkeley, Michigan, and Boston University) or now are considered part of the elite ranks (USC, UCLA, and NYU), have gotten bigger. According to Katzman, "There are 55 percent more seats available at top colleges than there were when this class's parents applied 30 years ago. Even considering the increase in international applicants, there are 44 percent more seats for every American student than the early 1980s." Moreover, on average, nationwide, four-year institutions accepted about 65 percent of all students who applied for admission.[2]

Ahem.

That's right, folks. The Culture of Crazy is built on a lot of media hype and stirring up fear in our college-going students. Not only does Katzman argue that getting into college has actually gotten easier in the last 30 years, but the fact is that the majority of students who apply to college are, in fact, accepted.

Additionally, there are more colleges in the U.S. than ever before. According to the U.S. Department of Education's National Center for Education Statistics, the number of U.S. four-year colleges has increased by over a thousand schools since 1980.[3] Of course, the frenzy is stirred up by the competitiveness at only a handful of schools. But because this flies in the face of what prevailing culture and the media might otherwise have you believe, it is really worth contemplating why the fact that most students get in and that there now are more available seats isn't more widely known.

The Global Age

Beyond this, given the competitive environment and the high, high cost of higher education, there is a significant rise of students applying to institutions to obtain their degrees outside of the United States. This is an important piece of information, but it's often something parents and counselors don't know much about because the information is not readily available. According to a 2013 report from the Institute of

International Education, more than 46,500 U.S. students were pursuing full degrees abroad, with 84% enrolled in bachelor's or master's degrees and 16 percent in doctoral degrees. The top fields for degree study include the humanities, social sciences, physical and life sciences, and business and management.[4]

Why does this matter? Because with the world of colleges and universities overseas opened up to you, it considerably changes the ways you might engage in the college admissions process.

I talk more about the compelling reasons to investigate this as an option—including free tuition at some of these institutions—in Myth #5.

Community Colleges

Likewise, community colleges (also sometimes called junior colleges) have begun to play a significant role in gaining applicant interest and are becoming formidable competitors to four-year schools. These two-year schools provide more affordable options for post-secondary education.

According to the American Association of Community Colleges, 1,167 community colleges in America enroll more than 12.4 million students and source almost half of all undergraduates in the U.S.[5]

Not surprisingly, since the economic crash in 2008, attendance at community colleges has jumped significantly. But even with this rise, unlike some of their four-year counterparts, community colleges have been able to accommodate the need. Further, barriers to access are far fewer in the case of community colleges. According to the *Community College Review*, the average community college acceptance rate was 76 percent. Maine had the lowest acceptance rate at 52 percent and Arizona the highest at 92 percent.[6]

Think this option is only for a few? Or for those in very particular circumstances? Think again. Nearly half of all students graduating with a four-year degree in 2013-2014 benefitted from enrollment in a two-year institution. Nearly half! And, according to a report from the National Student Clearinghouse Research Center, 46 percent of all students who completed a four-year degree had been enrolled at a two-year institution at some point in the past 10 years. And get this: 65 percent of these students graduating attended at least three semesters at a community college.[7]

In many cases, community colleges offer a much more economic, flexible, and hands-on experience than many four-year institutions.

To give you a sense of the economics of this, the average annual tuition and fees at community colleges is $3,260, whereas at its four-year public, in-state counterparts, it is $8,890.[8] And it is no secret that many private institutions charge upwards of $60,000 annually. Moreover, community colleges have become a viable pathway to a four-year degree; not only are the schools far less expensive to attend, but they also have a reputation for smaller class sizes and a hands-on approach in providing support to students.

Beyond the affordability, the flexibility offered at these institutions means that people can continue to work or fulfill other obligations that otherwise might inhibit them from pursuing their education. About 60 percent of students at community colleges are enrolled part time, making it an ideal choice for those who have to work or have families or other commitments. Further, 62 percent of full-time students work, and 73 percent of part-time students hold jobs. Finally, the location of these schools—where the name "community college" is derived—is also important, allowing people to remain close to home or not incur the expense of living and pursuing school elsewhere.[9]

Something else to consider is the relationship that many community colleges have with industry. Not only are these schools sometimes faster to incorporative classes or training relevant to current trends in the economy, but they also form partnerships with companies and industries that lead to job training that can serve as a pipeline directly to jobs in a field in which one is interested.

Myth #2: Getting a College Degree Guarantees Your Success

A college degree always has been one of the gold standards of accomplishment. Not only is it important to the student who holds the degree, but it's also thought to be valuable to the employer and to society generally. But there is something we aren't yet accounting for.

From interviews with more than 30,000 graduates, the Gallup-Purdue Index measured the degree to which graduates have "great jobs," through successful and engaging careers, and if they are leading "great lives," by thriving in their overall well-being. The poll shows that a staggering 25 percent of U.S. college graduates "fail to thrive in their overall careers and lives."[10]

Gulp. Though some are not shocked by this statistic, I sure am. With all this hype about the promise of a college degree, one out of four kids that we send off to college with the promise of a bright future, doesn't, in fact, thrive? We don't advertise this statistic, of course, because it would upend the argument that has been made about the value of a college education. But when 25 percent of college graduates are failing to thrive even after obtaining the degree—and likely the large debt load that comes along with it—we have to pay attention.

This poll supports the argument that the value of a college degree really depends not on just obtaining one, but on the *experience* the student has in obtaining the degree. As part of the poll, Gallup identified six experiences in college, or what they refer to as the "Big Six," which account for the improved long-term success of graduates.[11]

THE BIG SIX

1) A professor who made them excited about learning

2) Professors who cared about them as a person

3) A mentor who encouraged them to pursue their goals and dreams

4) Worked on a long-term project

5) Had a job or internship where they applied what they were learning

6) Were extremely involved in extracurricular activities

According to Gallup, those graduates who experienced all six of the Big Six were significantly more likely than those who did not to strongly agree that college had prepared them for life beyond college. Further, those who experienced all six strongly agreed that they were engaged in work and thriving in all areas of well-being. Another important fact? Those who experienced the Big Six were rated significantly higher in completing their degree in four years or less.

"...why wouldn't we use the Big Six as a way to measure the success of schools far more than the ways we have traditionally established college rankings..."

On the following pages, let's look at how having these experiences correlated to measures of success translates to key college, work, and life outcomes.

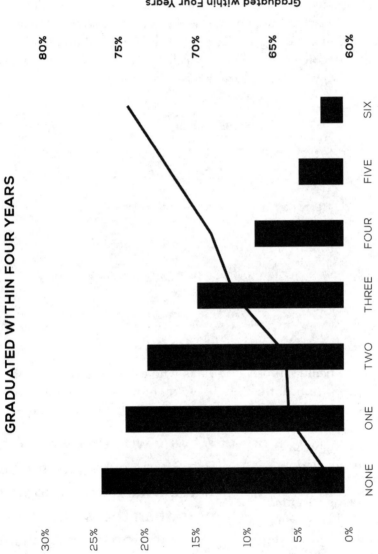

GRADUATED WITHIN FOUR YEARS

Graduated within Four Years

80%

75%

70%

65%

60%

Strongly Agree to "Big Six"

30%

25%

20%

15%

10%

5%

0%

NONE   ONE   TWO   THREE   FOUR   FIVE   SIX

Number of "Big Six" Experiences

Source: Gallup

ENGAGED AT WORK

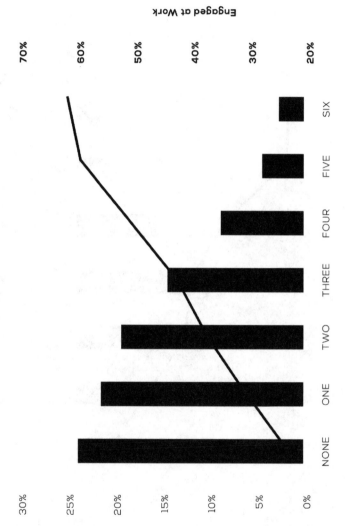

Engaged at Work

70%

60%

50%

40%

30%

20%

SIX

FIVE

FOUR

THREE

TWO

ONE

NONE

Number of "Big Six" Experiences

30%

25%

20%

15%

10%

5%

0%

Strongly Agree to "Big Six"

Source: Gallup

THRIVING IN ALL FIVE ELEMENTS OF WELL-BEING

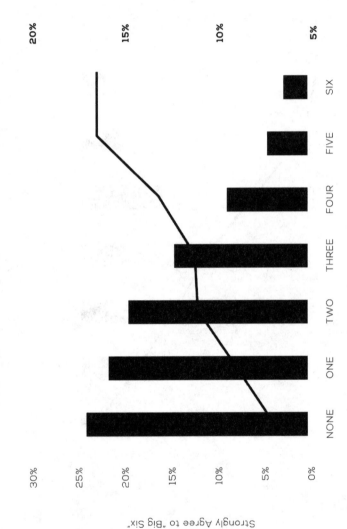

Thriving in All Five Elements of Well-Being

Strongly Agree to "Big Six"

Number of "Big Six" Experiences

Note: Free elements of well-being are purpose, social, financial, community & physical

Source: Gallup

If work engagement and well-being in life are two factors important to you in thinking about your future (and, boy, I sure hope they are), then all this hocus pocus hype around traditional college rankings needs a major facelift. According to Gallup, this data suggests that selectivity of a school or the myriad other ways we have traditionally measured college takes a back seat to "*what* students are actually doing during college and *how* they are experiencing it."[12] And, while these two areas are having the biggest impact on students' lives and careers, some students simply aren't experiencing these.

In other words, the world of excellent college experiences is likely much larger than you believe it to be! There are many, many places for you to have a successful college experience. This information should show you that the stress you feel from the pressure of getting into a certain type of school is unfounded. You can have the experiences described here at any number of schools.

At a minimum, this study should have far-reaching implications on how students make decisions about where to attend college, how colleges determine how best to serve their student bodies and how employers make hiring decisions. And one more question: why wouldn't we use the Big Six as a way to measure the success of schools far more than the ways we have traditionally established college rankings, which do not take into consideration the health and well being of students? Just saying…

Myth #3: You Have to Go to a Selective School to Be Successful

The Gallup-Purdue Index shows that the type of institution one attends matters less than the experiences he or she has there. The harrowing news: Only 3 percent of all the graduates studied had the types of experiences in college that led to stellar jobs and lives after college.

The study found that the types of schools graduates attended — whether they be small or large, very selective or less selective, public or private — "hardly matters at all to their engagement in the workplace or current well-being." Further, as many graduates from large, public universities as from small, private colleges are engaged in work and are thriving in all areas of well-being. The problem is there are very are very few people who fall into this category.

What makes the difference? Support and experiences in college. These had the most undeniable relationship to positive long-term outcomes for alumni. It wasn't the ranking of the school, not the number of times you took the SAT or your SAT scores, and not the stellar application résumé. Instead, the findings included the following:

- Just 14 percent of graduates strongly agree that they were supported by professors who cared, who made them excited about learning, and who encouraged their dreams

- Just 6 percent of graduates strongly agree that it was because of an internship or job that allowed them to apply what they were learning, they had worked on a long-term project, and had been actively involved in extra-curricular activities

- As mentioned above, just 3 percent of those studied strongly agreed that they'd had all six of these experiences during college.[13]

In 2005 and 2006, there were a number of articles published about the decline in CEO positions held by those graduating from the Ivies. A 2006 *Wall Street Journal* article reported on the results of a survey by executive recruiter Spencer Stuart that CEOs heading top Fortune 500 companies that attended Ivy League schools comprised only 10 percent. When the article was published, more CEOs had earned their degrees from the University of Wisconsin than from Harvard, the most represented Ivy school.[14] The same was true in 2008.

Moreover, several executives have argued that they were better prepared for business internally and externally in terms of customer relations by attending public universities. This is because such universities more closely represent the demographics of society, allowing students to form relationships and operate in an environment that may prepared them to meet the needs of a wider variety of individuals.

Successful businessman Warren Buffet has never been a fan of judging people by where they attended school. Says Buffet, "I don't care where someone went to school, and that never caused me to hire anyone or buy a business." Buffet himself graduated from the University of Nebraska—Lincoln.

Buffet's view of "name" schools reflects a growing trend nationally. A July 15, 2015 article in the *Huffington Post* served to underscore this point, profiling a law firm that actively does *not* hire Ivy League graduates. While there is still plenty of evidence to support that many of the U.S.'s top law firms recruit from Ivy League Institutions, there are some firms that are beginning to take a stand in a different direction — actively not hiring graduates from elite universities. Adam Reitman

Bailey, Founding Partner of Adam Reitman Bailey, P.C. and one of New York City's most prominent real estate attorneys—as well as a *New York Times* bestselling author—states: "Our hires come from the top of the classes of the second, third, or fourth tier law schools. We find these men and women we take under our wing to be more ambitious and more hungry to excel in the legal profession."[15]

Other recent books have addressed this myth. Deresiewicz more fully explores this in his book *Excellent Sheep: The Miseducation of the American Elite & The Way to a Meaningful Life.*[16] And Frank Bruni, in his recent book, *Where You Go Isn't Who You'll Be,* tells numerous stories of people who found terrific educations and created their own great futures at less selective schools.[17]

Current hiring practices also support this idea. In a 2014 Gallup Poll, business leaders were asked to rank the importance of four factors in hiring:

1) The amount of knowledge a candidate has in the field

2) The candidate's applied skills in the field

3) The candidate's college or university major

4) Where the candidate received his or her college degree

Any guesses on the two most important factors? Drum roll please…

A whopping 84 percent of the business leaders surveyed reported that the amount of knowledge a person has in a field was "very important," followed closely by a candidate's applied skills (79 percent). These two factors significantly outweighed the importance of one's college major—"very important" to only 28 percent—and where one received his or her college degree, which mattered only to 9 percent. In other words, U.S. businesses placed a far higher value on the amount of knowledge a candidate has in a field and his or her applied skills than where a candidate attended school or what his or her major was.[18]

But here is where it really gets interesting. The Gallup poll also posed the questions to the American public. While American adults agree with the importance of knowledge and applied skills (about 80 percent said that the knowledge and applied skills are "very important" to the managers making hiring decisions in organizations), an important distinction emerged. The prevailing public opinion is that

"

Taking the **SAT hardened me** and made me **determined not** to be **defined** by others, **especially** where **test scores** were **concerned.** When I **applied** to **graduate programs,** I applied only to **schools** that **didn't require** the **GRE.**

STUDENT VOICE

"

a person's college major and where he or she went to school matters much more than hiring managers believe it does; nearly half of American adults (47 percent) report that the major is a very important factor to managers making hiring decisions for organizations, and 30 percent—or more than three times as many as the 9 percent of managers—believe that where the candidate received his or her degree is "very important."[19]

This study indicates part of the reason for the prevailing culture of fear and also illustrates how things in the workplace have changed. Yes, it used to be that one's college major or where someone went to school was more influential in hiring decisions, but with the explosion of new ways to obtain knowledge and apply skills, hiring managers rely much less on these. It is time the American public recognizes that its perception does not match reality. It's time to update our thinking and to put those old mental models to rest.

Myth #4: You Have to be a Superhero to Get into College

Many of you believe that perfect SAT scores and a heroic load of activities determines everything. But this is not the case. In fact, a recent survey reports that more colleges and universities reduced or eliminated admissions testing over the past 12 months than in any other previous year. Many have no idea that there is a growing number of schools that do not require standardized test scores for admission. That's right! More than 850 accredited, undergraduate schools do not require the submission of ACT or SAT test scores. Beyond this, the ACT/ SAT optional list now includes more than 165 schools. And many of these schools are top-tier schools in their respective categories. Want more good news? More than one-third of the top-ranked national liberal arts colleges have test-optional policies, including Bowdoin, Middlebury, Wesleyan, Hamilton, Bates, Colby, Smith, Bryn Mawr, and Colorado College, all schools in the top 30 of *U.S. News and World Report's* college ranking list[20] (in case that sort of thing is important to you—though I hope by now, it isn't.)

Does this shock you? Not like electric shock, I hope, but shock you in a good way? I hope so. But, really, it shouldn't. This change in testing policies has been around for a while. What should shock you is the fact these changes are little known facts. Even worse, most students and college counselors don't know this is an option, and so we adhere to the status quo, continuing to run our students through the standardized testing mill.

Yep, that's right folks, the National Center for Fair & Open Testing (also known as "FairTest") has been around for some time, advocating for schools to rely less on standardized admissions tests and promoting the idea that "test scores do not equal merit."

One of the main arguments in favor of standardized testing is that the tests serve as a common yard stick by which we can measure student achievements, thus enabling admissions officers to compare students from different backgrounds. But, really, many now agree that this is quite silly. As Fair Test (1998) points out, even the Educational Testing Service, which makes the SAT, has criticized the "Myth of a Single YardStick," arguing that there is "no single, primary ordering of people as 'best-qualified' or 'most meritorious' as simple notions of merit require."[21]

In a press release from April 2015, Bob Schaeffer, FairTest's Public Education Director, added, "The test optional surge is a sharp rejection of the 'new SAT' and an embracing of better ways to evaluate applicants."[22]

Not only are perfect test scores not necessary, but you also do not need a never-ending list of extracurricular activities. Researchers suggest that there is a "belief that it is the volume of activities that provides a boost in the application process" and that "students need to shine in multiple domains to garner attention of an admission committee."[23] One student who attended the top magnet high school in New Jersey, says, "It was very unusual and looked down upon if you weren't involved in at least three activities at the same time."[24]

But, it turns out colleges admissions officers can tell when students add on activities simply to add another thing to their résumé—and they don't like it. Jeff Rickey, Dean of Admission at St. Lawrence University, says, "We admissions officers are fans of students with deep involvement in a few activities. We are not fans of students who pad their list of activities in their junior and senior year to look more engaged."[25]

In an 2013 article in the *Journal of College Admission*, Alexis Brooke Redding shares the story of how, in 2005, Marilee Jones, former Dean of Admissions at MIT, took serious action to significantly reduce "the number of spaces for students to list their extracurricular activities on the application in order to encourage students to list only their most meaningful activities." To alert students that MIT was as interested in "human being" as it was in "human doing," Jones also added a new question for applicants: "What do you do just for the pleasure of it?" As Redding describes, however, such action didn't amount to much; that is, student "beliefs about the importance of multiple activities have become so ingrained" that students just took to attaching additional pages to list their many activities and accomplishments.[26]

So, all this business with students overloading themselves? Not necessary. Even worse, they are getting engaged in things they aren't truly interested in for the sake of getting into college, with the main question becoming "Will this look good on my résumé?" But, the reality is that "college admissions boards want to see passion, dedication and involvement over the long haul. It's much more desirable to have two or three extracurricular activities to which you are truly devoted, than to load up on superficial activities that you don't care much about."[27]

Myth #5: The Only Way to Get an Education is Through the Traditional U.S. Approach

With the many different options in front of you, there is no reason to continue to believe there is just one path to college. As Jason Dewitt, a research manager with the National Student Clearinghouse Research Center, stated, "The idea that there's only one path through college is antiquated."[28]

Cross the Pond

In Myth One, I noted that students are increasingly looking overseas for college education. And with good reason. It's no secret that college in America costs money. A lot of money. Since 1985, the cost of college education in the U.S. has increased 500 percent.

According to College Board, the annual tuition and fees to attend a private, nonprofit four-year university in America last year averaged $32,231. And many Ivy League schools and research universities cost as much as $50,000-$60,000. But, at King's College in London, tuition is $23,470. In Canada, the second most popular place to pursue a degree outside of the U.S., the average tuition for international undergraduate students was $15,380.[29] Not surprisingly, according to the Institute for International Education, some of the most popular countries for foreign college enrollment have seen sharp increases in students enrolled in academic-degree programs overseas. In 2012-2013, for example, the U.K., which is the number one country for U.S. students, experienced an 8% annual increase. And, according to the

German Academic Exchange Service, Germany saw a 33% increase between 2010 and 2013.[30]

In an October 2014 *Washington Post* article, Rick Noack profiled "Seven countries where Americans can study at universities, in English, for free (or almost free)," in an article under the same title.[31] The article profiles such locations as Germany, Finland, Sweden, Norway, Slovenia, and France, among others.

While there are several wonderful location options for pursuing a degree overseas, I am going to zero in on Germany for a moment. That's because even though tuition rates in Germany have always been low, in early October 2014, Germany's universities became tuition free—even to foreigners. (As I write this, in fact, Bernie Sanders is campaigning across the country that college should be free for all Americans.)

A little known fact is that Germany is one of seven countries where American students are able to not only study for free, but also can do so in English. According to Noack, there are 900 programs offered in English, including such areas as engineering to social sciences, and in some cases, you don't even have to formally apply for some German degrees. Germany offers this astounding number of degrees in English for two primary reasons: 1) to prepare German students to communicate in English, and 2) to attract foreign students (because Germany needs more skilled workers).[32]

Germany is now one of the most popular places for Americans to study overseas. (The United Kingdom and Canada hold the first and second place spots respectively.) A recent article from NPR covered this emerging trend of students obtaining degrees abroad, examining Germany specifically.[33] At last count, there were approximately 4,300 American students studying at German universities. More than half of these students were pursuing degrees.[34]

Do you want in on a little secret? U.S. federal loans are available for Americans to study overseas. In fact, hundreds of overseas institutions participate in the U.S. student loan program, which you can apply for through the completion of the Free Application for Federal Student Aid (FAFSA).

Perhaps living in Germany (or any of the other countries offering such opportunities) wasn't part of the original mental model you held for your college experience. But with college costs on the rise, and the availability of excellent international programs and degrees at a fraction of the price, perhaps the ideas is worth more than just a passing thought.[35]

FOREIGN DEGREE

Market share of countries hosting U.S. students pursuing degrees abroad.

U.K.	36%
CANADA	20%
FRANCE	10%
GERMANY	9%
NEW ZEALAND	5%
AUSTRALIA	5%
CHINA	5%
NETHERLANDS	4%
IRELAND	2%
SPAIN	2%
SWEDEN	1%
JAPAN	1%
DENMARK	Less than 1%
MALAYSIA	Less than 1%

Source: New Frontiers: U.S. Students Pursuing Degrees Abroad report by the Institute of International Education

Online Disruption

If moving overseas to obtain your degree isn't your bag, then you need look no further than your computer at home. In recent years, the online schooling market has exploded.

To underscore this trend, consider teacher education programs. Greg Toppo and Christopher Schnaars' article "Online Degrees

Skyrocket," shows that four big universities, operating mostly online, quickly became the largest education schools in America as a result of their online offerings. In 2012, those four accounted for 1 in 16 bachelor degrees and nearly 1 in 11 advanced degrees, including master's and doctoral degrees.[36]

To get your brain wrapped around this growth, look at the statistics for the University of Phoenix: In 2001, the school awarded 72 education degrees to teachers, administrators, and school personnel; in 2012, the school awarded 6,000 degrees, more than any other university. And more traditional institutions are also diving into this space. For comparison's sake, from 2001–2011, the following growth occurred: Teachers College of Columbia University grew from 1,014 to 1,345 online degrees in education, Johns Hopkins from 597 to 805, Harvard from 57 to 700, NYU from 771 to 775, and University of Pennsylvania from 269 to 569.[37]

According to the authors, many of these online education programs have open enrollment, similar to that offered at community colleges, the value of which we have already addressed in Myth One. Not only do these programs accommodate those working and those who have families, but the institutions that offer these programs suggest that the classes offer that which does not always exist in traditional classrooms. According to the article, Meredith Curley, Dean of the University of Phoenix's College of Education, explained that the virtual classroom environment is one in which everyone participates and is engaged in the work. "You can't hide," she said. Though the schools are sometimes thought of as "second-class citizens" to their traditional counterparts, the schools argue they are accredited by the same certifying organizations that accredit other more traditional programs.

Think and say what you will about the prestige of some of the online schools, but the fact is that online programs are owning the market in several sectors, and many people are taking advantage of them. Even big schools such as Arizona State University and University of Georgia have added online programs.

MOOCs

A MOOC is a "Massive Online Open Course." You have likely heard of these by now. These online classes have expanded the traditional classroom through the Internet and allowed students from all over the world to join in the learning action. There is Coursera, Udacity, and edX to name only a few.[38]

MOOCs are causing significant disruption in higher education. Not only can MOOCs mitigate student loan debt, but they also can offer learners the ability to earn certifications or degrees while working. Not too shabby. Even the country's most elite institutions have joined the online party. Harvard, MIT, Princeton, University of Pennsylvania, Stanford, Georgetown, Brown, and Columbia have jumped on the bandwagon and already offer MOOCs or have partnered with organizations that deliver the courses.[39]

Though there is quite a bit of discussion about the completion rates of such courses and if MOOCs can, in fact, replace traditional college experiences, MOOCs give broad access to professors and education experiences that many, otherwise, would not be able to have. According to a recent article in *U.S. News & World Report*, "Champions of MOOCs believe they are the best higher education development in decades, a way of providing free, high-quality classes to students anywhere in the world. But skeptics worry the courses will have a devastating effect on the American university system."[40] Regardless of where you land in this debate, there is no question these disruptions to the traditional way education has been delivered or obtained are here to stay. In two days from the time I am writing this, I will sign on to my own edX experience (not my first and certainly won't be my last) with Dr. C. Otto Scharmer, Senior Lecturer at Massachusetts Institute of Technology's Sloan School of Management and co-founder of the Presencing Institute, who runs the U.Lab. Last January, he ran the same course with 30,000 students from 190 countries across the globe. You can find more on Dr. Scharmer and his work in the Selected Resources section of this book.

Unschooling and the DIY Education Movement

The culmination of these disruptions has led to another disruption: that of the unschooling movement. "Unschooling" was a term first coined by John Holt, an education reformer, in 1977. The movement has come to mean different things to different people, but at the heart of it was Holt's desire to see education that depends on the child for direction. The idea is there are no mandatory books, no formal curriculum, and no tests or grades. Holt was opposed to the notion of homeschooling in the sense of recreating a school-type environment at home; instead, he believed that education should follow the student and not be directive in nature. Thus the creation of the term "un-schooling."

While this may be too far out for some, with the explosion of modalities that are making education more and more accessible, including online programs and MOOCS to name only a few, unschooling and a new "do it yourself" (DIY) approach to education have become reality. People are piecing together the education that works best for them, their interests, and their professional goals, seeking opportunities to pursue educational opportunities outside of the formal setting of school, or even in spite of the formal setting of school. As just one example, look up the story of Dale Stevens, who founded UnCollege. org, and wrote a book entitled, *Hacking Your Education: Ditch the Lectures, Save Tens of Thousands, and Learn More than Your Peers Ever Will,* which is listed in the Selected Resources section of this book.[41] Or check out the Thiel Fellowship, which is a two-year program founded in 2011 by technology entrepreneur Peter Thiel. Fellows "skip or stop out of college" and receive $100,000 grant and support from the Thiel Foundation's founders, investors, and scientists "to build new things."[42] And you might also explore the stories being collected at #GenDIY, which is profiling young people who are taking control of their own pathways to careers, college, and contribution. The idea is this: Powered by digital learning, "GenDIY" is working to combat unemployment and the increasing costs of earning a degree through alternative pathways to find or create jobs they love.[43] See what I mean? Unschooling and the DIY education revolution is happening.

And, in case this notion isn't wild enough for you already, Sparks & Honey, a New York City-based firm of futurists, has predicted that one of the top ten jobs in 2025 will be an unschooling counselor. Yep, that's right. According to Sparks & Honey, in the future there will be plenty of people unschooling—so many that there will be a cottage industry that emerges to help those engaged in unschooling weave together the educational experiences and activities that are most compelling and useful to them.[44]

With these disruptive innovations, and there are many more on their way, it's a myth that you need to worry about applying for college or seeking your future plans in *one particular* way; instead, you need to be concerned with doing it *your* way. And I'm confident that as the years progress, there are going to be many more pathways than even the few I've outlined here for you to make your education your own and a vehicle to really live your purpose and offer your gifts to the world.

Story Busting: Reimagining Possibilities

The aim of addressing some of these prevailing myths is to start to call attention to the way we have mentally created a system that is failing us. The world we live in, the world of work, and our circumstances have changed, but our beliefs and practices in college admissions have not. The continued use of these thoughts, beliefs, and actions serves to reconfirm those old and outdated stories, processes, approaches, and long-standing beliefs. As previously discussed, this has become a snowball, or a reinforcing feedback loop, leading to an approach to college admissions that perpetuates itself; however, many of these practices do not reflect the current reality of the system and have not evolved to keep up with the pace of change. There is ample evidence for us to begin to question the prevailing approach and to begin to see that there are alternatives to how we have (or have not) been serving students.

The next part of this book offers an approach that is transformational. It is one that undoubtedly will feel illogical at times, especially given the prevailing attitude of how things in the world of college admissions operate. The purpose is simply to offer a new way to approach college admissions given the current conditions. Part of what is required—and what this book aims to do—is provide a total shift in beliefs, perception, and way of doing things.

A wonderful illustration of this comes from a nine-dot puzzle exercise in Rosamund Stone Zander and Benjamin Zander's book, *The Art of Possibility*.[45] The puzzle is to connect all nine dots with four straight lines, without ever taking the pen from the paper. Try it here!

As Zander and Zander explain, most people attempt to solve this puzzle by working within the space of the dots; that is, they use the outer dots as the outer limit of the space in which they will operate.

Though it is not said explicitly in the instructions, most people believe that in order to be successful at this puzzle, they must operate within the square that is formed by the outer dots.

The trouble is, however, that within that framework there is no solution. The world of possibility opens up when I tell you that you can use the space outside the dots. Suddenly, the puzzle is not so challenging to solve.

This graphic is an illustration of what I am suggesting in this book — to live in the universe of possibility that exists outside of the dots – especially in your pursuit of college admissions and your future.

The stories we tell are founded in the beliefs we hold about getting into college, a tangled web of hidden assumptions about what is or isn't possible. If you learn to recognize these stories and call them into the light, you can begin to see what underlying assumptions you hold (no, you aren't going to be homeless or jobless if you don't get into that big name school, and you won't be a failure and have let everyone down) and how they may be limiting what is possible for you. In this way, you can engage in what I like to call "story busting," and also in designing the admissions experience based on a new set of assumptions and criteria: those that work best for you.

In other words, it is our minds that create the constraints, or what we believe to be possible. Zander and Zander write, "Every problem, every dilemma, every dead end we find ourselves facing in life, only appears unsolvable inside a particular frame or point of view."

Zander and Zander also offer two questions to practice getting out of the box of your assumptions.

What assumption am I making, that I am not aware I'm making, that gives me what I see?

After you answer this first question, they suggest you ask yourself another question:

What might I now invent, that I haven't yet invented, that would give me other choices?

Because the old way of doing things is the current prevailing culture, it doesn't mean it is the one that should exist. Developing a level of certainty about any one thing "robs us of the capacity for wonder, that stifles our abilities to see new interpretations and new possibilities for action." According to Senge et al., "Such are the roots of belief systems that become rigid, entrenched, and ultimately self protective."[46] By putting yourself back firmly in the middle of this design process, you are able to define your own experience and pursue the path and the way that is just right for you.

You Are the Answer You've Been Waiting For

By now you know quite a lot about the system and about a new approach that has been successful with numerous students and will set you on a path — one of meaning and purpose — toward a promising and authentic future. In systems thinking, to make a change in a system, one must first know the "leverage points" of the system. A leverage point is "an area where a small change can yield large improvements in a system"[47] and "places within a complex system...where a small change in one thing can produce big changes in everything."[48] Such leverage points serve an important purpose as, through them, one can understand these issues in broader context for the purpose of evaluating the potential opportunities for improvement of the college admissions system.

So what are the leverage points for change in college admissions? While I, along with many others, call for the system to be redesigned, YOU are the key leverage point and the first step. Systems change is going to take a long time, but changes you make — in your mental models, patterns of behavior, and actions — can be instantaneous. That's right. YOU are the change we seek. By recognizing the negative impacts of the current system, and by seeing there is another way, the emerging reality of something different can take hold. When you embrace a way that places you at the center of the process, you become that leverage point, instantly creating change for yourself and for others. In designing a system that works for you rather than just adhering to the prevailing system that exists, you take your power back. By acting on your own behalf in this way, you interact with the system differently. You are no longer a passive recipient of what the system hands you; by taking the reins, you set your intentions and make the system work for you. As writer and thinker Thomas Merton said, "We don't have to adjust *to* the world. We can *adjust* the world."

Chapter Seven:
Designing You—The U Map

*"What lies behind us and what lies before us are tiny matters
compared to what lies within us."*
— *Ralph Waldo Emerson*

We've been on quite a journey together now, starting with exploring the culture of crazy and moving on to the ways the system is negatively impacting students. From there we explored mental models and upended prevailing myths to support a new way of approaching college admissions—one where YOU (rather than a school) is at the center of the conversation and the effort.

I've already said this is not your traditional college admissions book. It does not provide a formula or tips and tricks on how to get into an Ivy League school, or really any school for that matter. As previously pointed out, there are many of those books out there, several of which say a lot of the same things. This is a book about designing your process so that you can achieve your dreams (which I hope you know by now are a lot more important than achieving entrance to a "dream" school). The missing piece in doing that is conversation about YOU, including your values and beliefs, your deepest desires, and your purpose, and how to catalyze your big, bad self into action to bring your gifts to the world.

The Missing Piece

As a young child, I cherished books by famous author Shel Silverstein—so much, in fact, that I later read them to my daughter Sydney. One of my favorite Silverstein books was *The Missing Piece*.[1]

In *The Missing Piece*, a circle searches for its missing piece, believing finding its missing piece will make it happy. On its quest for the discovery of its missing piece, the circle has many enjoyable experiences, including hanging out with a butterfly, stopping to smell some flowers, and spending time with a bug. When it does eventually find its missing piece, it soon finds that it's not able to do many of the things it previously enjoyed; for example, with its piece, the circle now rolls by too quickly to engage with the flower, the butterfly, or the beetle. It doesn't take long for the circle to let go of the missing piece, realizing that the very thing for which it was searching did not, in fact, make it happy. When, at the end of the book, the circle again begins its search for the missing piece, the reader is gifted an important lesson: More than the finding of the missing piece, it's the search itself that is the most enjoyable.

This is a perfect metaphor for the college quest: Always searching for the missing piece that will make you whole can lead to missing the enjoyment in everyday life. By rolling along so fast that you don't enjoy the process of the search or the meaning it can provide, you lose important elements of the process. It's also critical to realize that there are many pieces that will fit; it's not just one "magical" piece—whether that be an activity, a test score, or an acceptance letter—that will solve all your problems or be the key to your happiness. And sometimes it is the quest, and not the finding, that leads to fulfillment. In my work with students, this is how I like to think of the college admissions process and of life. The quest itself is rich with learning and where we should place our focus. It's the idea that we never really "arrive"; instead, we continually evolve—on the journey to become better and better versions of ourselves.

"By putting yourself back firmly in the middle of this design process, you are able to define your own experience and pursue the path and the way that is just right for you."

This section of the book is focused on two questions that are critical to this conversation, and ones I believe should be at the heart of the college admissions process:

"Who am I?" and "What am I doing here?"

Based on my work helping thousands of students, I have discovered that by facilitating the asking and the answering of these two questions at this important juncture, we would help students to better find their way in an increasingly complex world. Rather than people asking these questions at midlife or even later, after years of life having mindlessly whizzed by, or after some major life event—a death, divorce, or a crisis—what if you instead had a method to actively step into this process in a way that helped you take the important step from high school to college and beyond?

"Who am I?" and "What am I doing here?" are not simple questions. They are not blanks that can be filled in on a sheet or entered into a computer in career class; they are questions that require thoughtful deliberation, reflection, and time for consideration. They are the makings of a crafting of a soul. Students turn to their guides — parents, guardians, teachers, counselors, and coaches — but these guides cannot answer these questions. These are questions that can only be answered by the individual who poses them for him or herself.

So what happens? The pace of life takes over, the prevailing ways of engaging in college admissions win, and we let the questions go. Laurence Boldt writes:

> It takes more courage than most can muster to stand amidst the crowd and return to the quest for a fully integrated life. The great mythic heroes are those who confront challenges as well as the shadow sides of themselves. As a result of this, they are aligned between who they say they are, who they wish to become, and their day-to-day actions. These individuals have a strong sense of self to the point that even when faced with wicked problems, they can stand strong and convicted.[2]

Designing Your Life

A process that evolves over time and actually involves students in the design of their lives and futures in a meaningful way is a place to start. At the heart of this process is not the sense of that clean and tidy, well-ordered beginning, middle, and end that so many of the college admissions books call for. And it isn't the idea that you have a certain number of achievements that you will rack up by a certain date. Rather, it is an open-ended, progressive narrative that encourages students to dig and reflect, to seek their own paths, and to author and co-create their own futures and conclusions.

We have failed to acknowledge students as the thinking, growing, evolving beings that they are. It is our job as adults to support you into a blossoming over time — and at your own pace — and to catalyze you to write your own story.

At this time in history, students have more access to information than we ever before believed possible. Not only is the world growing more sophisticated and complex, but so are the individuals who live in it. Students' views of the world today are much more multi-layered. It is no longer that you choose between *this* or *that*. Old binary ways of operating have given way to multidimensional views and multiple pathways. This is why there is no better time than now for you to design your own experience.

Designing Your Future: From University to YOUniversity

According to the Webster dictionary, the word "university" means "an institution organized and incorporated for the purpose of imparting instruction, examining students, and otherwise promoting education in the higher branches of literature, science, art, etc. empowered to confer degrees in the several arts and faculties, as in theology, law, medicine, music, etc."[3] Now read that definition again. Nowhere in this widely accepted definition is mention of a focus on developing the person. Certainly, many schools have incorporated this into their work and their purpose, but in the definition itself, it is markedly absent.

A little known fact is that an alternate (and less known) definition of "university" is "the universe; the whole." The reason that I like this definition is that it acknowledges a more complete picture, and one I am aiming to encourage through this book. I am proposing that we — individually and collectively — take a more comprehensive look at what is out there and at helping individuals grow into their best — and most complete — selves while designing their futures.

It is for these reasons that I suggest a slight twist on the word "university." Instead, "Youniversity" is what I use to encourage students to design the process as their own. "Youniversity" captures the notion of designing and creating your journey toward the results *you* most desire and to develop yourself toward the goals and purposes you choose. I have chosen the term to encourage you to embrace this experience and process as your own and to encompass a much wider view than the one you currently hold.

One of the disturbing trends I presented had to do with students not knowing themselves. If students are to be at the center of this process, they MUST know themselves, their strengths, their interests, their values, their callings and dreams, and their deepest selves. From there, they can design the admissions experience that best suits their needs and path forward.

Theory U

Because the system requires profound change, I have done a considerable amount of research in the area of systems thinking to understand how to affect change. I have also researched how to help students acknowledge their interior world as the foundation of the college admissions process. My development of this notion of "Youniversity" and of the U Map framework, to which you will soon be introduced, was influenced in part by the wonderful ideas of Dr. Scharmer, to whom you were introduced earlier in this book.

Dr. Scharmer's Theory U, first popularized in 2006, has become quite influential in helping people to understand that the results of any system—including, in our case, the system of college admissions—is the "function of the quality of awareness, attention, or consciousness that the participants in the system operate from."[4] Scharmer's ideas have helped me to solidify my own as I've helped students employ design to move forward toward the great promise of their future.

And to understand how design is used, let's turn to a discussion of design thinking.

Design Thinking

I have a fundamental belief that everyone has the ability to design. Having read many books on design and with experience in the industry, I find the design thinking methodology to be the most accessible and understandable in thinking about how to apply design to everyday life. It is for these reasons that I'm loosely using the framework of design thinking to help students think through and design their admissions process.

Design thinking is an approach for creative problem solving. In the words of Tim Brown, CEO of the design and innovation firm IDEO (which employs design thinking in its work with clients), "design has become too important to be left to designers."[5] The idea is that innovation is no longer limited to physical products; there must be innovations across many different disciplines and sectors. Design thinking uses creative tools to integrate three areas: that which is desirable from a human point of view, that which is feasible (often from a technological point of view) and that which is economically viable.

Design thinking relies on more than just the typical problem-solving activities. It incorporates intuition, the recognition of patterns, and the ability to express oneself beyond words or symbols. It seeks solutions that are emotionally meaningful *and* functional. And rather than an over-reliance on rational and logical approaches to problem solving or too much emphasis on inspiration, feelings, and intuition, design thinking incorporates both of these, creating an integrated "third" way.[6]

The process of design thinking is a system of overlapping areas more than sequential steps. In design thinking, there are three main categories: inspiration, ideation, and implementation. Inspiration is the reason that you are motivated to design in the first place. Ideation is the process of creating, building on, and testing ideas. Finally, implementation is putting your ideas into action.[7] Design thinkers cycle back through a process multiple times to strike the perfect balance of the elements that are required for their design. Moreover, design thinkers willingly and enthusiastically accept multiple and competing constraints. It is these principles and elements of design thinking—rather than any strict adherence to a design thinking framework—that we make use of in this book.

Beyond the information I have provided above about why design thinking is relevant to this matter, there are some specific reasons I've selected design thinking as the general basis for your approach to college admissions:

1) **Design Thinking questions assumptions:** Through the process of design thinking, it is normal to reconsider some of your most basic ideas about how things work. Every time you challenge one of your mental models, you open up new pathways of thought. This is a good thing. It is like upgrading your thinking.

2) **Design Thinking is customizable:** Rather than adhering to a system that takes a "one size fits all" approach, or working within a system that requires you to be a certain way to achieve success (even though we have already proven that's not true), using design thinking, you can design with your exact situation in mind.

3) **Design Thinking is open-ended and open-minded:** In design thinking, there are no easy or right answers. The answers come through the process of designing. And your design process will provide different answers than what another's design process brings.

4) **Design Thinking is iterative and non-linear:** Design thinking is a creative and exploratory process. It allows for discoveries to be made along the way and for those discoveries to be integrated into the overall design—in this case, the design of you.[7]

For all of these reasons, design thinking can feel really messy and chaotic when it is first experienced. In the case of college admissions, this can feel especially weird since there is a prevailing culture of the "right" way to do things. But moving away from the linear and milestone-based process can be liberating. Through your willingness to embrace possibilities and experimentation, you open many more pathways toward a satisfying future.

Divergent and Convergent Thinking

Design thinking incorporates two forms of thinking—divergent and convergent—both of which are important for the purposes of college admissions.

Divergent thinking is wide-open, expansive thinking. It is the kind of thinking you use when you are brainstorming or being creative. Divergent thinking usually happens in a free-flowing manner. In other words, ideas are generated in a spontaneous and random manner that can seem and feel unorganized. Divergent thinking is about opening things up to anything possible and beyond—to that which is so big and expansive that it seems beyond possible.

Convergent thinking, on the other hand, is much more linear and logical. It provides the balance to divergent thinking in that it's the narrowing, or finding the single best solution to a problem you are trying to solve. It is the type of thinking you do when you are trying to solve a well-defined and straight-forward answer to a problem.[8]

Here is how these two work together: You use divergent thinking to dream up as many possibilities as you can and then you use convergent thinking to narrow down the possibilities to the point of selection. In this book, we use both divergent and convergent thinking to explore ideas and opportunities. You need both. Where divergent thinking allows for expansion and growth of what you might imagine possible, convergent thinking will help you put your various ideas together in a structured and organized way so that you can act upon them.

What Am I Designing For? The Good Life

Often when I meet with students to support them on their journey to college, I ask them what they hope for in the future. The most frequent response I get from students is: "I want to have a good life." So, before we get started on the design of what I call your "U Map," we need to spend some time defining the type of life you are designing for, and what exactly is meant by a "good life." Before you get started on the U Map, it is important to understand what I have come to believe is meant by the "good life" and how the U Map I developed will get you there.

A "good life" means different things to different people, of course. Over my time counseling students, I have heard many answers to what constitutes a good life, but generally the definitions fall into the following three categories:

GOOD LIFE #1

"Good life #1" is achieved through feeling and pleasure. It is found through things like socializing, eating good food, hanging out with friends and family, and obtaining possessions and experiences (cars, houses, travel, etc.).

GOOD LIFE #2

"Good life #2" is based on achieving one's maximum potential. Often this means finding what you are good at, doing it, and enjoying it. (This is also called "Flow," which we will discuss more in depth later.) Students who want this type of good life usually also want a balance of work and play. Addtionally, they want time to engage in strong relationships with their family and friends.

GOOD LIFE #3

"Good life #3" occurs through seeking and finding fulfillment through helping others. Often this type of life is rooted in a desire to live for a purpose that is greater than one's self.[9]

It is important to note that liking one of these good life definitions does not prevent you from wanting or engaging in the other types of good lives, too. But there are important distinctions to be made. For our purposes, I am going to focus on "Good Life #3." The reason for this focus is because students – far more often than not – select this one as the life they are aiming for. So, here is how I see "Good Life #3":

This "good life" is an authentic one, not one in which someone follows a preconceived notion of the "right" path. The journey is also one of continual becoming, one in which the process of becoming fully oneself is not about external rewards, but about internal ones. It is about serving oneself in the truest sense, but also about serving more than only oneself. It is about designing your way forward to bloom into your full glory and to offer your gifts to the world—while also balancing the call and responsibility to serve as a citizen of the world.

Another way to understand this good life is through looking at Abraham Maslow's Hierarchy of Needs. Maslow, who is considered one of the greatest psychologists of modern times and one of the founders of the humanistic psychology movement, suggested that it is our needs that motivate us to do things. In *A Theory of Human Motivation* (1943), Maslow outlined the basics of human motivations, recognizing that there may be different kinds of needs, spanning from biological and physiological, which are at the very foundation of our human survival, to esteem needs, to self-transcendent needs, and he organized all of these into a pyramid.[10] It was Maslow's suggestion that after an area of need is fulfilled, a person seeks the next, which is why he arranged these needs in a hierarchy.

Maslow did a lot of work on this theory over the course of his life, building on his ideas over time, and adding more and more levels as his thoughts and ideas progressed. Without going into all of that here, what I want you to know about is his most recent version of the hierarchy of needs:

While I really love Maslow's theory, and I could go on and on about it, most important is to draw your attention to the connection between the model and the types of lives students often describe. At the middle of the pyramid are "Esteem Needs." These are often the needs that correspond to "Good Life #1." "Good Life #2" is really built on "Self-Actualization," or reaching your personal potential. Maslow himself said the following: "A musician must make music, an artist must paint, and a poet must write, if he is ultimately to be at peace with himself. What a man can be, he must be. This is what we may call the need for self-actualization."[11] Finally, "Good Life #3" is about striving not only for your own self-actualization, but for helping others to achieve self-actualization, too. "Transcendence" is acting for things that are beyond oneself.

The same system applies to the way one approaches college admissions. You can go for the "Esteem Needs"—the school that brings you power and prestige, the one that is a marker of achievement, etc. Or you could reframe the experience to think about the need for self-actualization or your desire for transcendence. Rather than concern with the prestige of the school, you might ask questions more along the lines of "Where am I apt to reach my greatest potential?" or "Where will I be able to grow to my potential and also learn to help others do the same?" Naturally, such questions may cause you to look at schools differently.

There are some other things that my definition of the "good life" presumes, too.

- That life is a continuous journey; you never "arrive"

- That your ability to progress toward self-actualization and transcendence is not about external rewards; it is about being inwardly driven

- That you can and should discover your own good life (rather than following a preconceived or "right" path)

- That you can be trusted to know what you are called toward and, with support, you can take action in the direction of your dreams

- That you can and should know both your areas of strength and your areas of improvement

- That regardless of where you are today, you can engage in continuous growth (We'll talk about the importance of a growth mindset later.)[12]

These ideas are the basis for the framework I have created for designing your admissions experience toward your "good life."

Meet the U Map.

The U Map

Over the next pages, you will have the opportunity to step into the U Map. The U Map is meant to help you answer the two questions that are most important to your present and your future: "Who am I?" and "What I am doing here?" As such, the U Map is meant to take you on a journey to knowledge of self and to the deepest parts of you and also to spur you to creative action based on what you want for yourself and your future.

By engaging in the admissions process in the way I am suggesting, you can indeed come to know yourself better and obtain a clearer sense of what you want, what you have to offer the world, and what action to take.

With the U Map in front of you, let's briefly walk through the process of looking within, discovering all of who you are, and then gathering your resources, dreaming big, and taking action to catalyze you toward your biggest and brightest future.

Starting with the questions "Who am I?" and "Where am I going?", your journey of self-discovery begins. The journey is set in motion with reflection, so Step One is to "Get Quiet." Step Two, "Discover," is where you take an inventory of all your raw material, recognizing the wonderful and unique things about you and your life to this point. In Step Three, you begin to assemble a Dream Team to support

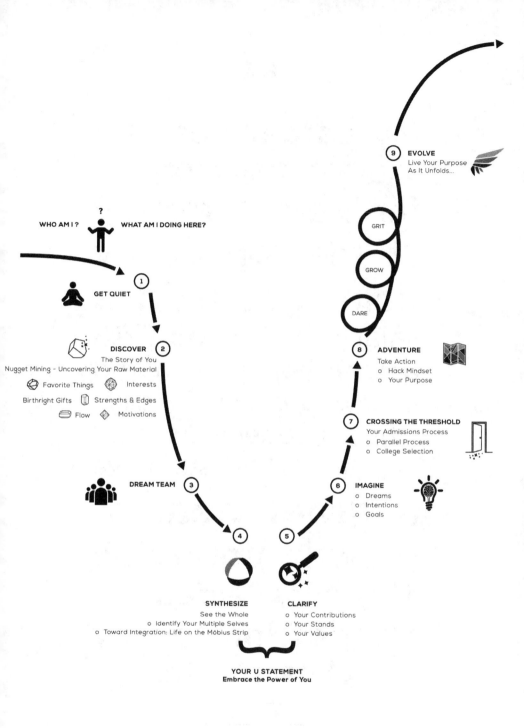

WHO AM I? **?** WHAT AM I DOING HERE?

GET QUIET (1)

DISCOVER (2)
The Story of You
Nugget Mining - Uncovering Your Raw Material

Favorite Things   Interests

Birthright Gifts   Strengths & Edges

Flow   Motivations

DREAM TEAM (3)

(4)

(5)

SYNTHESIZE
See the Whole
o Identify Your Multiple Selves
o Toward Integration: Life on the Möbius Strip

CLARIFY
o Your Contributions
o Your Stands
o Your Values

YOUR U STATEMENT
Embrace the Power of You

(6) **IMAGINE**
o Dreams
o Intentions
o Goals

(7) **CROSSING THE THRESHOLD**
Your Admissions Process
o Parallel Process
o College Selection

(8) **ADVENTURE**
Take Action
o Hack Mindset
o Your Purpose

DARE

GROW

GRIT

(9) **EVOLVE**
Live Your Purpose
As It Unfolds...

"

My **career** has had a **great trajectory** so far. I am **currently** at the **top** of my field, get **paid** a salary in the **top fifth percentile,** and can find a **new position** in days when needed. **Best** of **all,** I feel like I still have a **great deal** of growth **potential.** This was **aided** by **my passion** for my **chosen** path.

STUDENT VOICE

"

your efforts. In Steps Four and Five, you recognize the multi-dimensional and dynamic being that you are and engage in a process of integration. You also clarify your contributions, stands, and values. With this awareness—and at the mid-point of the U Map—you craft a U Statement and recognize the power you have. From there, in Step Six, "Imagine," you dream up what you want for your life and then create intentions and goals. It is only after you have engaged in Steps One through Six that you step into the actual process of applying to college. This point, Step Seven, is called "Crossing the Threshold." Here, I do not provide you with the nuts and bolts of how to complete the applications (check out the Selected Resources section for books directed toward that end); instead, I provide you with an inspired way to think about and approach the act of applying. And because many college admissions books do not address how to journey your way through college, I cover that in Step Eight, urging you to "adventure" your way into your future, through college and beyond, with some key mindsets. In Step Nine, the final step of the U Map, I encourage you to evolve toward your purpose by embracing emergence. The length of time it takes students to work through the U Map is widely varying. The point of the U Map is to make it your own.

This journey is not a one-time process; it's a process that happens over and over again throughout your life, each time placing you on higher ground. Of course, in this case, I am using college admissions as the catalyst for dipping into the U Map. On a grander scale, however, there is the larger experience of your life and all of these parts and pieces are but steps in your journey. You will journey through the U Map many times throughout your life.

When you embark on your journey, while you should know it will be rewarding, you also should know that it won't be easy. That is because the road toward your future, toward becoming the YOU you are meant to become can't be entirely clear or certain. Though this might freak you out, what should freak you out more is that you mistakenly have been given the sense it might be clear and certain. It just doesn't work like that. Life is much messier, and much more beautiful, than you can imagine. On your journey, you will face obstacles and complexity. And my hope is that you will welcome them for this is from where the greatest learning and growth come.

After a description of the particular focus for each section of the Map, you will find sections entitled "How." These sections are comprised of exercises designed to support you along your U Map path. They are to be engaged in thoughtfully, but they are not meant to take tons and tons of time. I have created them so that they shouldn't take you more than 10 minutes to complete though, should you desire, you can spend more time on them. I've designed the exercises this way so that you answer from the perspective of your soul, not your logical mind or your ego. When your logical mind and your ego start to interfere, they put limits and judgments on what is possible.

In thinking you "know" something, you are often using only the limited information available to you through sight and sound. For the purposes of the U Map, however, you really need to tune into the signals that are beyond your eyes and ears. Though you can see and hear what is happening, begin to experiment with other ways of knowing or sensing. As just one example, your body, heart, and mind might be telling you three different things, and you may be really only hearing the messages from one. Begin to check in with yourself to see if you are able to hear messages from each and all of these parts of you. Can you determine rational thinking from intuitive thinking? Can you feel where energy—your own or someone else's—is stuck or flowing? In addition to your thoughts, do you have a felt sense of your experience? These are all important things to consider.

It is my hope that these exercises also might stay with you and that you find you want to return to them from time to time. This is because your subconscious is processing the information you are bringing to the surface.

I also need to tell you that it isn't unusual for your answers to any of the exercises to overlap. Alternatively, you may find that your answers come from very different places and have no overlap at all. Either is fine. All of this is only meant to serve you to understand the many different sides of you so that you can engage in *Admissions by Design* accordingly. Let's get started.

Chapter Eight:
U Map Step One—Get Quiet

"It is the still, small voice that the soul heeds, not the deafening blasts of doom."
—William Dean Howells

In the frenzied atmosphere of college admissions today, the very first step in the U Map might seem difficult: Get Quiet.

My clients and their families often look quizzically at me when I first suggest this, and believe me, this isn't advice that you will find in most college admissions books. But not only is this the key to discovering the important things about yourself, it is also the key to ensuring you are living in the Green Zone, which we discussed earlier in the book.

Slowing yourself down and putting yourself on pause absolutely must be the starting point. Here's why: It is only through inner focus and quiet that you can access the still point at the center of yourself. Accessing this point is critical to discovering who you are, and being able to listen to that still, small voice will guide you toward your future. Also, finding this inner stillness frees you from the external distractions that can confuse you on your path.

Kris Carr, developer of the Crazy Sexy Cancer movement and one of my heroes (seriously, look her up, she rocks), talks about giving a wellness lecture at Harvard, where she taught students a simple meditation technique and encouraged them to engage in silence for five minutes. Afterward, she asked them about their experience. She describes one of the students as having reported, "I hated it! Half way through it felt like torture!" Though her intention was for students to improve concentration and focus, it was hard for students to even sit still for five minutes. She writes, "Harvard is an extremely competitive joint where the vast majority of the students experience major burn-out. What good is the expensive knowledge if you're too fried to use it?"[1] I understand that now she is developing a curriculum called Inner Harvard, and meditation is at the top of this list. I can't wait to get my hands on that.

The most important part of the getting quiet piece is that it is the fast track to getting to know yourself. At first, this is going to be HARD. And there are not going to be any rewards tied to it (except for that part about actually getting to know yourself and what you have to offer the world). You are going to just have your thoughts, wonder if you are doing it correctly, and maybe even fall asleep. This is why a lot of people don't stick with this. Sometimes slowing down and hearing what your mind is telling you can be too much to bear. But don't worry. If you wait that out, if you are able to let those thoughts pass by—like watching clouds drift by in the sky—eventually there will be space, and that is when the good stuff is going to start to come.

What do I mean by "the good stuff?" I mean the thoughts, images, and words that are going to lead you to the path that is most soul fulfilling for you. This can look like a lot of things, but at its core, it is the simple expression of your deepest self and your truest desires. If you are patient enough, the messages will start to come, and, when they do, you may be surprised at how remarkably faithful they are to you and your path. In slowing down, you will be able to hear what matters to YOU and what gifts you have to offer the world.

You see, as a little being, you came into this world knowing something about your gifts and what makes you happy. I have a nephew who has always loved cooking, and a neighbor kid who loves ballet. Both of their parents say it is as if these interests were delivered with them at the time of their birth; they have always had them. When you are young, you get lost when you lose the connection to the things you love. This doesn't mean that you can't add new things, but it does mean that there are some threads that have always been there, and the sooner you remember them, the more your life will catalyze you to express your gifts. (BTW: We talk more about this "remembering" later.)

If you can get yourself to get quiet and to actually listen to yourself, the answers or the remembering will start to come. You see, the tricky part of stepping into your future isn't the *doing* part, it is the *being* part. Really. It is getting quiet and still enough to listen to what you actually might want to do and what your dreams (and not those of your parents, or your teachers, or your coaches) are.

The reason for this is that while your teachers, professors, parents, and counselors will all be willing to give you lots of advice, what YOU have to contribute to this world can only, at the end of the day, come from you. When you slow yourself down enough to really listen—and I mean really listen—to what your heart and your gut are telling you, that is when you will be able to hear more and more input that is productive and that guides you correctly on your path. This world is bursting with an over-reliance on rational and linear thinking and with the belief that it is a straight shot from Point A to Point B. So before you go thinking slowing down and getting quiet is too "hoodoo voodoo," I suggest you try it. This stuff works.

What's important to realize is that getting quiet or surrendering is actually not a passive activity. This is the mistake most people make in thinking they don't have time for quiet reflection when they have so many things to get done. In this culture, we have an addiction to busyness. This certainly has made its way into college admissions, where students seem to embody the phrase "the busier, the better." The length of activity lists and number of extracurricular activities has been endlessly growing since I started my work with students many years ago, and each year it seems to get more insane.

The problem with this being busy all the time is that we make the false assumption that the activity translates to being productive. Running around and doing what everyone thinks is right and expects of you to get into college—joining clubs, volunteering, and winning awards—isn't useful if it doesn't come from the right place. These things may be good when they are in line with your passions, but when they don't enhance your life or are only adding more stress, or you are only doing them to please others or get into college, that's when the problems occur. In fact, when you become beholden to the "shoulds" and "ought-tos" in this process, you lose so much of what this process has to offer, and, in turn, so much of yourself. Moreover, the "shoulds" and "ought-tos" cloud the things that are of real importance to you.

When you slow down, you are left with empty space, something we are much too afraid of these days. Yes, as I've said, that empty space is going to give rise to a lot of stuff—everything from your dreams to your fears to your insecurities. You may realize that you are seeking fame and fortune only to justify your existence on this planet when really just being you and doing the things you love are ultimately the keys to your sustained happiness and success. Slowing down is the pathway to the intuitive insights that are yours to claim, but that you may be just too busy to hear. By taking this time to sit quietly with yourself, you will see how enhanced every aspect of your family, social, and school life will become and how you will know much more about yourself and your authentic path.

So, yes. I am suggesting that you begin to slay your own dragons and wrestle that mind of yours to stillness before you get out there to slay the dragons of college admissions.

"

Envision

what you **want** as
a college/**university**
experience and find
schools **that can**
give that **to you.**

STUDENT VOICE

"

HOW

1) Do you know your own personal style of relaxation? What is it? Does it allow for you to gain insight from a deeper part of you? (Watching TV or playing video games, for example, wouldn't count in this way.) Reflect: How do you already practice getting quiet or reflective, if you do? Maybe you journal or spend time in nature?

2) Make a "Get Quiet" Plan: Design your own plan to "get quiet" for a few moments every day. This can include going on a walk, sitting quietly on the couch, or writing in a journal. This is important time to give your brain a break and to listen to what your inner voice is saying.

3) Practice Mindfulness: Just 10 minutes a day will make a remarkable difference in your ability to get in touch with yourself and to manage your stress. If it is hard to stay still for that long, start with five minutes each day, and then move to eight minutes, and eventually to 10 minutes. A good way to practice mindfulness is to focus on the sensation of your breath. Whenever your mind wanders, just notice it, and then refocus your attention on your breath. It's that simple! If sitting in silence is too hard at first, try listening to music or using a mindfulness app like Relax Melodies, Buddhify, or Omvana. Start or end your day with these, or use them to relax before a test or going into a college interview.

Chapter Nine:
U Map Step Two—Discover

"Knowing yourself is the real journey."
—David Schwimmer

The second step in the U Map, Discover, is about looking inward to find out more about who you are. It's a review of your life to this point and also an opportunity to witness the "raw material" that is you.

The Story of You

Not surprisingly, your process of discovery begins with the story of you. Think back across the span of the history of your life—from the time of your birth to where you are at this moment. Think of this journey as a path you have been on—a path of peaks and valleys, of forests where you have become lost and of wide open fields or clearings where there is much space and room for opportunity. This path has had both wonderful and difficult twists and turns, and you have made many decisions, leading you to the place you are now.

You have become the person you are today not only because of who you are, but also because of the way this journey has shaped you. You cannot control all of the circumstances of your life. Between your birth and this exact moment of time, there are a variety of things that have happened to you that have helped to shape the very unique person that you are and that you've become.

In my many years of hearing the life stories of students, not only have I learned a tremendous amount about them, but I have also seen the way the students themselves have made meaning of the life experiences they've had. In exploring the unique story of you, you identify important moments and themes that will serve you to learn more about yourself and what's important to you. Through this process, you will likely make connections or have insights that will leave you reflecting for a long time to come.

HOW

1) Get quiet and spend time thinking about the significant events on your journey so far — from the high peaks to the low valleys, from the moments of being lost to the moments of great clarity to the moments you were heroic to the times you were vulnerable and afraid.

2) Retrace the events of your life, beginning with when you were a very young child. Think about where you were at each age; which groups, like family, homes, or religious or spiritual institutions you belonged to; which schools, places, or organizations influenced you; what the high and low points of those experiences were; and what insights you have as a result. In doing this exercise, record and share only what is comfortable for you.

Using the chart below, adapted from an exercise in Laurel Donnellan's book *Passion into Practice: The Path to Remarkable Work*, record as much of this as feels significant to the person you have become.[1]

Age	Influential Groups, Schools, Places, and Organizations, and People	High Points (list 3-5)	Low Points (list 3-5)	Insights (list 3-5)
Ages 0-5				
Ages 5-10				
Ages 10-15				
Ages 15-20				

3) Think about the meaning you made of these different life events (we will talk about this more later in the exercises). How have these events impacted you? What patterns of satisfaction or dis satisfaction do you see?

4) We all experience important decision points in the journey of our life. Using our metaphor of the path you are journeying on, you can think of these decision points as forks in the road, where you chose a particular path. What have been the most significant forks in the road of your life? What decisions did you make and why?

Important Forks	Why

Important Decisions	Why

5) Describe what things you want to carry forward with you as you head into the next phase of your life. And what things do you want to release or let go of?

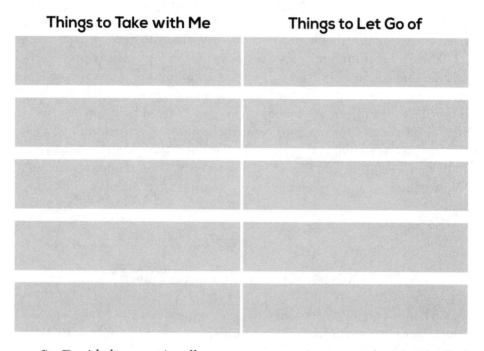

Things to Take with Me	Things to Let Go of

6) Decide how to visually represent your journey to here with all of life's highs, lows, twists, turns, and forks. One suggestion is to use an adaptation of the Life Line below, recording your high and low points chronologically.

In my many years of doing this, I have seen student representations of their journeys presented in many, many different ways—from models, to artistic renderings, to PowerPoints, to songs, to stories, to timelines filled with dates and people. All of these do the job. The point is simply to connect with the story of you. So go for it! Create something that lets the world know about your journey to this point in your life. Use your creativity!

Nugget Mining — Uncovering Your Raw Material

Your story is rich with raw material that comprises various parts and pieces of you, and that you need to understand more about you — everything from your activities to your skills to your values and beliefs. So, naturally, this begins with mining the "nuggets" of your story.

This "nugget mining" idea comes courtesy of one of my professors in graduate school, Dr. Mark Jones. Nugget mining is the idea that buried in what you do, say, or believe are some gems that provide important core information about who you are and how you see the world. Of course, for our purposes, these nuggets are essential.

But also essential is that this effort is your own. You, in wanting to live a more authentic life, are going to have to do the hard work of pulling these nuggets from your story to guide you on your most true path.

So let's start digging.

Nugget Mining #1: Favorite Things

When my daughter, Sydney, was a little girl, she loved the movie, *The Sound of Music*. In fact, she loved it so much, she watched it a lot. Like All. The. Time. Naturally, this meant that I, too, watched that movie 888,888 times. Remember the scene where Julie Andrews sings about a few of her favorite things? Well, that (and the rest of the movie) is burned into my brain, where it will likely remain forever. The good news is that since it has stayed with me, it's now making its way to you.

Whenever I ask students to explore more about what is important to them, I often give them the warm up exercise of identifying their favorite things. The cool thing about exploring your favorite things is that they are, in part, what make you the unique being that you are. Sometimes your favorite things are tied to your areas of passion, and sometimes they are not. An example is my pink and lumpy childhood pillow I lovingly call "Puddie." I would probably put my life on the line for that thing, but I can't say it really represents a passion so much as that it is really soft, just the right shade of pink, and it's been with me through thick and thin. Similarly, I cannot tell you why I am obsessed with Dr. Bronner's peppermint soap, hiking, cinnamon gummy bears, or office supplies. But I am. Somehow, these favorite things represent important things about the full picture of me. The list of your favorite things provides a more complete view of yourself and the things that are meaningful to you.

Your list of favorite things can be super funky, and it can and should bring up things you might have forgotten about yourself. Here are portions of lists from some of my previous students to give you an idea of what this looks like:

Bryan P.

Writing, hanging out with my friends, In-N-Out burger, helping animals, chocolate, painted fingernails, hockey, and coding.

Angela C.

Basketball, my childhood blanket named "Snuffie," the smell of deodorant, lemon cake, rainy days, and cooking.

Morgan J.

Cherry Jello, my cat Slinky, the blue color of my room, Frappuccinos, my chess trophy, weekend mornings, *The Onion*, and skateboarding.

Now, it's your turn.

HOW

1) In the box below, make a list of as many of your favorite things as you can think of in a minute period. (And if you want to get all "Julie Andrews" about it, feel free to sing the list!)

My Favorite Things Today

2) Now make a list of things you loved when you were a little wee one. Do your best to note the age at which you liked these things. If you don't remember the age, just take a guess. There is no perfect science to this. To gain insight, you can also engage your parents or another adult to help with this question.

My Favorite Things When I Was Younger	Age

By now, you may be starting to see a trend or some overlap between things. If you don't see any overlap, don't worry. This may mean you just have a lot of areas of interest. We're going to talk about that, too.

3) If you are a Pinterest user, take your present-day list and start to make a board related to it. You can even make two boards: one related to your younger self and one related to your present-day self. Some students put things from both the younger self and present day self together on the same Pinterest board, believing all of these things have helped to form who they are today. You also can decide to post things related to this on Instagram or make a collage of these things. Or you can simply keep this list near you, reminding you of the stuff you love and adding to it as you find more things that you love.

4) Spend an hour taking yourself on a "date" to do some of the things you loved to do as a child or bring some reminders of your favorite things from when you were a child. Maybe it is something you have lost touch with all together and want to bring back into your life. Or maybe it is something that you just want to do again to remember that time in your life. And, by all means, feel free to drag a friend along.

P.S. Some of my things were eating bubble gum ice cream (my favorite when I was 8!) and chowing down on some Count Chocula cereal. Both experiences were disgusting, actually, so I guess we can count these activities among those I grew out of, but I still had a heck of a lot of fun in the process.

Nugget Mining #2: Interests

In thinking about your life now and where you want to go, the next best place to really dig in and excavate is your current areas of interest. It is important to note that what is fulfilling today may look a lot different from what was exciting to you when you were younger and what is going to be fulfilling to you in your early or late twenties, thirties, and forties. With this said, it is necessary to take a look at all of it. It's also valuable to remember your passions don't have to be interesting to others; they just have to "wow" *you.*

Maybe you can recall a time when you thought it was all freaky that your science teacher became giddy talking about amoebas, but somehow, even though you don't really like amoebas, you also got excited? Passion is infectious, and by finding your interests, you will be infectious, too (and in a good way — not in the latest-and-greatest freaky virus sort of way). Your interests also are evidenced by the fact that you can get lost in those things for hours and hours and never get bored. These interests are what create the spark that can later turn into a full-blown fire of thrill as you pursue the things that most interest you.

To me, the best way to explore the topic of interests is by way of ice cream. I know this sounds a little weird (though also hopefully fun), so let me explain. First, you should know I am a major fan of ice cream. This stems from going to Little Annie's ice cream shop in my small hometown every Saturday night with my family for pretty much the better part of my childhood. I was the kid paralyzed by choice — there were always multiple flavors I wanted, but, naturally, I was permitted one scoop. (Lucky for me, near where I now live, there is an amazing ice cream shop I frequent that allows you to split one scoop into two flavors! Choice! What a revelation!)

I have the same philosophy about interests as I do about ice cream flavors: It is OK to have a lot of them. The purpose of this exercise, then, is to help you expand — rather than narrow — your interests.

HOW

1) Interest List: Using a sheet of paper or the space provided, and in no particular order, list all the interests that you find exciting. Consider things you would like to be doing, things that fascinate you, subjects that are calling to you. Be aware that this is a list of current interests. These are not set in stone in any way, and

they don't have to be from earlier times in your life, nor do they have to extend out into the future. I am only asking you to re cord what you find interesting right now. Of course, since you know I love choice, you can imagine that at any time it is totally OK to revisit this list, add to or subtract from it, or ditch it all together and start from scratch.

_____

_____

_____

_____

2) Ice Cream Cone of Interests: From this list, I want you to select five interests that are most interesting (Ha! Get it?) to you right now. Since I love ice cream, I have provided you with a sampler cone for your interests:

3) Your Previous Interests: You already know I'm a big fan of surveying the past because it can give you important clues about things that are important to you, either by way of recognizing some of the things that might be considered innate in you or through experiences that have shaped you into the person you are today. Your interests are an expression of yourself; they may very well be the things in which you can get lost for hours. Often I tell students to look at what they do with their free time or what hobbies they have because we sometimes carry our interests as children into adulthood through our recreational activities or hobbies, often believing that we couldn't possibly make a living at them.

Complete the chart below. See if you can gather any insight about patterns of interest. What interests have been lost along the way—either through growing out of something that was previously interesting or because you were too busy to continue or began something else? Determine whether or not there are things from when you were younger that you want to reclaim.

	My Younger Self (Pick any age for the question. Just be sure to note the age.)	Still an interest today (Y/N)? If yes, how has this interest shown up in your life today?
Things I love to do (that I can get lost in for hours and hours and are super fun)		
Areas of Interest		

4) Spend an hour taking yourself on a "date" to explore your current or previous interests. Like with your favorite things, maybe it is something you haven't explored in awhile or have lost touch with all together and want to bring back into your life. Or may be it is something that you just want to do again to remember that time in your life. If you feel like it, take someone with you.

Nugget Mining #3: Birthright Gifts

Now that you have done some thinking about your favorite things and your interests, critical to your effort to gather your raw material is the identification of what world-renowned writer, speaker and activist Parker Palmer calls your "birthright gifts," or those gifts with which we come into this world. Palmer writes, "We arrive in this world with birthright gifts—then we spend the first half of our lives abandoning them or letting others disabuse us of them." Rather than embracing these gifts that contain hints to the unique things we have to offer the world, according to Palmer, "as young people, we are surrounded by expectations that may have little to do with who we really are, expectations held by people who are not trying to discern our selfhood but fit us into slots." Perhaps this is no more clearly seen than in the case of college admissions, where the seeking for the particular "right" equation to get into the "right" school has led to a disfiguring of our original selves, our truest selves. Palmer writes, "Our original shape is deformed beyond recognition; and we ourselves, driven by fear, too often betray the true self to gain approval of others."[2]

The movie, *The Legend of Baggar Vance* provides a good illustration of why the past is something that is useful. Basically the story goes a little like this: A golfer, who isn't playing well, gets the help of Baggar Vance, an inspirational golf caddy, to help him improve his game. In one of the movie scenes, Baggar Vance remarks, "Inside each and every one of us is one, true, authentic swing. Something we were born with. Something that's ours and ours alone. Something that can't be taught to you or learned. Something that's got to be remembered."[3]

The movie line is an important reminder that your gifts are things you *remember* about yourself. Naturally, then, as part of the U Map process, I am suggesting you reclaim your birthright gifts because they may offer important clues about areas in which you naturally excel. Sometimes students ask me, but what if I don't have any birthright gifts? Impossible! You do! Everyone has them. Sometimes they get buried, which is why we are going through this excavation process.

HOW

1) Make a list of your birthright gifts. What are they?

2) If you are stuck or want more information, ask your friends and family members or adults, who knew you when you were young, what gifts you showed early in your life.

3) Have the expectations of others impacted the expression of your gifts either positively or negatively? How?

4) Find a time to honor or engage in one or two of your birthright gifts. Write, draw, or use Pinterest to capture your experience.

Nugget Mining #4: Strengths and Edges

Strengths are a combination of your talent, knowledge, and skills, as well as your investment in practicing, developing your skills, and building your knowledge base.[4] Even though you may be shy about your strengths, I find in my work with students that most people know the areas in which they have strengths. These are things you are good at, whether you have come by them naturally or whether you have grown into them over time. And you shouldn't be shy in claiming these things.

An "edge," on the other hand, is an area of improvement. I use "edge" instead of words like "weakness" or "flaw" or "shortcoming" because I like the idea of a growth mindset (more on that later in the book). I also have seen that with the right perspective and work and if you develop knowledge and skills related to that area, your edges can become strengths. Think of a knife edge, for example. At first just a piece of metal. It isn't until it's sharpened and honed and polished that the edge becomes a blade. And then to be made useful, it must be in a skilled hand. Edges are areas you are working to improve over time.

HOW

1) Make a list of three to five of your strengths here. For each of your answers, explain why you believe this is a strength.

_____

_____

_____

_____

_____

2) Make a list of three to five of your edges here. For each of your answers, explain why you believe this is an edge.

_____

_____

_____

_____

_____

3) Think about what actions you can take to use your strengths more often. Create a list of conditions under which you exhibit your strengths. Where are you? What are you doing? Who are you with?

4) Create a list of things that block you from exhibiting your strengths. Become familiar with this list, and know when you are heading down a road that isn't congruent with your best self.

5) Brainstorm actions that would help you make your best self even better. How could you really exhibit and maximize your strengths or become even better at applying your strengths?

6) What actions might you take that will help you to hone and im prove your edges?

7) What do you do when you are hitting your edges? How do you know when you are up against your comfort zone boundary? How can you stay more in the learning that happens in this place of discomfort?

8) Now that you have done some thinking about your own strengths and edges, go and interview those who are close to you. Talk to your friends, your girlfriend or boyfriend, your siblings, and your parents. Talk to your grandparents, your employers, and your neighbor lady. Ask your coaches, your teachers, your counselors. Basically, track down the people who know you best and ask them what they think your strengths and edges are. Reflect on what you learn.

A WORD OF CAUTION

Be careful not to give others too much power in telling you what your strengths and edges are. Why? Because sometimes how people view you has a lot to do with them and not as much to do with you. Nonetheless, it is good to know how people see you. This is also why it is a good idea to take a wide sampling and notice the themes.

Additionally, to become the best version of yourself, you need to become really good at taking feedback. But remember, this is not a chance to morph your identity and how you see yourself into what others think is best or right or even true about you. It is also not the time to take the feedback and then think you are the King or Queen of the Universe or a miserable piece of trash based on what you've been told. The judgment piece needs to stay out of it. This is a chance to understand where you are at this moment of time and to practice taking feedback. You are a growing human being, and you can and will change. You are collecting information because it is a helpful part of this process. The themes you uncover may help you understand more about yourself.

9) Create a plan about how you might create a system where you check in with these people or others over time to continue learning more about your strengths and edges. Balance this with your own perspective on what you know your strengths and edges to be.

Nugget Mining #5: Flow

Have you ever become so lost in an activity that you lost track of time or that time stood still? If so, you have experienced the state of "Flow." Flow occurs when you become so absorbed in an activity that you forget yourself and begin to act fully and effortlessly in the present moment. You may have heard of such a concept, especially in the case of athletics, as "being in the zone," but it's not just athletes who experience it. Musicians, artists, teachers, scientists—you name it—all experience Flow.

Mihaly Csikszentmihalyi is a Distinguished Professor of Psychology and Management at Claremont Graduate School and the Founding Co-Director of the Quality of Life Research Center, a non-profit research institute that studies positive psychology. Csikszentmihalyi is considered one of the pioneers in positive psychology and has popularized the notion of Flow.

Csikszentmihalyi first discovered psychology after seeing Carl Jung speak in Switzerland when Csikszentmihalyi was just 15 or 16 years old. He then read everything he could find on psychology, and due to the lack of psychology programs in Europe, he came to the United States to study psychology at the University of Illinois (he later finished his studies at the University of Chicago). An accomplished painter before the age of 22, he was first interested in studying the cognitive processes of artists, specifically how they formulate problems and decide what to paint. But in observing these artists, he started to see something else: The activity was so enjoyable to them that they become completely enraptured with it. So he changed course and developed a theoretical conception of the positive joy artists experience when creating. He then studied people who did things for which they received no external rewards. All of this was the foundation for what would later become his work on Flow.[5]

Csikszentmihalyi describes Flow as "a state in which people are so involved in an activity that nothing else seems to matter; the experience is so enjoyable that people will continue to do it even at great cost, for the sheer sake of doing it."[6]

The following are the conditions Csikszentmihalyi has described as related to achieving a state of Flow:

CONDITIONS RELATED TO ACHIEVING FLOW

- There are clear goals each step of the way.

- There is immediate feedback to one's actions.

- There is balance between challenges and skills.

- Action and awareness are merged.

- Distractions are excluded from consciousness.

- There is no worry of failure.

- Self-consciousness disappears.
- Sense of time becomes distorted.
- The activity is an end in itself.

Csikszentmihalyi found that people are genuinely satisfied in a Flow state of consciousness; however, a Flow state is not characterized by positive feelings. In Flow, there is no interference of the cognitive mind. During such an experience, people feel "strong, alert, in effortless control, unselfconscious, and at the peak of their abilities."

However, it is important to note that a state of Flow should not be confused with ease (like "going with the flow"); that is, a state of Flow is dependent upon the establishing of challenges that are neither too difficult nor too easy. Csikszentmihalyi believes satisfaction with one's life is the result of action toward your higher aims and aspirations and that "the best moments in our lives are not the passive, receptive, relaxing times ... .The best moments occur if a person's body or mind is stretched to its limits in a voluntary effort to accomplish something difficult and worthwhile."[7] In other words, you can be active in your achievement of Flow. Rather than passive acceptance of a future seemingly determined by external forces, achieving Flow is the act of setting challenges for yourself, achieving them, and exercising control over the way you think about things. And everyone is capable of this.[8]

HOW

1) When have you experienced Flow? Where were you and what were you doing?

2) When was the last time you experienced Flow?

3) Are there areas of your life where you Flow? What are they?

4) What does Flow feel like to you?

5) Pay attention to your activities. Notice if there are times you are in a state of Flow and what you are doing and who you are with at those times.

Nugget Mining #6: Motivations

Motivation is your reason or your drive for doing something. Without it, well, you'd probably just want to lounge around in your pajamas and Big Bird slippers all day, every day. Simply put, you need motivation to accomplish the things in life you want to do.

There are two kinds of motivations: extrinsic and intrinsic. I like the way P.M. Forni describes this in the book, *The Thinking Life*.[9] He states, "Humans tend to function either more like weather vanes or more like clocks." Forni means that for some people, life experience is driven by the external world—the way others react or respond to them. These are the "weather vanes." Just like a weather vane, these folks rely on an external force—the wind—to get them moving or take their cues from the external world for their self-worth. This is an out-side-in approach to life and success, and it's precisely what the current college admissions system is built on.

Forni explains that clocks are different than weather vanes be-cause clocks (and these are old school clocks, mind you, not the fancy new Apple Watches) move based on internal forces, or the wind up mechanism of the clock itself. When you have the ability to rely on an internal mechanism, or your own self-awareness, as the foundation for your self-worth, what is happening on the outside matters less. This is an "inside-out" way of living.

Forni's description of people as weather vanes or clocks highlights the difference between extrinsic and intrinsic motivation. Extrinsic motivations are those that are measured by the external standards of the external world. They are things that are motivating you outside of you, which could be things like pleasing your parents, or getting money for chores, or getting good grades because you will get some reward, like getting into college. Intrinsic motivations, on the other hand, are rooted in your deep desires, or the things you find most per-sonally rewarding. These are things you would do whether you were recognized or not. There are a variety of reasons and ways we become oriented toward one of these types of motivation over the other, and these can range from our genes to our life experiences to the modeling we have by those around us.

Extrinsic Motivations	Intrinsic Motivations
• Financial compensation	• Personal meaning from efforts
• Having social status	• Expressing one's values and beliefs
• Public recognition	• Having a positive impact on the world
• Power and title	• Helping others
• Over-focus on getting good grades (instead of the act of learning) to get into college	• Experiencing satisfaction in doing a good job
• Reading a book because it makes you look smart	• Learning because it is interesting to you or you are passionate about the subject
	• Reading a book about a subject that interests you

We have placed a lot of value on extrinsic achievement, especially when it comes to college admissions. External measurements of success and visible achievements often trump inner desire and motivations in our education system. The issue with extrinsic motivation is that it sometimes defines a leader: That is, self-esteem comes from what you have achieved externally rather than what has been achieved internally. What makes this hard is that it will be difficult to achieve what you set out to do in your own unique way if you are placing all the power to define that success in the external world. Again, this is about being self-aware.

There isn't anything wrong with external motivation per se, but you want to be careful to not get caught in the snowball of peer or parental pressure to follow a pre-determined path to happiness, which is often rewarded by externally-motivated factors. The best ways to avoid this is to be very clear about where it is that you find happiness and fulfillment internally.

As I have already mentioned, for your college admissions process to be supportive of helping you to become the person you are meant to be, you must have more than just an externally-focused orientation. You must work hard to get beyond the voices of what the external world says success is, and move closer to those things that call to you. Your intrinsic motivations are important and should be cultivated.

When you share who you are and what you want for your life with others, as vulnerable as it can be, it helps you to take action in the direction of your dreams. It also helps people know how to support you and to connect you to others who might help.

HOW

1) Reflect upon the insights you gained from the reviewing of your story and the taking stock of your raw material. What are the qualities of people who might best be able to support you?

2) Make a list of the most important people in your life right now. Do any of these people exhibit these qualities?

3) Make a list of the most important people in your past. What was your most important relationship?

4) Identify at least one or two people you can talk to about the insights you have as you walk this road exploring who you are and your dreams, goals, and intentions. This is your chance to be really specific with that person. Ask him or her to be to be a member of your Dream Team to help realize your dreams, goals, and intentions.

5) Begin to think of others who might be willing to do the same.

"

Please know that **college is not** the **end** goal.
It is a place to **develop** about things, the way in which **you talk about things** and where you can **broaden** your perspective on the **world**. But **it is no longer** the place **where** you define **who** you're **going to be** or **what** is your life is going to be about because **that happens** all **throughout your life.** It's **not** just college.

STUDENT VOICE

"

HOW

1) Fill out the chart below, listing your activities, your motivations, and whether the motivation is intrinsic or extrinsic. If it is only being done to please someone else, think about why you are participating in the activity.

Activity	Description of Motivation	Extrinsic Motivation (E), Intrinsic Motivation (I), or Both Extrinsic and Intrinsic (B)
Piano lessons	I love music, and this brings me a lot of joy.	I

2) Consider your findings. Are there more externally motivated activities or internally motivated activities on your list? How do you feel about this? Consider if there are changes you want to make in your activities as a result of this insight.

3) Compare how you feel when you do each of these activities. Do you notice any difference between the ones that are extrinsically motivated and those that are intrinsically motivated?

Having gathered your raw material, which we will draw from as you continue your journey, it is now time to turn from your internal investigation to those who will support you.

Chapter Ten:
U Map Step Three—Dream Team

"Surround yourself with only people who are going to lift you higher."
— *Oprah Winfrey*

Having surveyed your life and collected many nuggets of raw material, you now turn your attention to those who can provide you support on this journey. Being boldly yourself is an exciting act, but it can be a lonely one. At the heart of being your biggest, baddest self is stepping out, stepping up and embracing the next courageous step toward the authentic version of you. This is not for the faint of heart. Being yourself is an act only you can do and no one can do on your behalf; however, it is much, much easier to be yourself when you have a tribe that supports you.

There are several reasons to create this tribe. Your tribe makes all the difference when you are working to live the bold life that represents you. Not only will these folks provide support, encouragement and enthusiasm, but also they will offer you feedback, challenge and accountability toward your goals. By engaging a group of people to help you realize your dreams, you will be supported in being the truest version of yourself.

Organizations have boards of advisors, so why shouldn't you? This is why you create your Dream Team. Who should be on this Dream Team of yours? You add people to your Dream Team slowly throughout this process because as you learn more about yourself and what is important to you, you need to make sure the people on your Dream Team are aligned with who you are and with that which supports you on your path.

One of the traps of bold acts is doing them to please or to impress others, whether this be family members, friends, mentors, kids who look up to you, or the cute boy or girl you are dying to date. You can engage in bold action but not be any closer to the truest version of yourself if your actions are aimed at pleasing or impressing others. These actions aren't about acting on behalf of the truest form of you; they are about performance.

"

I'd say where you **go doesn't have** to be a **top,** top **school** to **provide** you with the opportunities **you need.** If you have a **specific passion,** look for a school or a **professor** that **excels** in that field.

STUDENT VOICE

"

Chapter Eleven:
U Map Step Four—Synthesize

"Wholeness is not achieved by cutting off a portion of one's being, but by integration of the contraries." – Carl Jung

Now that you have gathered your raw material and started to identify people to support you, it is time to put it all together to begin to make meaning of what you have gathered and to begin to frame the opportunities ahead of you from the place you now stand. This requires steps to interpret where you are based on the learnings you have experienced through surveying the landscape of you and through your nugget mining.

Identify Your Multiple Selves

One of the chief complaints students have about their experiences in applying to college is that there exists the expectation they have to know what they are going to do or be. Most students feel enormous pressure to know what they will major in and what job or career they will pursue. Unless you are one of the (very) few people on this planet born knowing exactly what you will do with your life, you will likely have to go through a relatively robust process of discovery before you can know such things. To me, college is one of the places this type of activity should happen. More than only a single track to a job, college is an opportunity to explore and learn more about yourself and the world around you. This is one of the many ways the current process is destructive to your budding interests. By implying you must know this at the time you head off to college is, well, nuts. You are going to learn a lot more about yourself and the world during that time.

Moreover, believing that you have to be just one thing or find that one true calling can be a trap. There are some folks who knew from a young age what they wanted to do or be, but most didn't. At all. For most, it is a process of discovery over a period of years, and it is an ongoing process. Just ask some adults in your lives about how they got where they are in their careers, and I promise that you will find that there are plenty of people who took a very crooked path to where they are today.

One of the big problems that I have with the system as it stands today is the fact that students don't believe they have the room for being and doing different things. And all of this just as you are starting out on your path! Here is the deal: There is room for you to experiment and discover, and I suggest you take it. This is why I have included this section on celebrating your many selves.

I want to make clear that part of the intent of this journey is synthesis. Another word I use often to invoke the same meaning is integration. Often I find that people have experienced a fracture—a separation from parts of themselves longing for expression—and this is the root of discontent or of the stress they are experiencing. It is for this same reason that while working with students I often hear they have different voices running inside of them. Sometimes it is a critical voice, or a voice of self-compassion, or a voice coaching them to be their best selves, shouting, "You can do it!" Sometimes students can tie these voices to particular people in their lives, and other times they are voices that seem to come from another place.

As crazy as this may seem, all of these parts of you and these voices play a very important role in leading you closer to an understanding of the complexity of you. You are not a one-dimensional being; there is far more depth to you than we in society tend to acknowledge. Sometimes you may do your best to shoo away these various voices—the voices of parts of yourself trying to find expression. But if you are to be in search of your deepest and truest self, this is a dangerous act.

In his wonderful book, *Your Signature Path*, Geoffrey Bellman describes the concept of "three selves"—the public self, the private self, and the reflective self.[1] I often use these "selves" in my work with students, especially in the process of applying to college. Here they are:

Public Self: This is the you that people see on the outside. It's the actions you take and the words you say.

Private Self: This self includes your thoughts and feelings and even what you seek through the actions your public self takes.

Reflective Self: Often confused with the private self, this is the self that actually observes your public self and your private self and makes meaning of them.

Many students apply for college admissions using only their public selves. They do this because this is how we as a society communicate they should behave when applying for college admissions. Sadly, this often then carries into their adult lives until they can no longer handle the lack of the alignment between these three selves. This is often the reason I see people in mid-life; they have been wearing the mask of the public self for a long time—or sometimes the masks of a variety of public selves—and they are now ready to cast off the mask, but they are afraid of exposing what is behind that mask—their private and reflective selves.

In fact, the most successful admissions path is a blending of these three selves—and it is this effort toward synthesis or integration that must be at the heart of your design process. Students often think it is far too risky to expose their private or reflective selves, but, really, this is where all the good stuff is. Through the process of integrating these three selves, students become more human and something far beyond the standard words and numbers on a page—even their essays become far more powerful because students share with authenticity who they really are.

HOW

1) Have you noticed times that your three selves are split apart? When does your public self come out? Your private self? Your reflective self?

2) What are the characteristics of each of these selves?

3) Take time to notice from which self you are operating at different times of the day and week. When does your public self show up? Your private self? Your reflective self?

4) When was the last time you noticed that these three selves were integrated? Where were you and what were you doing?

One-Person Play: Your Cast of Characters

Though I often reference the three selves I described above in my work with students and their families, in my experience, there are usually many, many more than only these three selves. I call this the "one-person play" because in a one-person play, all the characters are contained in just one person—in this case, you! This crazy cast of characters is comprised of many creatures eager to get your time and attention—and to be in charge. When I recently engaged in an exercise exploring different selves with a student, we found she had an evil troll, a sad dog, a big white elephant, an ogre, and a 1990s rock star among her cast of characters—all with different voices saying different things.

You likely have a number of these characters inside of you, too; however, there are a few particular voices I want to highlight.

The Saboteur

Sadly, I have yet to meet someone who does not have a Saboteur. In fact, most people have more than one. The Saboteur loves to tell you all the reasons you are not good enough and all the reasons your plans to achieve your goals or to express your full and best self are trash. Yep, the Saboteur is mean, mean, mean. The Saboteur likes to make you believe things like, "You should be working harder" and "You aren't very smart." Usually with the Saboteur, you are too much of something (too fat, too loud, too stupid, too much) or not enough of something (not pretty or handsome enough, not smart enough, not successful enough, not old enough). You get the point. The Saboteur loves to make sure you are playing within the confines of the box and by the rules—and not stepping out of line of any prevailing rules and beliefs.

My own Saboteurs (yes, I have two) are alive and well—and super wicked! There is a nasty, warty troll with a matted white beard and a White Witch (much like the witch in the movie version of *The Lion, the Witch and the Wardrobe*). As I work on this book, it has been mostly the troll with me, telling me all kinds of rotten things—about how this book is a dumb idea, about how no one will read it, about how this whole section doesn't make sense, about how I don't know what I'm doing, about how people will find it hokey . . . and I could go on and on (because he goes on and on). I am really sick of that little troll (maybe the mean, nasty witch is on vacation? I am sure she'll be back soon), but because I know the troll thinks he's doing what is best for me, we have come to a mutual understanding. I do my best to either comfort him, telling him things are OK, or I just let his voice slide right on by, like chatter from the other room. Sometimes, if I am lucky, he takes a nap.

Most think the Saboteur is there to ensure nothing bad happens, which is, in part, true—it's just that the Saboteur becomes extra loud and kicks it into high gear when you make a choice to lead a more fulfilling life. You can rest assured that the Saboteur will be shouting at you as soon as you start to dream and scheme in line with your interests and values or when you start to follow your heart and your callings. It is also the Saboteur running the show when you believe that you are a fraud and do not deserve the attention or success you are having. In short, the Saboteur is bad news. Though it thinks it has your best interest in mind in keeping you right where you are, if you want to be on the path to the fullest and most authentic expression of you, the Saboteur needs to be watched out for and put on a pretty short leash.

Your Wise Self

Gratefully, you have a counter to your Saboteur: Your Wise Self. Your Wise Self is wickedly cool. Your Wise Self is you in 20 years, confident in what he or she has achieved (i.e. your dreams) and giving you information about how to get to that place. Your Wise Self doesn't give a rip about the opinions or judgments of others (it is so refreshing!). Your Wise Self is only interested in seeing you become the person you are meant to become and to help you fulfill your dreams. Your Wise Self is accomplished and fulfilled in all the best ways—and is available to guide you to the best version of you.

HOW

1) The Costume Shop—Explore Your Different Selves: Imagine yourself in the biggest costume shop of all time. See yourself trying on the costumes and actually becoming the character you were dressing up to be. Who would you dress up as? And why? How does this character display something that is present in your life? Or how does it display something you don't have enough of in your life? What is the costume for your Saboteur? For your Wise Self?

2) Throughout the day, as thoughts come into your mind, try to assign the voices of those thoughts a name and an identity. I like to create a whole cast of characters with faces and names (yes,

some of their faces are from popular culture, for example), so I can become friendly to them. In particular, name your Saboteur and give it an identity. (Of course, like me, you may have more than one.) Also name Your Wise Self and give that character an identity. See if there are others who can be identified and given a face and a name.

3) Use a Pinterest board to give images to the cast of characters that live inside of you. Or create a collage or some other artistic representation of some of the key characters. As I write this, I am staring at two figurines, a troll and a unicorn, which represent my Saboteur and my Wise Self. Cheesy? Probably. But, I'll tell you what: It's helping.

Are you a Multipotentialite or a Specialist?

Just like you may have many areas of interests, you also have many areas of potential. One of my favorite TED Talks is Emilie Wapnick's "Why some of us don't have one true calling." Wapnick defines someone with many interests and creative pursuits as a "Multipotentialite."[2] Such individuals are also called "Renaissance Souls" by Margaret Lobenstine[3] and "Scanners" by Barbara Sher.[4] In her talk, Wapnick states, "It's easy to see your multipotentiality as a limitation or an affliction that you need to overcome. But what I've learned through speaking with people and writing about these ideas on my website, is that there are some tremendous strengths to being this way." Many of the greatest thinkers and contributors to society have been Multipotentialites. Wapnick cites three Multipotentialite super powers: idea synthesis, rapid learning, and adaptivity. And guess what? All of these skills are badly needed today and in the future.

One of the many ways in which we are destructive in the process of college admissions is through suggesting to students that they have to know what they are planning to do or to be once they hit college. We often send messages to you that you have to choose—and that there is just one "true" calling, a notion that has become highly romanticized in our culture. If you don't fit into this mold, you feel like something is wrong with you. In fact, in our rapidly changing world, Multipotentialites are everywhere and growing in number all the time.

Alternatively, there are Specialist tendencies. Specialists are those who often are very clear on the direction they are headed, and rather than span several subjects, they deep dive into one. Of course, this, too, is a great strength; huge contributions have been made by people who have been in their fields gaining deeper and deeper knowledge.

In fact, according to Wapnick, Multipotentialites and Specialists make great team members because of their diversity in thinking, approaches, and views. In short, there is no wrong way. And, rather than engaging in "either-or" thinking (like someone is either Multipotentialite *or* a Specialist), think of these qualities on more of a spectrum. If you are running around thinking that you have to be just one thing, this is a completely false notion. If, however, you are clear on what you want to do, and that is just one thing, embrace that. There is nothing wrong with you except that you think something is wrong with you. Celebrate your natural way of being. In a perfect world, you would be designing your experience based on how you are wired.

HOW

1) Think about the qualities of Multipotentialites and Specialists. Where do you think you fall on this spectrum? If you don't know, don't worry! You can hold them both in your mind as you learn more about yourself!

2) Below is an image of several frames I have adapted from the work of Margaret Lobenstine in her book, *The Renaissance Soul*.[5]

   a. If you resonate with the description of a Multipotentialite, use the various frames below to identify your various areas of potential. As a Multipotentialite, begin to translate your interests into frames of work you might do.

   b. If you resonate more with a Specialist, use just one or two of the frames and explore where your interests might lead you. As you deep dive—as a Specialist would—you may find yourself using more frames to explore the various depths of your interests.

   c. Switch identities: If you consider yourself a Multipotentialite, see what it feels like to narrow your focus like you would if you were a Specialist. If you are a Specialist, see if you can push yourself to try on the identity of a Multipotentialite by identifying more than one area you like and want to explore.

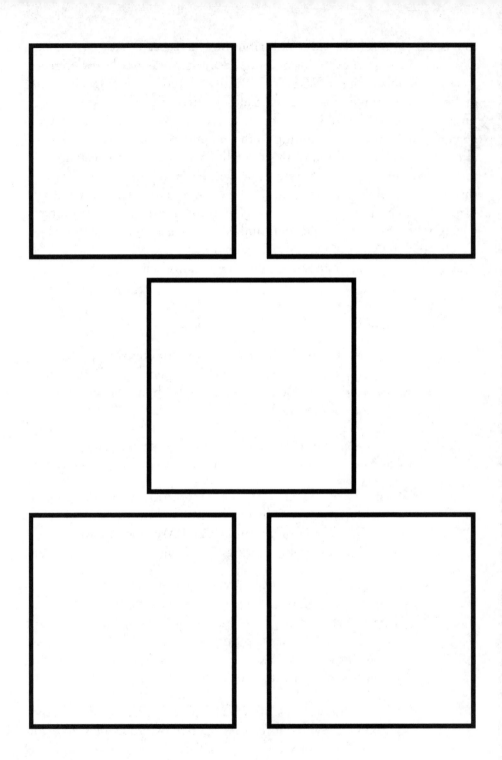

Toward Integration: Life on the Möbius Strip

Now that you have identified some of the many aspects of yourself and your potential, you are ready for an exercise in integration.

Ultimately, what you are aiming for at the bottom of the U Map is the integration of all these parts and pieces of you that you've identified. Integration is "to form, coordinate, or blend into a functioning or unified whole." The best way to understand this integration is through Parker Palmer's metaphor of life on the Möbius strip. The premise of the Möbius strip is perhaps best digested while thinking of a strip of paper. If you attach a strip of paper end to end, you get a circle, something like the paper chains you may have created as a child. If you were to trace your finger on the circle, there is a clear inside of the circle and a clear outer portion to the circle. These two sides—inner and outer—do not touch. This is often how we live: We have an external part of ourselves that face the world, but we keep our soul selves—our true aspirations and dreams—locked away in the inside circle. Often, there is no reconciliation, no meeting, and no integration of our external and internal worlds.

If, however, you take that same strip of paper and twist it a quarter turn and then attach the ends, you get something called a Möbius strip. Tracing your finger along the surface of this strip, there is no distinct inside and outside of the strip; it is one continuum. Our finger flows from the inside to the outside surface without interruption, or, in the words of Palmer, "The two surfaces keep flowing into each other, co-creating each other, in an endless cycle of a form that has only one side."[6]

On the Möbius strip, the inner and outer selves are integrated, complementing one another, feeding one another. There is a healthy tension; not a destructive separation. There is a dance between the inner and outer worlds. And, as Palmer states, "Much depends on what we choose to send out into the world from within ourselves—and much depends on how we choose to internalize what the world sends back to us."[7] It is, indeed, a choice.

In thinking about how you might consciously choose your path as an act of deep respect and honor for the person you already are, choice is paramount. Consider ending the frenzied pursuit to be somebody "colleges want" and move toward the expression of what you want — your deepest longings and knowings. Thinking about this, I am struck by Palmer's powerful question: "How can I travel the Möbius strip so keenly aware of this constant co-creative exchange of the inner and outer that can make choices about it — about what I send out and what I take in — in ways that are life giving for the world, for other people, and for me?"[8]

HOW

1) Pay attention to how your inner and outer worlds are or are not integrated. If they are integrated, why do you believe they are? If they are not, why do you believe they aren't?

2) Where is there the "co-creative exchange" of your inner and outer worlds? And in what areas is this nourishing for you, for other people, and for the world?

3) Are there areas where your favorite things, interests, strengths, and/or gifts are integrated or overlap? If so, where?

Your Brain Needs Integration, Too!: The Left and Right Sides of the Brain

Even your brain loves integration! You likely already know something about the left and right sides of your brain, having heard remarks along the lines of how so-and-so is really "left brained" and is good at math, but not very creative. Or how someone who is more emotional and creative is really "right-brained."

The fact is that it is more complicated than this in that your left and right sides of your brain are always talking to each other. The left and right sides of the brain are communicating all the time through something called the corpus callosum, Latin for "tough body," which is a flat and wide group of neural fibers which is like a horizontal highway back and forth between these two sides. This is also the largest area of white matter in your brain.

Reflect back to when you were a wee little one. The development of your brain is dominant on the right side in your early years. You probably don't remember this from when you were just a tot, but you have likely seen this if you have ever seen or been in contact with a little baby: Your early years were pre-verbal. In other words, you got your needs met through using your body—crying, cooing, and being generally just, well, cute. The right side of your brain is responsible for things like your emotions and relationships. It is also where things like images, metaphors, non-verbal and autobiographical memory are stored. Interestingly, the right side of your brain has the primary role in stress reduction and your sensing of your whole body and your intuition.

Later on, like at the ages of two or three, you began asking a lot of "why?" questions. You know the ones I'm talking about: Why is the sky blue? Why does the dog have fur? Why does a bicycle have wheels? The reason for this is because that is the stage of development in which the left side of your brain is coming on strong. The left side of your brain is in charge of reasoning and rational thought. It's the side of your brain that really digs on all things linear and predictable patterns like cause and effect.

There is a big difference between these two sides of your brain, and in the best of cases, they are complementary to one another, but they can also compete. Dr. Dan Siegel writes, "The right mode creates an "AND" stance, while the left creates an "OR" point of view."[9]

The reason the discussion of left and right side business is so critical is because we have made college admissions primarily a left-side brain process, when really you need the right side of your brain online, too. The thing is that your brain really wants to be integrated; that is, the right wants to work with the left, and vice versa. The integration of these two sides is the mind's natural way of being, which is called, not surprisingly, "bilateral integration." Without bilateral integration, it is tough to write essays that answer questions like, "What matters to you?" and "What has been your biggest challenge so far?"

"

It may be hard to **differentiate** a **passion** for something from a **random whim, but** if the student is **adamant,** and **pushes back** on your **advice,** you should **accept their choice** and **attempt** to **find** them **the best** location to go to **school** for what they have **decided** to do. **Even** if that is being a **game developer** when **you don't** think that that is a **"real job,"** or **even** if they **really want nothing more** than to be a **tradesman** or an **artist**. Not **every** student **needs** to go to a **prestigious school,** and some may **in fact** be **better off** if they **don't**.

STUDENT VOICE

"

Chapter Twelve:
U Map Step Five—Clarify

"Today you are you! That is truer than true! There is no one alive who is you-er than you!" – Dr. Seuss

Now that you have spent time seeing and investigating the multidimensional being that you are and synthesizing and integrating the many parts of you, it is time to distill and clarify that which is important to you.

Your Contributions

In their book, *The Art of Possibility*, Rosamund Stone Zander and Benjamin Zander offer a reframing of the living of one's life to "being a contribution." They suggest that by declaring oneself a contribution to the world, suddenly the traditional trappings of ego, money, and fame fall into the background, becoming secondary to the offering you are providing to others and to the world by embracing the contribution you make. They write, "Naming oneself and others as a contribution produces a shift away from self concern and engages us in a relationship with others that is an arena for making a difference."[1]

For the purposes of your journey, it is important to understand the areas in which you are a contribution and to declare yourself as such. By doing this, you begin to see the impact—in both big and small ways—you have on the lives of others.

HOW

1) Identify your contributions. Make a list of the ways you currently make a difference in the following areas:

- Your family
- Your friends
- Your school community
- Your larger local community
- The global community

If you don't make a significant contribution to all of these areas, don't get worked up about it. There is plenty of time. If you would like to be a contribution in more areas than you currently are, that's something to reflect upon and think about changing.

2) Dream of the ways you would like to be a contribution in the future. If you could do anything at all, how might you contribute to the following areas?

- Your family
- Your friends
- Your school community

- Your larger local community
- The global community

3) Believe you are a contribution. Throw yourself into life as someone who makes a difference, accepting that you may not know how or why, but being open to the many possibilities.

Your Stands

Next, let's explore your stands. The very best way I've discovered to identify your stands is to think about the things that really make you angry. I am not talking about the kind of anger you might feel if your sister uses your toothbrush or someone cuts you off at the traffic light. I am talking about the kind of anger you experience when something is really important to you. It is the fiery passion you feel for a cause or for something larger than yourself. Sometimes these stands are rooted in your personal experiences and something you have witnessed; other times, they are areas you feel strongly about just because.

I love this one because this is where you get to be your baddest, maddest self. Somehow, these stands tend to get the blood to a boil in under a minute. They are your hot button issues. I personally can become quite a dragon lady when I am angry, and I love to let her out to play when it comes to my stands. Just one of my stands (yep, I have several) has to do with the injustice and destructiveness that exists because the way we approach college admissions is SO DARN WRONG. I am mad enough—and inspired by the potential in all of you enough—that I have to say something about it, which is the very reason I am writing this book.

Sometimes people describe their stands as things they cannot help but do, so that can be another clue to your stands. There may be things that ring your bell so loudly, you feel you don't have a choice but to act.

Of course, taking a stand or feeling passionately about a topic doesn't actually mean you have to be angry (though it might). But, like I said, it's often a good place to start. Usually in the case of stands, you feel you have a duty to say or do something. That fiery passion you feel for the environment, children, poverty, politics, women's issues, or health-related matters, for example, can (and should) be used as a force for good. In taking a stand, you are an advocate for something bigger, larger, and more meaningful than yourself alone.

HOW

1) Make a list of things that really make you angry related to larger world themes. How do these connect to your personal experiences? Think back to the surveying of your life to this point. Were there particular experiences that have influenced you to the point of wanting to take a stand for something?

2) Where do you see unfairness in the world that you feel passionately about and want to somehow get involved?

3) What are the areas in which you have felt a duty to say or do something about a particular topic?

Your Values

Before we can talk about what success actually might be, we need to take a closer look at that which we value. Though most people start with values and beliefs, I start with an investigation of your life and some of its key components because I believe your values should stem from the things that you are naturally drawn to and express. If the way you are living lines up with the life you hope to lead, good for you! But if it doesn't, this is the time to consider what changes you would like to make. Often in my practice, I see students who are so harried, there is no time to clarify their values. This can lead to a deep feeling of emptiness, and a lot of *doing* without direction or satisfaction. Success can be defined in many different ways, and most often we feel success when our life reflects the values we hold most dear.

The reason to get in touch with your values is that at your core, as a human being, you need to be motivated by something larger than you. You need to know, and not just "at the end of the day," what you stand for. And, you need this to connect to a larger community with members who stand for the same thing. Beyond this, it is connection to your values that allows you to sustain motivation to realize your dreams, and it is your values that help ensure you are on a path to a fulfilling life. When you are out of line with your values, and you know what those values are, it is just a matter of course correction. If you don't know your values, it is like taking a journey without a map. Another thing? Your values help you deal with your Saboteur. When you have your values in place, it is much easier to weigh your values more heavily than the voice of your Saboteur; that is, your Saboteur is probably going to lose that battle every time.

Without even knowing it, most of us act on and honor our values without the awareness that we are even doing so. It sometimes isn't until something goes really well or right—or until something goes really badly—that your values become evident. By more explicitly identifying your values, you can use them as a compass for your decision making and for living the way that is most fulfilling to you. It is for this reason that this section contains many exercises to help you identify and clarify your values. Becoming conscious of your values is an essential part of this process.

HOW

Life Line Highs and Lows

1) Look back at the highs and lows on your Life Line. Often when things go really well, it is because there is an expression of one's values embedded in the event. When things don't go well, or we experience loss, it often has to do with something we value being negatively impacted.

2) For our purposes, I've adapted the following exercises from Co-Active Coaching:[2]

   For the highs, what values were present at that moment in time? (List three values, if possible.)

   _____

   _____

   _____

For the lows, what values were lost or hidden at that moment in time? (List three values, if possible.)

_____

_____

_____

3) Make a list of "Must Haves" for your life. Beyond the basic requirements of things like food and shelter, what MUST you have in order to live a life that is fulfilling to you? Think about things that are non-negotiable. What are the values you absolutely must honor for your life to have meaning?

_____

_____

_____

Throw Yourself a Birthday Bash

When my wonderful grandfather, "Pop Pop," was 90 years old, we threw him a big ol' birthday bash. We wore t-shirts in his honor, and many people spoke kind words about what he had meant to them. It occurred to me that when I am 90, I hope people say those same nice things about me.

So, imagine, just like my Pop, you live a remarkable, healthy and full 90 years, and life had unfolded for you beyond your wildest dreams. People are throwing you a raging birthday bash to celebrate. Naturally, because you have lived such an awesome life, there are many people who want to give you a toast. Representatives from the following five groups step forward to honor you:

- A member of your family
- A friend
- Someone you worked with
- Someone you helped
- Someone from your community

1) What does each of these people say about you? You can choose only some of them, but hearing from all of them is pretty powerful! And you are 90! So, of course, you want to hear them! Write down what they say about your inner traits, skills, and accomplishments. Since each knows you in a different con text, what sides of your personality have they seen?

2) After you have heard from each of these individuals, see if you can identify from their words what values they've suggested you hold.

The Cover Story of You

The following activity is adapted from *Business Model You*.[3]

It is five years from now, and you have just been featured in a major news story.

1) What is the name of the newspaper, magazine, or program that featured you? Choose an actual publication in which you would like to be featured.

2) Why were you featured? What is the story about?

3) Write down some quotes from the interview or the news story. What did you say? And what was said to you?

4) Share and discuss your cover story with a member of your Dream Team.

5) Mine what you uncovered for your values. What does the story indicate about what is important to you?

People You Admire

Now its time to turn your attention to people you admire. Using the grid below, fill in the values of different types of people you admire—and also the values of someone you don't admire.

	Name	Value 1	Value 2	Value 3
A person in your family, chosen family or network of friends whom you admire				
A public figure whom you admire				
A person from another environment whom you admire				
A person who drives you nuts and/or whom you do not admire				

1) What values from the grid resonate with you most? Are they values you want to claim as your own?

2) What do the values you recorded about the person who drives you nuts say about your own values? Sometimes it can be easier to identify the values you don't want to exhibit, which ultimately can assist you to find the ones you do.

Values Shop

Having completed the exercises above, it is now time to "shop" for some values.

1) Select eight values from the following list that represent the values you hold and express in your life or values you *would like* to hold and express in your life. When you are selecting these values, do not use your thinking mind; instead, choose the values that resonate with you. See if you can even get a felt sense of each word, and select the ones that you are most drawn toward.

For you to know what your priorities are in life, you must know what you value.

Achievement	Accountability	Advancement
Affection	Adventure	Appearances
Authenticity	Autonomy	Arts
Beauty	Challenge	Balance
Harmony	Having family	Commitment
Helpfulness	Honesty	Health
Honor	Independence	Humor
Inner harmony	Integrity	Influence
Involvement	Supervising others	Intellectual status
Communication	Competence	Community
Competition	Cooperation	Compassion
Creativity	Ecological	Courage
Effectiveness	awareness	Economic security
Expertise	Efficiency	Excitement
Fairness	Excellence	Ethical practice
Family	Faith	Fame
Financial gain	Fast living	Freedom
Growth	Friendship	Fun
Joy	Happiness	Job tranquility
Leadership	Justice	Knowledge
Loyalty	Location	Love
Money	Meaningful work	Merit
Order	Nature	Openness and honesty
Power and authority	Personal development	Pleasure
Purity	Privacy	Public service
Relationships	Prosperity	Recognition
Resilience	Religion	Reputation
Tolerance	Responsibility	Time
Truth	Tranquility	Trust
Work quality	Wealth	Wisdom
	Work with others	Work alone

2) Do your best to narrow your list down to your top three to five values. Write them below:

_____

_____

_____

_____

_____

Interview Those Close to You

It can be very hard to identify your values, so another way to uncover them is to ask your friends and family members what values they see you expressing through your actions. Though you might not always be able to recognize the values you live by, those around you might be able to provide some insight. If you'd like, you can also share a blank copy of the list above with those close to you or members of your Dream Team and ask them to circle the five qualities that they see in you.

1) Look at the information they provide with curiosity. Are there overlaps? Are there words you hadn't considered?

2) Have a conversation about why a particular word was circled. You might also ask them to be specific about what caused them to choose a particular word. Ask for the reasons behind the selection of that word.

A WORD OF CAUTION

If the values others provide you don't resonate (even if they are values you have previously held or expressed), don't feel pressure to take them on or to use them. You don't want to get sucked into the vortex of other people's values. The identification of your values isn't a crowdsourcing exercise, and not everyone needs to have a say about your values. But by checking in with others, you may gain some important insight. The purpose of this is simple: to have mirrored back to you some of the values you may be expressing without even realizing it. By asking those around you what values you are exhibiting, you may become more clear on what is important to you and values you are expressing without even knowing it.

Select Your Values

Now that you have selected a handful of values, the next important part of this is exploring the way you define your values. "Love," for example, means different things to different people. Your job is to give this a definition, as best you can, based on what the meaning is to you.

The easiest way to do this is to back into a definition. This is through thinking about people you know directly or people you have seen (in movies or on TV) that represent this value to you.

In doing this exercise, don't limit yourself to those who are only in your life now because the truth is that you may not be surrounding yourself with people who best reflect your values. If this is the case, your job is to go and find those people. Set an intention to draw these folks into your life, and then watch for them. Before you know it, they will begin to show up. And when they do, you can then ask them to be on your Dream Team.

1) On the grid below, write down one of your values. Then write down a name of someone who represents that value.

2) What is it that this person does that represents this value to you? What are the specific actions they take that let you know they are living this particular value?

3) Write down your ideas on how you might express the value. What actions could you take?

Value	Name	Things they do to express it	Things I might do to express it

A REMINDER: HOLD THESE LIGHTLY

Values are really important to your process. Be certain to dig into these, but also know that over time, you may experience some modification in your values or what is important to you. Not only is this normal, it is good. It means you are a growing and evolving human being.

Mine/Theirs: Values in Action

I now want to introduce an excellent tool from Margaret Lobenstine's *The Renaissance Soul: How to Make your Passions Your Life*.[4] For this exercise, review all of the activities in which you are currently engaged. Using the grid below, in the first column, place the name of the activity. In the second column write down why you do this activity. In the third column, write down whose values its expresses—an "M" for "Mine, a "T" for "Theirs," or a "B" for "Both Mine and Theirs." In the fourth column, identify which values are expressed through this activity (you can use the long list of values on the previous pages if that is helpful), and finally, in the fifth column, determine if it is something you might want to continue.

Activity	Justification for activity— Why do you engage in this activity?	What values?	My Values (M), Their Values (T), Both Mine and Theirs (B)	Continue? (Y or N)
Piano lessons	I love music	Creativity, Growth and Fun	B—I love it, and my parents are in support of it	Y

The results of this may be astounding to you, or they may not surprise you at all. You may be doing things just because it looks good or because you think it is what others want for you or because it expresses their values. You may also find that activities that you have been on the fence about actually very much line up with your values, and you may begin to feel differently about them.

The goal of this exercise is not for you to go home and stir the pot with your parents or other adults in your lives about the things they want for you or have "forced" you to do. In fact, you may be surprised to learn that later in life you may look back fondly on these activities. But the point is for you to recognize if it is something you are doing for yourself or if you are doing it for someone else. This is where we are connecting the dots between internal and external motivation, your values, and the activities where you spend your time.

A WORD ABOUT PARENTS

Sometimes students are shocked to hear that parents (yes, parents) really do have their kid's best interest at heart and, in fact, do know a lot about what makes their child tick. Yes, there are parents who are reliving their own dreams (for lack of pursing them), but that is the exception more than it is the rule. Try having a conversation with your parents about the results of your chart, and see what agreements you can come to about how to move forward and be engaged in activities that are meaningful to you and express your values.

Putting It All Together

Now you should have a number of values with which to work — all of those that have come from the exercises above. Revisit the various values that you uncovered, and make a master list of these values below.

_____

_____

_____

_____

1) Looking at the list, consider if there are any values you hold that have not been expressed through your activities or these exercises that need to be incorporated, and incorporate them.

2) After you have compiled your master list, see if you can narrow the list down to the three to five values that resonate most with you. If you don't want to narrow down the list and you prefer to just sit with the values you have identified, that is fine! In that case, you can pick three to five values to work with to answer the following questions:

- How and where do these values show up in your daily life?

- Are there values on the list that you are not currently expressing? Where are there gaps?

- What are some ways you might start living to express those values?

Moving forward, a good benchmark for living your values is to ensure at least two of your values show up in the projects, activities, and jobs. This doesn't have to be a hard and fast rule, but it will help you be more consistent with living the values that are important to you.

You have been doing a lot of work to get yourself to this point. Now it's time to take all this rich learning and consolidate it into a statement that represents you. Say hello to Your U Statement.

Your U Statement

Your U Statement is a statement about yourself and what is important to you. It's a combination of the things you uncovered about yourself up to this point in your journey. The draft statement below is only a starting point. It is not meant to be prescriptive. What students often do is use this statement to create a first draft of their U Statement and then they modify and craft the statement into something that is fully expressive of themselves. There is no wrong way to do this; you are simply working to articulate what you have learned about yourself and what is important to you into a statement.

YOUR U STATEMENT

Standing in
[INSERT STRENGTHS OR BIRTHRIGHT GIFTS],

working to improve
[INSERT EDGES],

and expressing my interests and passions, including
[INSERT INTERESTS OR PASSIONS],

I step more fully into my values of
[INSERT VALUES].

I recognize my contributions of
[INSERT CONTRIBUTIONS].

I take a stand for
[INSERT STANDS].

Using the previous model as a guide, create the draft of your statement below:

_____

_____

_____

_____

_____

This is just a draft, and it is something you will continue to craft and hone over time. So, having created this, which is no small task, stop and take a breath. Honor what you have accomplished. It is now time to embrace the power of the unique and wonderful you.

Embrace The Power of You

Now that you have arrived at the center of the U Map, it is going to be more important and relevant than ever before for you to really become friends with your power. Power might seem like an odd section in a book about college admissions, but, hang tight, because especially now that you are armed with the knowledge of things that are important to you, it is one of the most essential.

I am not talking about the cheap kind of power—you know, the fake kind where people pretend they are better than you. That's not real power. I am talking about the kind of power that comes from deep within you, the kind you have when you are your most true and authentic self.

What is True Power?

True power is not the golden ticket to one of the Ivies or any other "name" school. It is knowing yourself and creating a pathway to your future that supports your interests, ways of learning, and your dreams. Of course, part of the point of this book is to redefine the way we view and engage in college admissions by redefining power. True power is about knowing who you are, knowing what you want, and expressing that in the world unapologetically. As Maria Shriver shared with a *Newsweek* reporter: "I now understand that true power has very little to do with what's on your résumé. It's about being true to yourself and finding your own voice and path in the world. The way you come to your power is through your life's experiences and knowing who you are."[5]

Claiming Your Power to Choose What is Right for YOU

Armed with the self awareness you have gained up to this point in your journey (aka your true power), and your U Statement, it's now time to take back the power of your decision-making process. With this information, the process of selecting schools becomes considerably easier. If you know what makes you tick, you are more likely to find an environment to support you in that, one that also will help you achieve your dreams.

Pulitzer Prize-winning novelist and poet Alice Walker said, "The most common way people give up their power is by thinking they don't have any." True power does not look like you running around acting all crazy to get into a "name" school or have the "right" job, house, or car. And it's not achieved by becoming Ms. or Mr. Sassy Pants and acting (which is often pretending) you are "all that"; it comes by legitimately looking at experiences through the lens of what will work best for you. In the case of college, this means you are in touch with things like your strengths and areas you could improve.

You know your values and what you stand for. You know what contributions you want to make. As such, you are interviewing schools as much as they are interviewing you. That's right. You have a lot of research to do to see if the school is the right fit for you.

True power is understanding what you seek in your college experience beyond the name, and going out there to find it. It is playing a more active role in shopping colleges and finding out what they have to offer you, and not just what you have to offer them. Let me provide you with the little reminder that you are the consumer. So act like one.

> **"True power is understanding what you seek in your college experience beyond the name, and going out there to find it."**

Finally, I want to remind you that true power doesn't just relate to the college admissions process; it is a life-long endeavor of being true to yourself. True power means embracing your authentic self. It is not being afraid to own who you are and what you love. That's the power in being you.

And true power is exercising choice. So get out there and do some exercising.

HOW

1) Notice the areas in your life where you do exercise authentic power (the power of being completely you). What are those places? And what are the conditions?

2) Where are the areas you are more reluctant to act powerfully? Where do you hold back?

3) Work with a member or members of your Dream Team and have them describe when they have witnessed you embody your most powerful self.

4) Do something this week that feels powerful—from that place of authenticity. Then record the feelings you have. (BTW: It isn't uncommon for it to feel vulnerable and weird. If you feel that way, good for you! You are on the right track!)

5) Write down some thoughts about how you can feel powerful in this college admissions process. What do you have control over? Focus there.

"

The **application process** was **fulfilling...** **largely** because it was an **opportunity** for me to **define** who **I was**, on my **own** terms.

STUDENT VOICE

"

Chapter Thirteen:
U Map Step Six— Imagine

"Imagination is the beginning of creation. You imagine what you desire, you will what you imagine, and at last you create what you will."
— George Bernard Shaw

Your next step in the U Map process is to embody the notion of throwing the doors wide open to what is possible. Here is where you get to really imagine what it is you want to create with your life. Remember that business about divergent and convergent thinking? Here's a quick reminder: Divergent thinking is the expansive possibility thinking, where not even the sky is the limit. And convergent thinking is the narrowing-type thinking, the type you use to select options from what you have generated during the divergent thinking process. You are going to be using both in this section.

Dreaming and Scheming

When we only recognize certain aspects of ourselves, dreaming and scheming can become very one dimensional. If you haven't been given the opportunity to recognize all these different forms and sides of yourself, you may be only giving the typical answer to the awful question about what you want to study or do with the rest of your life. But, if you've recognized the multi-dimensional being that you are, you've also recognized that just one path or one vision of your future might be limiting.

Your Brand New Life

One day, someone arrives on your doorstep with a letter from your long lost Aunt Mildred.[1] She has left you $20 million dollars, but to receive the money, you must complete two tasks over two years, during which time all your living expenses and any expenses related to the accomplishing of the tasks will be completely covered.

1) **First Year and Task:** You must spend this year gaining knowlege. You do not have to attend any formal institution of higher education, but you just must focus your energy on learning new things. What things would you learn and why? At the end of the year, $10 million dollars will be deposited into your account.

2) **Second Year and Task:** You have one year to discover, investigate, participate in, and choose a cause or a project that you really care about that will help humanity or the world in some way. What would you choose and why? At the end of the second year of your task, you will be given the remaining balance of $10 million dollars as well as a matching $10 million to donate to the cause of your choosing. What cause will you select and why?

3) **Third Year — Your Brand New Life:** After you have completed these two tasks, you will have $20 million dollars and much experience. What sort of lifestyle will you have? What will you do? Who will you be with? Where will you live? How will you spend your time? What will you do and work to accomplish?

Be a Cat: Explore Your Nine Lives

Having explored a couple of ways you might spend your life if you were given an abundance of resources, you may have recognized there were several things you wanted to do. This activity gives you the chance to plan several perfect lives for yourself. That's right. I said lives. Like a cat. Oh, yes, I am asking you to embody your inner cat and dream up as many as nine different lives for yourself. In doing this, give yourself permission to want exactly what you want. Write down everything that appeals to you in terms of your dream life. Don't worry about what is and isn't possible; just dream really, really big. This is not the time for practicality. Blow up your existing universe and create some new ones. Ready. Set. Go.

Life 1:

Life 2:

Life 3:

"

A **passion** is something that is **built** over a **lifetime**... I **expect** not **everyone** has a **clear passion in life** at the **end** of **high school,** but if you **do, don't let anybody's advice** steer you **away** from it.

"

Life 4:

Life 5:

Life 6:

Life 7:

Life 8:

Life 9:

Now pick three of these lives, and fill out the following chart on what your life would look like in these areas. Try to be as specific as possible.

	Life #1	Life #2	Life #3
Self			
Family			
Friends/Relationships			
Work			
Money			
Location/ Community			
Other 1 (Spiritual, Physical, Mental, etc.)			
Other 2 (Spiritual, Physical, Mental, etc.)			

What are the lives that appeal to you most? What insights did you gain as a result of this process?

The Genie Be/Do/Have List

In the next exercise, adapted from Barbara Stanny's book, *Sacred Success*, you are going to build on one of the lives from the previous exercise.[2] Pick just one life and pretend you have a genie's lamp in your hands. Conjure up that genie, and by this I mean really kick in your fantasies here and dive deeply into this life you've imagined. In this exercise, there is no reason to be realistic or practical. Again, this is a place to let your dreams fly.

Think about what you might want to be, do, and have for that life in each following categories. Start making a list, but take your time. This is not something you have to knock out quickly. This is your future life we are thinking about! Most importantly, avoid putting down what you think you should do, and stick with what feels right to your soul and to the life you've cooked up.

If you are having trouble with the "shoulds," you are not alone. In this case, I often recommend you make two lists, one with the "shoulds" or "ought tos" and a second with what you really want for yourself. Try to be as specific as possible.

	Be	Do	Have
Self			
Family			
Friends/Relationships			
Work			
Money			
Location/ Community			
Other 1 (Spiritual, Physical, Mental, etc.)			
Other 2 (Spiritual, Physical, Mental, etc.)			

In doing this, how do you feel? Liberated? Terrified? All such feelings are normal. Creativity and dreaming is often accompanied by fear (more about that in a bit). For now, enjoy the good news that when you are able to imagine what your life will look like in all aspects, it is easier to begin to set your intentions and goals.

Now that you have busted things wide open, we are going to begin to employ the convergent thinking, or the narrowing and refining, toward action.

Intentions and Goals

One of the reasons that we build intentions and goals from the bottom of your U Map is so that you don't spend a lot of time in your life chasing after goals without having a clear vision of yourself and some clarity about what your purpose(s) might be. By spending time thinking about who you are, what you value, and what you truly want, you can bring many of these pieces into alignment. The truth is that you will probably reach your goals much more quickly having become clearer on these things. I've had many students report as much to me. This is precisely why I've created the U Map: so that you can integrate and align more effectively and at an earlier point in your life than you otherwise might and save yourself a potential heartache and headache down the road.

Everyone has heard about the importance of goals. In school we like to give you a heavy dose of this, making the case for why goal setting is so important and giving you structures like the SMART framework for goals (Specific, Measureable, Attainable, Realistic, and Timely) to achieve your dreams, and so on.

I used to be one of those teachers and counselors, encouraging students to set short and long-term goals and to work toward them, and while I still think there is a lot of value in this, I have come to like something else much more: intentions. An intention is "a thing intended; an aim or a plan." Hmmm, you might think, this sounds a lot like a goal. Well, it is and it isn't, and it's the subtle difference that makes the distinction so important.

Goals are a set point. They are things like "Get into Harvard," or "Win the tournament," They are usually about ploughing through at whatever cost and achieving something that is concrete. But this goes back to motivations where I talked about "outer-focused" versus "inner-focused" motivations. Sadly, on the other side of these goals is rarely the happiness people think.

This is why I prefer the word "intentions" to the word "goals." Intentions are loftier than goals, and goals sometimes don't leave room for the expansive thinking that intention allows. You know what I am talking about: the heart-felt passionate view of your future—or what I like to call "where all of the good stuff is."

To me, the notion around goals is misguided. And yes, I know, I know—for many this will be considered some type of blasphemy. But hear me out. The fact is that a lot of times once goals are set, you think that you cannot undo them. I suppose this is good if you want to achieve the goals, but it also can create a nasty tension with your evolution. I have seen this time and time again with students, which is why I stopped setting goals with them and started setting intentions.

There is something about setting goals that triggers a response in people, which can range from emotional reactions to outright revolution. As much as people think they want to achieve this very measurable and specific act, unless it is in the context of their larger vision of their life, it really isn't all that fun. And then there is this notion that you can only achieve your goals through intense, crazed effort. Now, I am someone who believes in the power of hard work, but I also know that with intention setting, there is more gentleness to moving in the direction of your dreams. Yes, success takes hard work, but it also requires rest and allowing things to happen. We hear all this talk about sustaining our earth but not nearly enough talk about sustaining ourselves. This is why focusing on intention—on what you want to see happen—is a good way of balancing what you want in your life with what your life has in store for you. Additionally, when you set intentions, it is as if some magical dust suddenly appears, and the whole universe is conspiring to make your dreams a reality.

So, let's start with intentions. Intentions are more integrated; they are more reflective of the life you want to be living and direction toward your higher purpose and calling. They are loftier and more magical than goals. Beyond that, they are about leaning into the future you want to create. In the words of author Shakti Gawain, this is the "If I could be, do and have everything I want, this would be my ideal scene."[3] And this is precisely why we started this section with your ideal scenes.

The thing about intentions is that they open you up to what you see as your dream scenes, so don't be afraid to really stretch yourself and to have fun. The purpose is expansiveness, reaching beyond the limits that you have set or others have set for you. What if you really could have everything you wanted?

AN IMPORTANT NOTE OF CAUTION

The key to this is making sure that what you list is actually everything YOU want—not what you think you "should" want or what others have told you to want or what you think will make some family member happy that you want. It is what you, in your current form in this present moment, want for yourself and your future.

Now this is risky! I know it! While getting clear on what is true for you can be really tough, it is essential. It will help you to step onto your own path rather than someone else's. And do you really want to be on someone else's path? Some intentions I have heard are, "I want to make a difference in the world," or "I want to help people," or "I want to be a really good person."

It is once you have set your intentions that the goals can come in. These are the concrete actions steps you can take to walk in the direction of those dreams of yours. But they are not all that useful unless you have placed them in the context of the larger dreams of your life. Without that, goals just become boxes you have checked, not adding necessarily to your happiness or your understanding of the role you can play in co-creating your life.

The cool thing about starting with intentions is that the goals that follow can be more fluid and flexible. If you consider that you are setting those goals to achieve the vision you have for you and your future in a larger context, the goals become less important than the future you are working toward. That is, everything will be moving in the direction of the vision you have for yourself and things will reorganize accordingly.

There is a flow to life and some unpredictability that we cannot avoid. Here is my promise to you: Your vision will change and so will your goals. The key is for it to be an active and adaptive process, one that you return to with frequency rather than goals you set and return to later.

If you are not achieving the steps toward your future, there are usually one of two things at play: 1) Your future vision and the actions you have recorded aren't actually yours, or 2) You are afraid to go and get what you really want.

And heed these words: How this is all going to come together is only partly your business. The rest of it is up to the unpredictable but marvelous flow of life that I mentioned earlier.

HOW

1) Take one of your Dream Scenes and convert it into intentions. From there, see if you can transform it into goals. The idea is to hold the scene lightly enough so that you remain on path toward where you believe you want to head, but also so that the life's natural flow can do its job.

2) Really examine the goals you've had for yourself, and try to get to the heart of what is behind these goals. Ask yourself, why do I want that? And then when the answer comes, ask yourself again, why do I want that? And so on. Pretty soon, you will start to unearth some really "out there" stuff about why you are going after certain things. Answers I have heard often are "because it is important to my parents," or "because it will make my father proud of me," or "it will finally show all those people who made fun of me." There isn't anything wrong with any of these, so no judging – just noticing. It is an important part of becoming an adult to understand why you are doing what you are doing. It's this kind of self awareness that you need to find your unique path to offer your gifts to the world.

3) For each of your intentions and goals, think about specific people you know—or even would like to know—to ask to help make these things happen. These people may be members of your Dream Team, for example, or they may be others who will support you in achieving everything you want for yourself.

4) Pick a small action to tackle. Make it something specific to take on and to enlist the support of people above and make it happen.

Prioritizing your Intentions and Goals

An important thing to do is prioritize your intentions and goals. The best way I have found to do this is through an exercise I have adopted from Margaret Lobenstine's *The Renaissance Soul*.[4]

Take the intentions and/or goals you have set for yourself, and make a list of them again here below:

1)

2)

3)

4)

5)

6)

7)

8)

9)

10)

Pick any of the intentions you have set, and selecting from the circles below, place it in the circle size that feels most appropriate. The more important something is, the larger the circle you should place it in. These can obviously be moved around, but the key is that the most important thing to you right now is what goes in the largest circle, and the next important thing goes in the next smallest circle, and so on.

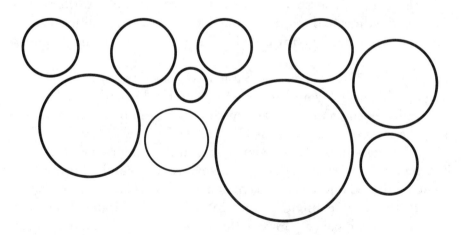

1) In looking at the circles, what insights do you have? What is really important to you now? What can wait?

2) What "aha" moments have you had in looking at your goals and intentions this way?

Chapter Fourteen:
Opening the Door to New Possibilities:
U Map Step Seven—Crossing the Threshold

"Follow your bliss and the universe will open doors
where there were only walls."
—Joseph Campbell

We have now arrived at the point of applying to college. In my work with students, I call this step "crossing the threshold."

The crossing of a threshold is a highly symbolic act. The crossing represents commitment and change, a leaving behind of the old and an embracing of the new. In mythology, such a crossing proves that a hero can follow his or her intent with positive, forward action. In engaging in this act, you are stepping into a brand new world, moving from what you have known through the doorway to something new and unknown. Of course, this is why it is both scary and thrilling. Crossing the threshold—opening the door to new possibilities—is your first active decision toward claiming independence and responsibility.

It is for all of these reasons that it is so critical to know yourself and your dreams for your future before you hit this juncture. This preparation ensures that you are much better equipped to meet and make the most of what is on the other side of that doorway.

At this point in the U Map journey, you are equipped with a U Statement that represents the person you are today and who you aspire to be. Based on that, you have done some dreaming and scheming and developed some intentions and goals. This is the foundation from which to apply to college. I know this feels like a significant departure from the traditional college exploration process, and that's OK. It can be very difficult to let go of long-held assumptions about the "right" way to go about it and instead approach this milestone differently.

By going about it this way, you become more aware of who you are and what you want from your experience. This is what I love about using the U Map with students: You really learn about yourself. Soon the "aha" moments come, and things start to make sense. Through the process itself, and the symbolic act of crossing the threshold on your path to independence and responsibility, regardless of where you go to school, your life is changed.

The Parallel Process

I want to take a moment to highlight what I call the parallel process of admissions; that is, while you are having your experience of applying to college, the adults in your life (your parents, a mentor) are also having the experience of sending you off to college. This is a big deal for all of you.

Over the years, I have found that while the experience of applying to college should be the student's alone, there are parts of the overall process that can and should be completed in dialogue and in partnership. Moreover, by completing these pieces together, you and your parents will have a much smoother time navigating the process. The following activities are those meant to be completed in partnership between you and your parents or another supportive adult. I use the word "parents" throughout this section, but I mean the term to represent a much wider definition, including that of any caring adult who is helping you through your process.

Letter of Intent

One of the best ways to explore this parallel process is through the authoring of letters. For students, there are two letters. First is the letter you write to yourself about this process and your future. But there is a twist. You write it from the voice of your still, small voice (the one you have been listening for while getting quiet) or from the voice of your Wise Self. I don't provide much more direction than this for a reason. In my experience, it is important there is plenty of room for whatever these voices bring. You may be surprised at the insights you will have through the authoring of this letter. This letter is for you to keep to yourself. The second letter is the one you write to your parents, the details of which are outlined below.

For parents, there are also two letters. The first is a letter you write to yourself about your own process to self discovery. What were the moments and events that were the most significant, challenging, and informative? Reflect on if they were planned or unplanned. This letter is meant to provide a foundation of understanding between you and your child about your own journey. The second is the letter you write to your child, the details of which are outlined below. The second letter contains the hopes, dreams, and wishes you have for your child as he or she steps into this next stage of life. It also contains important information about the process and how you will approach it together.

The following are topics that should be included in the letters from students to parents and from parents to students. Having worked with many students and parents through this process, I find the best way to complete the letter is first to do the exercises and then to draft the letter based on your responses.

Why College?

Before you even start on your college path, both you and your parents need to answer the question: Why College? Without the answer to this question, it is simply impossible to design for an admissions process that is going to meet your needs.

To this end, I want to again introduce the comments of David Brooks about the three purposes of a college education that I mentioned earlier in the book:[1]

1) Commercial Purpose: To prepare to start a career—where you go to gain skills and develop earning power to apply to the work place.

2) Cognitive Purpose: To learn things and to learn how to think. At a higher level, this is more than just learning about specific disciplines; it is a chance to take time out to really reflect upon and make sense of the world around you.

3) Moral Purpose: To develop the ability to make your own choices—to determine your beliefs and way of life independent from the pressures of peers, parents or influential adults, and society. Really, the moral purpose is about building and becoming a "self." It is through the things you learn and the experience that you are able to begin to mold yourself further into the unique being that you are. This is the process by which you craft a soul. In the words of William Deresiewicz:

It is only through the act of establishing communication between the mind and the heart, the mind and experience, that you become an individual, a unique being—a soul. The job of college is to assist you to begin to do that. Books, ideas, works of art and thought, the pressure of the minds around you that are looking for their own answers in their own ways.[2]

HOW

In your letters, answer the questions, "Why college?," and "Why now?" And are there other options to also explore? A gap year? An international program?

Students:
1) What are your reasons for attending college? And why now?

2) What do you want out of the college experience?

3) Which of the three purposes for attending most resonates with you and why?

Parents:
1) What are your reasons for having your child attend college? And why now?

2) What do you want them to get out of the college experience?

3) Which of the three purposes most resonates with you and why?

The D-C Conversation

In my work with students and parents or other caring adults, I find there are often two conversations not had: the one of dreams and the one of constraints. Since these two conversations are often very closely related, and often very hard to step into, I combine them and call it the "D-C Conversation." I also refer to it as the D-C Conversation because it lies at the intersection of divergent (D), or expansive, thinking and convergent (C), or narrowing, thinking.

Dreams

Rarely discussed in this process of admission are your dreams—the dreams you have for yourself and the dreams your parents or the supportive adults in your lives have for you. You have already done some dreaming and scheming, so I won't spend much time here so much as to say that it is important that you share these dreams, but with people who support your dreams and your visions for your future. In their early stages, dreams are fragile things, and must be cared for as such. And regardless of other's reactions to them—whether those reactions come from friends, family members, or even your self—you should hold on to them because your dreams are windows to your soul.

We often criticize parents for imposing their dreams on their children. I think this is ridiculous. Of course parents do—at least to some extent. Your parents have been with you for a long time, and they want what they think is best for you, whether or not that matches exactly with how you see the world. Having an open discussion about dreams is the surest way to understand where there is crossover and where there are departures. Neither is good or bad. It just is. But these things must be recognized and discussed openly for the admissions process to be all it can be.

To parents and other caring adults, one of the most effective and concise ways for me to suggest that you step into the conversation with your child about dreams are the wise words spoken by Harry S. Truman: "I have found the best way to give advice to your children is to find out what they want and then advise them to do it." This can be difficult, of course. But so is the process of discovering oneself. The more support your child has to chase his or her dreams, the better equipped he or she will be to explore and engage in the world from an authentic place. Rather than approaching the dreams discussion with "what is practical," leave that to the discussion of constraints. Use this opportunity to engage without restraints in your own dreaming about what you want for your kiddo.

HOW

Students:
1) Make a list of all your important dreams. You can use the work you already did in the "Dreaming and Scheming" section.

2) Now rank your dreams. Which are the most important to you? What are your top three?

3) How might these dreams be incorporated into your admissions design process?

Parents:
1) Make a list of as many of the dreams you hold for your child as possible. You can create this list independently or together.

2) Now rank the dreams. Which are the most important to you? What are your top three?

Constraints

In design, constraints are a reality. They can range from cost to availability. As a designer of your life, you must establish which constraints are important, establish a framework for evaluating these constraints, and design accordingly.

This is, in part, the reason that it doesn't work to provide a prescribed process in how to get in to college. You are a unique being with unique circumstances; therefore, only you can know the factors and constraints for which you have to design; for example, perhaps you have a sick parent, or money is tight, or it is important to you to be at a school that is by the beach. All of these things must be considered as you design.

A design thinker embraces constraints. Rather than viewing constraints as limitations, a designer designs with constraints in mind, making the most of even difficult situations. As Tim Brown, CEO of the design and innovation firm IDEO, said in an interview with Forbes.com, "Design thinking is all about upgrading within constraints."[4] In fact, many of the best ideas and design are created from having to design within really difficult constraints. The key is to recognize constraints as the opportunities they can be and become.

In design thinking, constraints are often presented in three overlapping categories: feasibility (which is possible in the foreseeable future), viability (what can happen in terms of a business model), and desirability (what you and others want or need).[5]

A design thinker does not necessarily try to solve for any one of these areas of constraint so much as to bring these areas to a place of balance. Get this: In design thinking, they say these three things must be appropriately balanced so that *sustainability* can be achieved.

What does this mean in practical terms? Sometimes you must give something up in one area to make room for another area. An example is that you may want to go to an elite school, but the one to which you have been accepted is more affordable and you don't want to take on more student debt than you have to. In this case, you may need to balance the desirability of the school with the viability of actually paying for it. It may also not be feasible for you to attend a certain school at this time based on your test scores, but you could find a school that was still desirable and financially viable while perhaps working on the piece of feasibility by applying to a school that doesn't require test scores or by improving your academic performance to later apply to transfer to the school of your dreams.

The point of bringing in design thinking is for you to make the experience your own. Yes. Your. Very. Own.

It is important to know that in design, the solution is not hidden somewhere, inaccessible to you or waiting for you to find it. The solution is found through the actual process of your design and discovery.

HOW

Students:
1) Make a list of all the constraints within which you must operate.

2) Now rank the constraints. Which are the most important to you? What are your top three?

3) How might these constraints be utilized to come up with an even better admissions design?

Parents:
1) Make a list of all the constraints within which you must operate.

2) Now rank the constraints. Which are the most important to you? What are your top three?

3) How might these constraints be utilized to come up with an even better admissions design?

The following note to parents, taken from Dr. Kastner and Dr. Wyatt's book, *The Launching Years*, provides great questions to consider in clarifying if it's parents own "needs, vulnerabilities, or dreams"—rather than those of their child—that are directing the college admissions process and decision.

PARENTS: BE AWARE OF THESE THINGS

Are you measuring success in college choice externally, by what other's define as success (i.e. solely on college ranking), instead of how a choice might enhance qualities that make for a successful life?

Are you so attached to a choice that you're possibly living through your child?

Do you see your child as vulnerable in some way (depressed, anxious, has learning differences or previous illness, for example)?

Is there anything in your background that makes you care too desperately about a choice?

How is where you did or didn't go to school affecting your hopes for your child?

Is your preferred college choice "perfect" because of issues related to vulnerability, but your child wants to take a risk?

Has your own competitiveness blindsided you to your child's needs in any way?

Some of My Favorite Memories

In writing your letters, include some of your favorite memories from being together these past years. What have been some of the highlights? What have you learned from each other? Record those as an honoring of this important transition time. Students, perhaps discuss some of the important lessons or values you will take with you. Parents, perhaps note how you have seen changes in your child as he or she has matured.

Letter Sharing Ritual

After you have authored your letters, decide how you will share them with each other. If you can, avoid just handing the letters to each other and reading them alone. Create a letter sharing ritual, and make a conversation of it. Perhaps do it over a meal or find some quiet time to devote to it. Find a way to make it a celebration of this very important transition time and your partnership in this process.

Choosing Where to Apply

I have already told you several times this is not a traditional admissions book in which the typical advice is provided. (You may want to check out the "College Guides" portion of the Selected Resources section at the end of this book as you prepare for and work on your applications.) That said, I do want to provide some guidance that is in alignment with the design philosophy I am proposing on how you might engage in the admissions process. It is simple really. In choosing where to apply and in selecting a college, the most important question to ask is "Where will I flourish?"

Where Will You Flourish?

In thinking about what will ensure your well-being long into the future, you need to take into consideration things far beyond SAT scores and elite schools. Life is comprised of so much more—from the ways we engage in our communities; to the way we maintain and promote our health; to the relationships we develop with our families, romantic partners, and friends; to the work we do in the world. All of these things make a difference in the quality of lives we lead, far more than the process of applying to college.

To help underscore this point, I want to call upon the work of Dr. Martin P. Seligman, the Zellerbach family Professor of Psychology at the University of Pennsylvania. Seligman, building on his original ideas of the "Authentic Happiness Theory," has recently expanded on some of his ideas and changed it to "Well-Being Theory." In his book, *Flourish*, he writes:

> I used to think that the topic of positive psychology was happiness, that the gold standard for measuring happiness was life satisfaction, and that the goal of positive psychology was to increase life satisfaction. I now think of the topic of positive psychology is well-being, that the gold standard for measuring well-being is flourishing, and that the goal of positive psychology is to increase flourishing.[7]

So, today, Seligman's interest is something more far-reaching than happiness alone—he is interested in seeing people flourish. In his Well-Being Theory, Seligman uses a framework he calls, "PERMA," a mnemonic device to remember the five elements he has identified: positive emotion, engagement, relationships, meaning, and accomplishment.

PERMA

- **Positive Emotion**: Experiencing positive emotions more frequently than negative ones

- **Engagement:** Being absorbed in activities

- **Relationships:** Being authentically connected with others

- **Meaning:** Having a purposeful existence

- **Accomplishment:** Having a sense of achieving goals and of success

It is fascinating to connect the manner in which PERMA corresponds to the Gallup Poll's findings on student engagement and success, which I discussed earlier in this book. Remember the Big Six? Here they are again:

THE BIG SIX

1) A professor who made them excited about learning

2) Professors who cared about them as a person

3) A mentor who encouraged them to pursue their goals and dreams

4) Worked on a long-term project

5) Had a job or internship where they applied what they were learning

6) Were extremely involved in extracurricular activities

An important insight: The Big Six are easily tied to the PERMA framework. As just a few examples, "Professors who cared about them as a person" and "A mentor who encouraged them to pursue their goals and dreams" can be tied to positive emotion and relationships. Engagement easily can be seen in "work on a long-term project" and/ or while "extremely involved in extracurricular activities." Both meaning and accomplishment can be tied to "had a job or internship where they applied what they were learning" and so on.

So what about this "off the beaten path" approach: Instead of placing emphasis on the prestige of the schools to which you apply, think instead about where you can fully express and develop the unique being that you are, where you can achieve your dreams, working within the constraints you have identified, and where you can best experience PERMA and the Big Six. This will not only help you to make the most of your college experience, but it will also help you achieve and sustain your well-being.

If you take this approach, much more than needing answers to questions like "How do I get a higher SAT score?" or "What will it take for me to get in?," you should be seeking answers to questions like these:

Where can I be fully myself and be encouraged to explore my interests?

Where is there good support for my growth and my mental and physical well being?

Where can I best take action in the direction of my dreams?

Where can I best balance my dreams and constraints?

Where can I experience PERMA?

Where can I experience the Big Six?

- Where can I work with a professor who gets me excited about learning?

- Where can I work with professors who care about me as a person?

- Where can I find a mentor who encourages me to pursue my goals and dreams?

- Where can I engage in meaningful work on a long-term project, and one that is aligned with my interests?

- Where can I find a job or internship where I apply what I am learning?

- Where can I be extremely involved in extracurricular activities that are meaningful to me?

If you think about it, it really doesn't have to be more complicated than this.

Match Maker, Match Maker

When I was younger, my grandmother, Edna Rudnick, was forever telling me to put on some lipstick to help me find a date. Though lipstick helps a lot of things, I am sorry to report some of my sweet granny's guidance was all wrong.

About matchmaking, that is. (As it turned out, the lipstick didn't help that much.)

But all the business with the lipstick did help with something: my thinking about college admissions. You see, sometimes, we get excited because a college seems "hot." The college is all dressed up and seems dreamy. In this way, college admissions is a lot like dating.

You know how the story of dating goes. You like her or him, but he doesn't like you. He likes you, but you don't like him. In fact, not even a little bit. You like his friend.

Finding the right college is a little like the magic of finding someone you like to hang out with—there is the liking each other, and then there is the getting to know each other. Then there is a decision point, right? It really isn't as scary as it seems. Again, remember the myths I shared earlier in the book! Most students get into colleges.

But here is an important tip (you'll thank me later, I promise): Just like in the case of dating at its very best, it isn't until after you have done the hard work and soul searching about who you are, your strengths, your passions and what you want to offer this world, that you can determine your match. Really. As I've said many times, we have this process all mixed up. We start with the school as the focus when really, as I have already noted, the process should start with you, the student. With an increased knowledge of yourself and what matters to you, and now having put that into a statement that can help guide you, you are much better equipped to design the college experience that will work best for you. It is in this act of creation—more than acceptance to a particular school—that your greatest opportunities exist.

Break Up with the "One"

So that takes me to my next important tip: You need to break up with the "one." This notion that there is only one and true perfect school for you and you absolutely must get in is, I hope you realize by now, complete nonsense. Remember what I shared with you earlier in the book? While it may be harder to get into just one school, it is easier than ever to get into a top college. But, breaking up with the "one" requires a slightly different approach, which I've consolidated into five simple steps.[8]

1) Don't narrow your options too early. Instead, think about all the things you have learned about yourself, including your fantasy lives and your dreams. You know what's important to you. Then think about the questions I have provided above and apply them to your search. Go figure out what people at that school really

do. Inquire. Research your options. Act like a buyer (because you are one).

2) Make a portfolio of 12-15 schools that would make you happy. Make sure every school on the list is a school you would like to attend (because you might), and apply to them all.

3) Think outside the box. Consider the many different possibilities for your next step, including two-year or four-year colleges, a gap year, vocational school, college overseas, or traditional on line institutions or certificate programs. In addition to the 12-15 schools, list five different ways you could go about this rather than the traditional way you may have always thought about it. Consider those possibilities.

4) Be Yourself. Being your most authentic, real self will only help you find the school that will help you realize your dreams and potential. Don't worry so much about your imperfections. We all have them. Acting like someone you're not and trying to be perfect is so overdone and past its due date. Be fresh! Show up as the real you.

5) Let go. Don't obsess over the "one." You can only attend one school, after all. You likely will not be a match for all 12-15 schools, but you will be a match for one. Plan to hang any rejection letters like badges of honor. You'll show them what they missed out on. Just wait! Ha!

SOME THOUGHTS ON APPLYING

I have given you a lot to think about here in terms of how to engage in applying to colleges differently. Armed with this knowledge, this is the point in the U Map at which you complete your applications. As I mentioned previously in the book, I do not walk you through the nitty-gritty of the actual process of authoring and submitting applications to colleges. Though this is a significant and complex undertaking, you will get through it! I encourage you to check out the "College Guides" portion of the Selected Resources at the end of this book, which may be helpful to you as you apply.

Fortunately, based on the U Map journey on which you have embarked, you are now well-positioned and well-equipped to apply, knowing yourself and what is important to you. Moreover, you will more readily be able to identify colleges you know will be a "fit" because you have engaged in this journey of discovery. And, most importantly, you will be presenting the authentic You. Yeah, baby.

"

My **advice** to **students** going through the **process** **now** would be to **follow** your **passion.**

STUDENT VOICE

"

Chapter Fifteen:
U Map Step Eight—Adventure

You can't get there by bus, only by hard work and risk and not quite knowing what you're doing. What you'll discover will be wonderful. What you'll discover will be yourself."
— Alan Alda

The U Map journey is designed to prepare you for much more than just the act of applying to college; it is meant to help you ready yourself for life. Step Eight, "Adventure," one of the last two steps in the U Map, marks the stage of discovery and exploration that follows your crossing of the threshold. Whether you read this chapter at the time you are applying to schools, at the time you are awaiting word from colleges, after you have been accepted, or even when you are in college, it is both important and useful to approach your college years with a sense of adventure.

Take Action

Adventure is about doing. And this is a good thing because most people learn by doing. Sitting around dreaming up what you will do is nice, and it's an important first step, but what is much better is sinking your teeth into the juicy experience of actually trying something. Not only do you learn a lot about the activity through this process, but you also learn a lot about yourself.

Further, this action must be coupled with reflection. The personal discoveries you make about yourself and the process are critical to your continued growth. The insights you gain must be applied. It is through action and reflection that you learn more about yourself and your relationship to others and the world. For this reason, there are some questions I want you to hold in your mind as you adventure forth and try new things that call to you. We will use your answers to these questions later, so be certain that you are both thinking about them and recording your insights as you engage in your adventures. These questions will help you begin to answer the question, "What am I doing here?"

The Why: What problems/issues are important to me?[1]
Make note of the issues or problems that you feel passionately about and you want to help solve. (You may want to go back to your "Stands" to help you think of problems that are important to you.)

The Who: What kinds of people do I like to spend time with?
Think about the people or groups of people with whom you most like to spend your time (or you think you might like to spend your time).

The How: What are the ways I like to help?
Consider how you specifically like to help.

The What: What activities do I enjoy?
Record the activities you most enjoy doing.

And here's another thing to keep in mind: Experience is measured by iteration and cycles of growth, so you must try, regroup, and try again. Every time you cycle through, you gain more skill, knowledge, and insight. It is for this reason that I have coupled taking action and reflecting on that action with the questions I've outlined above.

And in addition, to make your adventuring successful, you need the "three keys"—Dare, Growth, and Grit.

First Key: Dare

The first key in the U Map is Dare. If you are going to pursue the things that are meaningful to you and adventure and try new things as part of your experience in college, you are going to have to be brave and take risks. Being a beginner and stepping into the pursuit of something meaningful is not for the faint of heart. Most people don't like being uncomfortable in that way; they prefer the safety of sticking with what they know. Your years in college are precious, however, if you are going to discover more about who you are and what you are doing here, those years should be used to discover and to try new things. But to do this, you are going to have to face your fears.

To know more about the courage and vulnerability required to squarely meet your fears, you need to know about the research and work of Dr. Brené Brown, a professor at the University of Houston Graduate College of Social Work, who has spent the last 13 years studying vulnerability, courage, worthiness, and shame. Not only is she the author of three #1 *New York Times* Best Sellers: *Rising Strong, Daring Greatly,* and *The Gifts of Imperfection*, but her 2010 TEDx Houston talk, "The Power of Vulnerability," is one of the top five most viewed TED Talks in the world, with over 25 million viewers. I, like many others, am in love with her work and her message.

The epigraph in Dr. Brown's book, *Daring Greatly*, is a quote from Theodore Roosevelt's 1910 "Man in the Arena" speech, which I have provided for you here:

> It is not the critic who counts; not the man who points out how the strong man stumbles, or where the doer of deeds could have done them better. The credit belongs to the man who is actually in the arena, whose face is marred by dust and sweat and blood; who strives valiantly; who errs, who comes short again and again, because there is no effort without error and shortcoming; but who does actually strive to do the deeds; who knows great enthusiasms, the great devotions; who spends himself in a worthy cause; who at the best knows in the end the triumph of high achievement, and who at the worst, if he fails, at least fails while daring greatly.[2]

This quote expresses exactly what I hope for you. That in your adventures, you will dare to step into the arena, and in the pursuit of your dreams, take the necessary risks.

Taking risks isn't so much about being fearless as it's about welcoming and embracing your fear. Writer Elizabeth Gilbert states, "Creativity can ONLY coexist alongside fear. I have always lived a creative life, and I know that you can't be creative without being vulnerable. And you can't be vulnerable without experiencing fear."[3]

If this is true, and making friends with fear is the only way that you are going to be able to realize your most awesome self, then a deep understanding of fear is required. By far the best way that I have heard fear described has been by Tara Mohr. In her book, *Playing Big*, she explores fear by making the distinction between the two Hebrew words for fear: pachad and yirah.[4]

According to Mohr, pachad is "projected or imagined fear"; that is, the type of fear that the boogey man is made of—it is the irrational, hyperactive Saboteur-type fear that wants to keep us safe at all cost. This is the fear that doesn't want us to take a single step outside of the nice comfort zone we have created.

The other Hebrew word, yirah, is the fear that you find yourself in when something big is in front of you that provides opportunity. This fear is expansive rather than constrictive. And usually when you feel this fear, you know you are on to something important. This fear is more like excitement; it is the fear you feel before doing something that thrills or inspires you.

Unfortunately, in English, we just have just one word for fear. Because of this, we can confuse the two types of fear, when one is more representative of dread and the other is expressive of the excitement you feel when there is an opening to something new. If you begin to distinguish between these two types of fears, you will be able to uncover which fear you are experiencing and then effectively manage that fear so you can embrace it, like in the case of yirah, or make sure it doesn't get in your way, like in the case of pachad.[5]

HOW

1) What are the times in your life that you have been "in the arena?" What was that like?

2) What are examples of times you have been willing to risk and be vulnerable for the sake of your dreams?

3) The next time you experience fear, ask yourself, "Is this pachad or yirah?"

4) Write down your pachad fears. These are the often irrational fears that come from that lizard brain and seems life or death (though they are only imagined). Write down as many as you can think of.

5) Write down the times when you've experience yirah. What has that felt like? What have been the conditions or circumstances? Actively seek out experiences that provide you with the yirah type of fear.

6) Get out there and take some risks on your own behalf! Dare!

Still Have Too Much Fear to Chase Your Dreams?

If you still are having a hard time facing your fears and being brave in the ways you want to be while adventuring your way toward your future, then maybe some lessons from the dying will help.

Bronnie Ware, a writer who worked for many years with the dying, has outlined some of the themes of the dying and the things they would have done differently.[6] Though she uncovered several themes, here is a sampling to help drive home the importance of designing a future that expresses you:

> **I wish I'd had the courage to live a life true to myself, not the life others expected of me.**

Looking back, people realized how many of their precious personal dreams had gone unfulfilled. Rather than taking the risks to fulfill their own dreams, they prioritized the expectations others placed on them or they themselves embodied. If you believe you have this tendency, get to work on upending it. Like I have said, the world needs your gifts and passion more than ever. Don't risk having to count yourself among these people. Ware writes, "Most people had not honored even a half of their dreams and had to die knowing that it was due to choices they had made, or not made." Uncover and follow your dreams and make choices in the direction of them.

> **I wish I hadn't worked so hard.**

Work can be deeply fulfilling or it can be a grind. You know the difference. By discovering your work in an area you love, by pursuing your dreams and your purpose, you can count yourself among the fortunate folks who have discovered the winning combination that makes work feel like anything but, well, work. By all means, work hard, but do so at a job you love so that it never feels like work.

> **I wish I'd had the courage to express my feelings.**

Many people live unfulfilled lives or settle for lives that do not express their deepest selves. And in living such lives, they stuff their feelings about their unfulfilled hopes and dreams. This often leads to things like anxiety, depression, and resentment. Avoid this if you can. Stay in touch with yourself, find your center, and express yourself.

> **I wish I'd valued my relationships with family and friends more.**

Though in our culture, it can seem like the person with the most disposable income wins: in fact, it is relationships and love that trumps all. Do what you must to find and remain in meaningful relationships with those important to you. It is in your relationships that true wealth is found.

While I know the regrets of the dying can be sad to read, these lessons present incredibly important insights. Don't let your fears prevent you from chasing the life of your dreams.

HOW

1) Which of these regrets might you be a candidate for? Why do you think that?

2) Pick one or two of the lessons, and write down a plan for how you might rebel against being one of the people who experience these regrets. What could you do now to not face these regrets in the future?

3) Share these insights with one or all of your Dream Team members.

Second Key: Grow

The second key in the U Map is Grow. Dr. Carol Dweck, a world-renowned Stanford University psychologist who has researched achievement and success, argues that it isn't just our abilities or talent that is the basis for our achievement. Dweck's conclusions, as shown through her extensive research, is what she terms "fixed or growth mindset." In her book, *Mindset*, Dweck describes the difference between these very different ways of approaching the world.[7]

According to Dweck, those with fixed mindsets believe that they have been born with some "fixed" prior ability and talent; that is, that you really have no ability to change the gifts or the flaws that you were born with or that somehow have been instilled in you. It's the notion that these things are predetermined or that they are "carved in stone." On the other hand, those with a growth mindset believe that you can cultivate the qualities and talents you hope to see in yourself through our own efforts to do so. The cool thing about this? You can become conscious of your mindset and then decide the mindset you want to adopt.

Dweck writes that those with a fixed mindset have an urgency to prove themselves, sometimes over and over. Unfortunately, I know from my many years of counseling students, this mindset often steers students away from things they think they aren't good at, even if they love them, because they are afraid they won't be "good enough" or that it won't "look good" on their college applications. Some aspects of our education system are built on this notion of a "fixed" mindset—take IQ tests, for example. Much of this is the fuel behind the fire of "Imposter Syndrome," which we addressed earlier in the book. That is, students become consumed with proving themselves because if your intelligence and gifts are pre-determined, well, then, you better darn well prove you have them. Dweck writes, "Let's take a closer look at why, in the fixed mindset, it's so crucial to be perfect right now. It's because one test—or one evaluation—can measure you forever."

> **"It is actually impossible to know what someone is capable of achieving. Nothing is pre-set or predetermined."**

A growth mindset, on the other hand, looks much different. Dweck argues that part of having a growth mindset is plunging into something precisely because you love it and you aren't good at it. In other words, you don't have to come out fully formed in your ability to do something; you just have to have the desire to want to do it and to improve at it.

Because Dweck's growth mindset is based on growth and on evolution, it introduces a very important element to the ground that we are covering in this book: that it is actually impossible to know what someone is capable of achieving. Nothing is pre-set or predetermined. Dweck writes, "Each person has a unique genetic endowment. People may start with different temperaments and different attitudes, but it's clear that experiences, training, and personal effort take them the rest of the way."[8]

Certainly there is nowhere this is more clear than in the case of college admissions.

The challenge in light of Dweck's research is that we are sending messages to our kids that they have to be perfect, infallible, and, well, super human, to be accepted to an elite college. As a result, parents and students are obsessing over how to appear to be the "right way" to get into the schools. Snore. This is such an "all or nothing" way of thinking. You are a success or a failure. You're either smart or you're dumb. You win or lose. You are accepted or rejected. None of this type of thinking allows for the complexity of what truly is. You are not fully formed. These messages are damaging to your future self and what you are capable of becoming. Worst of all, it doesn't honor the very unique human being that you are, nor your potential for growth and success, wherever you may be at this point in your journey. So often intelligence is not expressed through the experiences we have in school. One of my favorite lines from Dweck's book is: "Remember, test scores and measures of achievement tell you where a student is, but they don't tell you where a students could end up."

Don't believe me (or Dweck) that a growth mindset makes a difference? Here are just a few examples to inspire and motivate you.

Michael Jordan got cut from his high school basketball team. Today he is considered one of the greatest basketball players of all time. His NBA career statistics that include 6,672 rebounds, 5,633 assists, and 32,292 total points.

Oprah Winfrey was fired from her first job as a television reporter because she was "unfit for TV." Her first boss told her she was too emotional. The Oprah Winfrey Show became one of the highest ranking shows in television history.

Steve Jobs not only dropped out of college, but he was fired from Apple, the company he co-founded in his garage with his friend and partner, Steve Wozniak. He later returned to Apple as its leader and transformed the entire computer and phone industries.

J. K. Rowling was broke, severely depressed, and a single parent attending school while writing her first novel. The manuscript was rejected by more than a dozen different publishers, and when it was accepted, Rowling was advised to get a day job since she had little chance of making money in children's books. She went from depending on welfare to becoming one of the wealthiest people in the world as a result of the success of her *Harry Potter* books, which have sold more than 400 million copies.

Steven Spielberg, who is famous for directing such movies as *Jaws*, *Saving Private Ryan*, *Indiana Jones*, and *E.T*, applied and was denied two times to University of Southern California's film school due to poor grades in high school. He attended Cal State University, Long Beach instead. In 1994, he received an honorary degree from the film school that twice rejected him. Two years later, he became a trustee of the university. Spielberg has directed 51 films and won three Oscars.

These were regular people who faced adversity before they grew into the extraordinary people they are today. And, of course, as evidenced here, this is in large part because they embraced a growth mindset.

Try this on: Wherever you are today, and wherever you have been previously, is just the beginning of your future development. The growth mindset suggests that the qualities you have or want to have are not just bestowed on you and are not subject to change. The idea is that you, through your hard work, effort, and attitude, have the ability to impact this. There is a lot of research out there that shows you are at the prime of your life to pursue the things that you love, and with a growth mindset, you have plenty of time to be successful at whatever you choose.

In fact, at this moment, you likely have no idea about the incredible things of which you are capable. And the adults in your life don't know either. Let me repeat this: NOBODY KNOWS. It is amazing what can be accomplished with drive and passion, and you, my dear, are no exception to this rule. So, rather than hiding your areas of vulnerability, how about you embrace them and become a student of that which is exciting to you. Go figure it out. You don't have to be perfect. You just have to be YOU.

HOW

1) In *Mindset*, Dweck makes a wonderful suggestion to grow your mindset: Step into the thing in your past that you think measured you and that you consider really painful. She suggests you reflect on that time and welcome all the emotion that comes with it. Really stay in that place.[9]

2) Now apply a growth mindset to the experience. Take the time to understand what happened, but change your story away from how this one moment defines you. You make your own future.

Ask yourself what you learned from that experience and what growth you can take with you as you move forward.

3) Wherever you are today, or wherever you have been previously, is just the beginning of your future development. The growth mindset suggests that the qualities you have or want to have are not just bestowed on you and are subject to change. The idea is that you, through your hard work, effort, and attitude, have the ability to impact this.

Third Key: Grit

The third key in the U Map is Grit. Angela Lee Duckworth, professor of psychology at the University of Pennsylvania, has made a study of why people succeed. Her findings might surprise you. Her research has demonstrated scientifically that the most successful people, from middle school students to corporate salespeople, aren't those who are the most talented, most intelligent, the most physically fit. In research study after research study, she asked, "Who is successful here and why?" Studying groups as wide ranging as spelling bee contestants and military cadets, Duckworth discovered that the primary marker for success is *grit*. She defines grit as "passion and performance for long-term goals."

During her April 2013 TED Talk on grit, Duckworth explained, "Grit is having stamina. Grit is sticking with your future, day in day out, not just for the week, not just for the month, but for years, and working really hard to make that future a reality."[10]

Duckworth is the first to admit that building grit in a person is still a notably indefinable process. In her TED Talk she shared that when queried by parents of students about the grit-building process she routinely offered, "So far the best idea I have heard about building grit in kids is something called 'growth mindset.'"

"Growth mindset" is now familiar to you as it is the second key to your adventuring. Remember Dr. Dweck's work you learned about above? Now you are getting how these pieces fit together!

Duckworth has said this about the relationship between growth mindset and grit:

It is the belief that the ability to learn is not fixed, that it can change with your effort. Dr. Dweck has shown that when kids read and learn about the brain, and how it changes and grows in response to challenge, they are much more likely to persevere when they fail because they don't believe that failure is a permanent condition. So growth mindset is a great idea for building grit, but we need more. We need to take our best ideas, our strongest intuitions, and we need to test them. We need to measure whether we have been successful, and we have to be willing to fail, to be wrong, to start over again.[11]

In short, grit is good. Grit is the rugged strand that can connect your passions to their fruition.

HOW

1) What are some times you expressed "grit." What was the circumstance and what were you doing? Why?

2) Now mine the times you expressed grit for some qualities you exhibit when you have your "grit" on. Then remember these when you need them. Living your dreams, following the calling of your heart is going to take some grit.

Try It

By embracing a spirit of adventure —trying new things through daring greatly, employing a growth mindset, and showing some grit— you are going to continue to move toward the most authentic version of you. Like I have said, I cannot tell you what to do, only how to think about approaching it. By thinking in terms of design, you are better positioned to imagine how things might unfold.

Hack Mindset

Sometimes you just get bogged down in the details of making something happen. This is where the design thinking's "hack mindset" can be really helpful. As I write this, the design firm IDEO and the Stanford Design School are collaborating to help school leaders redesign school culture using small, scrappy experiments called "hacks."

The hack mindset is pretty straightforward. It's just three simple things:

1) Start small. Do something small that moves you forward in a short timeframe.

2) Bias to action. In other words, get moving. Don't think so much. Just try it out.

3) Fail forward. This is the idea that through trying something and it not working, you can quickly adjust and try again.[12]

In using the "hack mindset," your mantra should be: Try it and see what happens. It is only through action that you will come to know if it is a good fit and you enjoy it and if you have the energy and disposition for it. Look back to the lives you dreamed up and find mini ways to experiment with trying them out. And, as you are trying, don't give up on yourself and your ideas of how these things you try might fit into your life. Try to remember that these ideas about who you are becoming are fragile and require support and tenderness. Your job is to create an environment of growth for these experiments to flourish. Don't give up. Stick with it. Try. Fail. Try again. And carry this spirit of adventure with you throughout your life.

Move Forward Toward Your Purpose (as it unfolds)

Given the many things you learned about yourself in answering the question, "Who am I?," and in having engaged in adventure to discover more about you and what you love, you are now prepared to begin to tackle the second question: "What am I doing here?"

The Changing Face of Purpose

In my work with students, I have identified five camps that students generally fall into with regard to purpose:

1) They knew their purpose early, and they are going with it.

2) They know their purpose, but they fight it because of family pressure or because they believe it somehow isn't legitimate.

3) They don't know their purpose, and they are in search of it.

4) They have many, many different interests and purposes (see the information on Multipotentialites), and it is hard to choose.

5) Purpose? Who cares?

The reason that I share these categories with you is because, more often than not, purpose is not immediately clear. And, guess what? Just like your answer to the question "Who am I?" will evolve, your answer to "What am I doing here?," or your purpose, likely will undergo many iterations in your life. I have found in my work with both students and adults that an individual's idea of purpose can change over a span of only a few months. This is especially true for younger people; as you gain more life and work experience, you become more familiar with what calls to and resonates with you. As Tim Clark, Alexander Osterwalder, and Yves Pigneur, authors of *Business Model You*, share:

> It's helpful to recognize that Purpose changes over time — and for different reasons. Life stage is one reason: Age 20 concerns (establishing a career, finding a significant other, etc.) are completely different from age 55 concerns (seeing children make the transition to adulthood, leaving a legacy, etc.). Big life events (marriage, divorce, births, deaths, new jobs, illness, etc.) are another reason for changes in Purpose. Finally while our core interests and abilities tend to remain stable over time, the form of their expression may evolve."[13]

This is why your purpose statement should be held lightly. It is an ever-evolving work in progress, and it should be treated as such. That means while you have created a first draft of it here, you will revisit it frequently as your life and experiences unfold.

Your Purpose Grid

The Purpose Grid is a tool designed to help you uncover what some of your purposes might be.[14] As you already know, I am not a fan of the notion that you have a single purpose so much as you have a direction in which you may be drawn.

Remember how I told you to keep some questions in mind as you engaged in your adventures and to record your insights? This is where we are going to make use of them. Here they are again for your reference, coupled with some descriptions of ways to answer the questions. We are going to use your answers to the questions to place in the Purpose Grid below.

The Why: What problems/issues are important to me?
What are the issues or problems that you feel passionately about and you want to help solve? (You may want to go back to your "Stands" to help you think of problems that are important to you.)

The Who: What kinds of people do I like to spend time with?
Describe the people or groups of people with whom you most like to spend your time (or you think you might like to spend your time).

The How: What are the ways I like to help?
Consider how you specifically like to help. Use verbs (action words) to describe the ways in which you enjoy being a contribution.

The What: What activities do I enjoy?
Record the activities you most enjoy doing.

The Purpose Grid is meant to help you make sense of what you have learned about yourself through the U Map journey, including your most recent adventuring and the answering of these questions. In completing the chart below, do not overthink your answers. Try to fill in the chart with an act of feeling more than thinking. Your completion of the chart doesn't have to be perfect or final; it needs only to represent what might resonate with you now that you have had some new and different experiences. Write down whatever comes to mind, and trust your intuition. And go for quantity here: Write down as many things as come to you.

PURPOSE GRID

Issues Important To Me	Groups of People With Whom I Like to Work/ Spend My Time

Ways I Like To Help (Action Words)	Activities I Enjoy

From Grid to Statement

After you fill in the grid, you are ready to begin to craft what at first will seem to be some very awkward statements.[15] Don't try to make the answers from your grid above make perfect sense line by line below. Just load the answers, and then you can mix and match them into statements below. In fact, it is often through the mixing and matching that new and better ideas come.

Issue (Noun)	Helping Word (Verb)	Groups of People (Noun)	Activity (Verb)
Hunger	Supporting	Children	Volunteering

The creation of your statements will look something like this:

I want to address
[ISSUE]

by
[HELPING WORD]
[GROUPS OF PEOPLE]

through
[ACTIVITY]

EXAMPLE

I want to address hunger by supporting children through volunteering.

At first your statement may seem very awkward, but it will contain the main ideas that provide direction toward your purpose. Once you have your awkward statement, you can work on it to make it less awkward and more of what you want it to be.

Adding Purpose to the U Statement

Now it's time for you to enhance the U Statement you created in Step Five of the U Map based on the many things you have experienced and learned about yourself and what you have uncovered about your purpose.

To do so, return to your U Statement. In reading it, does it still resonate? Has anything changed for you? You may even want to go back and do some of the exercises from earlier in the book to make any adjustments to get it just right. You can use the outline below to make any adjustments.

YOUR U STATEMENT

Standing in
[INSERT STRENGTHS OR BIRTHRIGHT GIFTS],

working to improve
[INSERT EDGES],

and expressing my interests and passions, including
[INSERT INTERESTS OR PASSIONS],

I step more fully into my values of
[INSERT VALUES].

I recognize my contributions of
[INSERT CONTRIBUTIONS].

I take a stand for
[INSERT STANDS].

Your revised U Statement:

_____

_____

_____

_____

_____

Now, you are going to take your revised U Statement and add what you have uncovered about your purpose to the end of it.

Recognizing purpose does not have to
be just one thing. I take action toward
purpose in several ways. One way
I express my purpose is to address
[INSERT ISSUE]

by
[INSERT HELPING WORD]
[INSERT GROUPS OF PEOPLE]

through
[INSERT ACTIVITY].

Another way I express my purpose is to address
[INSERT ISSUE]

by
[INSERT HELPING WORD]
[INSERT GROUPS OF PEOPLE]

through
[INSERT ACTIVITY].

Write your new U Statement complete with your purpose here below:

_____

_____

_____

_____

_____

_____

Remember! There isn't just one way to create your enhanced U Statement, so feel free to make it into whatever works best for you. The U Statement is for you. It serves as a North Star, guiding you toward the truest version of yourself and outlining some of the ways you will take action to share your gifts and purpose with the world.

What if I Still Don't Know My Purpose?

At this point I am sometimes asked the question, "What if I still have no idea what my purpose is?" That's ok! Actually, it is only a very small number of people who are "on purpose" in their work today. The uncovering of purpose is a life-long activity. And even if you cannot identify it through these exercises, by setting your intention to continually move toward it, you will get closer to an understanding of it, and that will help guide you forward. Remember, flowers bloom in their own time. Keep listening to your still, small voice, practice patience, and, as I outline in the next chapter, stay open to the possibilities.

Chapter Sixteen:
U Map Step Nine—Evolve Toward Purpose

Until you spread your wings, you'll have no idea how far you can fly.
-Unknown

Live the Question and Stay Open

After all this talk about discovering the things you do know about yourself and encouraging your adventuring to learn even more, this business about living the question and staying open may seem a bit odd, but it is key to living your purpose as it unfolds. By engaging in your future through action and through embracing emergence, new insights will start to form. Armed with the things you can control, there will be plenty of things that you cannot control. This is not meant to be disturbing; in fact, much of this you cannot and should not want to control to allow life to unfold in the wonderful and mysterious ways that it can.

One of my favorite TED Talks is Uri Alon's "Why truly innovative science demands a leap into the unknown."[1] While studying for his Ph.D. in physics, Alon thought he was a failure because all his research paths led to dead ends. But, by applying principles he learned through improv theater, he came to realize that there could be joy in living the question. In his talk, Alon calls for scientists to stop thinking of research as a direct line from question to answer, but as something more creative—and to allow the space and structure for collaboration and new possibilities to emerge.

To begin to experiment with a new way of doing things, you must stay open to the question. By embracing "not knowing" you allow for many more possibilities to come forth.

Emergent Strategy

In allowing life to unfold in its many magical ways, you have to have a different approach than the traditional one that suggests you can just plan everything. In this case, not only do you account for what you have dreamed, schemed, and intended, but also for the factors not yet known. The following graphic, adapted from *The Strategy Process* by Henry Mintzberg, Sumantra Ghoshal, and James B. Quinn, expresses the balance.[2]

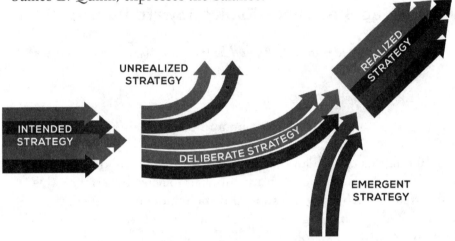

The idea is this: You have an intended strategy (this is what you identified with your intentions and goals, which were rooted in your dreams). But in your adventuring, there are going to be things that you find you don't like or things that don't resonate with you; for example, you may have believed you wanted to go into banking, but now that you've taken action and tried it, you've come to realize that it's not for you. This is where you move from intended strategy to deliberate strategy: You are taking action, and in that process, you are letting go of things that you find do not work for you, while also allowing new things to emerge and to inform and direct your path. The dance between these various factors—what you intend, what you let go of, and what you allow to come in—results in your realized strategy. Your initial intentions must accommodate to a changing current reality.

This is why it really isn't an option to have only the traditional five- or 10-year plan. It doesn't account for what might emerge along the way, and given the pace at which you are changing and the world is changing, you need room for emergence.

"

I think **I thought I could teach** because it was the **only tangible job** with **which I'd ever been** in contact. **I admired** teachers, and having **just graduated college**, I felt **sentimental** and **nostalgic** about my professors. **Turns** out I **hated teaching.** Turns out **my fatal flaw** is **impatience.**

STUDENT VOICE

"

The following table outlines the difference between traditional and emerging ideas:[3]

Traditional Ideas	Emerging Ideas
Focus on the predictable, controllable	Focus on the mysterious from a foundation of what we understand
Ensure there are no surprises	Experiment, learn from surprises
Build/construct/manage	Invite, open, support
Follow the plan	Follow the energy, using the plan as useful information
Manufacture	Midwife the birth of novelty and cultivate its development
Handle logistics	Cultivate welcoming logistics, including handling logistics
Classical	Classical skills that also support jazz and improvisation
Declare/advocate	Inquire/explore, using what is at the heart of advocacy as a resource
Top down or bottom up	Multi-directional

Remember that I am not a fan of "either-or" thinking? This is yet another case of that. It isn't that you select one or the other of these; you allow them to co-exist. You set intentions *and* you allow things to emerge. You declare what you think you might want, *and* you explore to learn if that still rings true as your life unfolds. You have a plan, *and* you also follow the energy of where life and your interests take you.

And you must recognize that you can't really control emergence and how it arises in your life. It is that chance encounter or that random phone call. It can be puzzling and overwhelming, but it also can be beautiful and provide breakthroughs. Emergence is going to happen no matter what, so to welcome it, I suggest that you take the following three actions:[4]

1) **Embrace Mystery:** Ask questions in addition to knowing answers

2) **Follow Life Energy:** Use your intuition in addition to making plans

3) **Choose Possibility:** Attend to your dreams and aspirations, not just your goals and objectives

"

I think **any** other number of **mistakes** and **wild decisions** **would have** put me on **an equally** **satisfying** and **surprising** path...

STUDENT VOICE

"

By engaging in these three actions—embracing mystery, following life energy, and choosing possibility—you will remain alert to who you are in this moment and how you are evolving. You will be rooted in that which is important to you and remain alive to life, actively engaging with all that it has to offer. You will evolve toward purpose.

HOW

1) Do you feel more comfortable with planning or with emergence? Why? How can you make more room for a balance of both of these things in your life?

2) Think of a time when something unexpected, mysterious, and cool occurred. Maybe it was a chance encounter or an incredible opportunity that just fell into your lap. What meaning did you make of that experience and how did it change your life?

3) Make a list of things that took place this past year that were planned and unplanned.

REFLECTION ON THE U MAP JOURNEY

You now have traveled through the final step of the U Map. I hope your journey through this process has inspired excitement, curiosity, and an understanding of your own power when it comes to designing your future.

And, most of all, I hope you keep in mind that every ending is really just a new beginning presenting another threshold to cross. And so I offer you the wise words of of T.S. Elliott: "We shall not cease from exploration, and the end of all our exploring will be to arrive where we started and know the place for the first time."

Conclusion

"The bad news: There is no key to the universe.
The good news: It was never locked."
—Swami Beyondananda

As I hope you've come to realize by now, there are bountiful benefits to approaching your admissions process through the lens of thoughtful design. By stepping into the designing of your future, and by allowing for a balance of what you have planned with what emerges, you uncover the enormous promise of what lies ahead. The following list represents just some of the changes you may experience through the U Map process:[1]

1) **You truly see, in vivid color, the incredible You:** By getting quiet, you connect with your "still, small voice." Through the discovery phase of design, you witness yourself in new ways, integrate these many parts, and celebrate and engage the "whole" of you.

2) **You acknowledge and embrace the power of You:** By approaching admissions with a design framework, you recognize you have power and choice in the system and can shape your admissions experience to be in line with who you are and what you want for your future. You "cross the threshold" with the confidence you can meet what is on the other side.

3) **You recognize your contribution and the contribution of others:** Rather than existing in a dog-eat-dog world, you discover community among a diverse mix of students. Through intention, you and others are joined together in the effort to discover the deeper meaning of your lives in your journey to college and beyond. Through this, lasting connections will form and a deep sense of connection grows.

4) **You experience important breakthroughs and insights:** Your willingness to explore new things and to take action in the direction of your dreams inspires more and more creative action. By adventuring, you get closer to what you want for yourself and for the world around you.

5) **You connect with your purpose:** You feel inspired to pursue that which matters to you. You begin to see how the work in which you are engaged impacts not only you, but also the community of which you are a part. This inspires more confidence in you to act.

6) **You exceed your boundaries and step into your pure potential:** You feel more courageous and supported to stretch your ideas of what you believed possible. With new ideas, and mentors to support you, you are spurred to action from a place of authenticity and purpose.

7) **You make room for emergence:** By allowing room for your life to unfold in the mysterious ways that it will, you'll be able to see and step into opportunities you may not have otherwise imagined.

8) **The culture begins to change:** Through your action and the action of others, things begin to shift. Over time and with new understanding of a different way to approach admissions, the culture surrounding college admissions will begin to change and a new narrative about the experience will form.

As I've said previously, your ability to act on your own behalf, as an advocate of yourself and your dreams, and to engage in the process in a different way than the system currently promotes will make all the difference in ensuring the expression of your gifts and talents and your sanity on the path to an authentic, promising, and purpose-filled future.

In short, YOU are the change.

A Final Message to Parents

"Life is either a daring adventure or nothing"
— Helen Keller

As I complete the final drafting and editing of this book, my own daughter, Sydney, has begun her ninth grade year—her journey to high school and beyond. As she begins to navigate the process I've outlined here, and her path toward the life that fulfills her, I stand at the ready, a member of her Dream Team, to support her as she embodies the richness of navigating the next steps on her journey.

In doing so, I quiet my own mind to listen deeply for the knowledge and awareness of that which will best support her on her path forward. This, ultimately, is the role we as parents have to play—one of coach and mentor—to build the foundations and bridges under the dreams and visions of our children, honoring their hopes for themselves and for this world.

And so I embrace this transition time—the crossing of this threshold—with the hope I can be the type of parent that will best support my daughter as she moves to this next stage of life. And I do my best to listen, truly listen, to what she hopes for her life, placing all my support behind helping her to realize her gifts and potential as she imagines it. I do this trusting that her innate wisdom and the still, small voice of her soul offer the truest callings.

In thinking about the realities I and so many other parents face as we walk this journey with our children, I am reminded of Kahlil Gabran's poem, "On Children":[2]

ON CHILDREN
Kahlil Gibran

Your children are not your children.
They are the sons and daughters of Life's longing for itself.
They come through you but not from you,
And though they are with you yet they belong not to you.

You may give them your love but not your thoughts,
For they have their own thoughts.
You may house their bodies but not their souls,
For their souls dwell in the house of tomorrow,

which you cannot visit, not even in your dreams.
You may strive to be like them,
but seek not to make them like you.
For life goes not backward nor tarries with yesterday.

You are the bows from which your children
as living arrows are sent forth.
The archer sees the mark upon the path of the infinite,
and He bends you with His might
that His arrows may go swift and far.
Let your bending in the archer's hand be for gladness;
For even as He loves the arrow that flies,
so He loves also the bow that is stable.

As you step into this next phase of life with your child, my invitation and wish for you is that you embrace your role of the bending, steady bow as you let fly the arrow.

A Final Message to Students

"Tell me, what is it you plan to do with your one wild and precious life?"
—*Mary Oliver*

To the students who have been with me on this journey and who stand on the threshold of something new, I hope this book has provided you insight into how to gain more knowledge about yourself, your dreams, and your purpose. I invite you to pursue, bravely, this self-knowledge and apply it in making your decisions about how you want to design your experience and your life. Look deep within yourself. What will carry you across the threshold and into the light of the unknown that contains your dreams and your future?

It is with this question in mind that I encourage you to step confidently and boldly into your next stage. Regardless of what you want to do with your "wild and precious life"—whether it is creating digital art, going to medical school, writing books, saving trees, coding, dancing, managing money, painting, dribbling, traveling to space, making movies, telling jokes, or howling at the moon—please (and, yes, now I am begging), go do it. And believe you *can* do it. Design your way toward it. And when the going gets tough, *stick with it*, because this is how you really learn about yourself and what is important to you. You deserve to put forth the many gifts you have to offer this world. We need the real you and your unique contributions now more than ever.

And on this threshold, take that first step to designing and authorizing your own vision for your own future. Stop participating in the nonsensical trap of competing with others. It really makes no difference what they are doing. *They are not you.* Abandon any fear that you and what you have to offer are not enough. It's simply not true. That's scarcity thinking, and the world already has too much of it. And it's a big part of how we got into this mess in the first place.

Imagine if all the people who believed faithfully in their own abilities and vision—from the Michael Jordans and the Oprah Winfreys to the Steve Jobs, J.K. Rowlings, and Steven Spielbergs of this world—had instead listened to the naysayers or to those who thought their ideas were too crazy and unconventional. Think of how robbed the world would have been. As I shared earlier in this book, all of these people showed up unapologetically as themselves and took action in the direction of their dreams. They dared, grew, and practiced grit.

And you can, too.

You must know yourself and your dreams and connect with and design your vision for your future regardless of what anyone—your friends, your teachers, your parents—thinks is right or possible. Only you—in knowing your true self and deepest callings—can know that of which you are truly capable.

And finally, as Howard Thurman said, "Don't ask what the world needs. Ask what makes you come alive, and go do it. Because what the world needs is people who have come alive."

My blessings to you. The world is waiting for you.

Now go come alive.

Endnotes

Introduction

1. Cohen, M.L. (1996, July). Great transitions, preparing adolescents for a new century: A commentary on the health component of the concluding report of the Carnegie Council on Adolescent Development. *Journal of Adolescent Health.* 19(1), 2-5.

Chapter One: Admissions By Design

1. Frankl, V. (2006). *Man's Search for Meaning.* Boston, MA: Beacon Press. 77.

Chapter Two: A Culture of Crazy

Issue of Supply and Demand
1. Clinedinst, M. (2014). State of college admission. NACAC. Retrieved from http://www.nacacnet.org/research/PublicationsResources/Marketplace/research/Pages/StateofCollegeAdmission.aspx
2. Clinedinst, M. (2014). State of college admission. NACAC. Retrieved from http://www.nacacnet.org/research/PublicationsResources/Marketplace/research/Pages/StateofCollegeAdmission.aspx
3. Paul, P. (2011, November 4). Being a legacy has its burden. *The New York Times.* Retrieved from http://www.nytime.com/2011/11/06/education/edlife/being-a-legacy-has-its-burden.html

Common Application
4. Clinedinst, M. (2014). State of college admission. NACAC. Retrieved from http://www.nacacnet.org/research/PublicationsResources/Marketplace/research/Pages/StateofCollegeAdmission.aspx
5. "About." (2015). Common Application. Retrieved from http://www.commonapp.org/about-us
6. Bruni, F. (2015). *Where you go is not who you'll be: An antidote to the college admissions mania.* New York, NY: Hachette Book Group.
7. de Vise, D. (2011, June 10). On Common App, Georgetown now stands alone. *The Washington Post.* Retrieved from http://www.washingtonpost.com/blogs/college-inc/post/on-common-app-georgetown-now-stands-alone/2011/06/10/AGDLY4OH_blog.html

Increase in International Applicants

8. Jordan, M. (2015, March 24). International students stream into U.S. colleges. *The Wall Street Journal*. Retrieved from http://www.wsj.com/articles/international-students-stream-into-u-s-colleges-1427248801

9. Jordan, M. (2015, March 24). International students stream into U.S. colleges. *The Wall Street Journal*. Retrieved from http://www.wsj.com/articles/international-students-stream-into-u-s-colleges-1427248801

Selectivity: Great News for Colleges, Not So Great News for You

10. Snider, S. (2015, November 3). 10 universities where the fewest applicants get in. *U.S. News & World Report*. Retrieved from http://www.usnews.com/education/best-colleges/the-short-list-college/articles/2015/11/03/10-colleges-and-universities-with-the-most-competitive-admissions-rates

Yield

11. College Board. (2015). Early Decision and Early Action. Retrieved from https://professionals.collegeboard.com/guidance/applications/early

12. Baskin, M. (2015, February 7). As 'yield rates' fluctuate, colleges work to protect reputations. *USA Today*. Retrieved from http://college.usatoday.com/2015/02/07/as-yield-rates-fluctuate-colleges-work-to-protect-reputations/

13. Abrams, T. (2013, May 13). Colleges report 2013 admission yields and wait-list offers. *The New York Times*. Retrieved from http://thechoice.blogs.nytimes.com/2013/05/30/college-admits-2013/?_r=1

14. Abrams, T. (2013, May 13). Colleges report 2013 admission yields and wait-list offers. *The New York Times*. Retrieved from http://thechoice.blogs.nytimes.com/2013/05/30/college-admits-2013/?_r=1

Self-Reporting

15. Wang, M. (2013, April 23). The admissions arms race: Six ways colleges game their numbers. *ProPublica*. Retrieved from http://www.propublica.org/article/the-admission-arms-race-six-ways-colleges-can-game-their-numbers

16. Anderson, N. (2013, February 6). Five colleges misreported data to U.S. News, raising concerns about rankings, reputation. *The Washington Post*. Retrieved from https://www.washingtonpost.com/local/education/five-colleges-misreported-data-to-us-news-raising-concerns-about-rankings-reputation/2013/02/06/cb437876-6b17-11e2-af53-7b2b2a7510a8_story.html

Test Prep

17. Weston, L. (2014, April 21). Resist the urge to go overboard on college test prep. *Reuters*. Retrieved from http://www.reuters.com/article/2014/04/21\us-col-umn-weston-testprep-idUSBREA3K0J120140421

18. Clark, P. (2014, October 8). The test prep industry is booming. *Bloomberg Business*. Retrieved from http://www.bloomberg.com/bw/articles/2014-10-08/sats-the-test-prep-business-is-booming

19. Clark, P. (2014, October 8). The test prep industry is booming. *Bloomberg Business*. Retrieved from http://www.bloomberg.com/bw/articles/2014-10-08/sats-the-test-prep-business-is-booming

20. Briggs, D. (2009). Preparation for college admissions exams. NACAC. Retrieved

from http://www.nacacnet.org/research/PublicationsResources/MarketplaceDoc-cuments/TestPrepDiscussionPaper.pdf

Shortage of School Counselors
21. Clinedinst, M. (2014). State of college admission. NACAC. Retrieved from http://www.nacacnet.org/research/PublicationsResources/Marketplace/research/Pages/StateofCollegeAdmission.aspx
22. Pratt,T. (2013, December 3). The high school counselor shortage. The Hechinger Report. *TIME*. Retrieved from http://nation.time.com/2013/12/03/the-high-school-guidance-counselor-shortage/
23. Pratt,T. (2013, December 3). The high school counselor shortage. The Hechinger Report. *TIME*. Retrieved from http://nation.time.com/2013/12/03/the-high-school-guidance-counselor-shortage/
24. Clinedinst, M. (2014). State of college admission. NACAC. Retrieved from http://www.nacacnet.org/research/PublicationsResources/Marketplace/research/Pages/StateofCollegeAdmission.aspx
25. Bruce, M., and Ridgeland, J. (2012, October). 2012 National survey of school counselors. True north: charting the course to college and career readiness. *The College Board Advocacy and Policy Center National Office for School Counselor Advocacy NOSCA*. Retrieved from http://www.civicenterprises.net/MediaLibrary/Docs/2012_NOSCA_Report.pdf
26. IECA. (n.d.).The new rules of the admissions game. Retrieved from http://www.iecaonline.com/news.html
27. Kaufman, W. (2005, October 27). Interview by R. Montagne. [Radio broadcast]. Seeking college admissions help with pricey counselors. Morning Edition. New York. *National Public Radio*. Retrieved from http://www.npr.org/templates/story/story.php?storyId=4976703

Chapter Three: The Ten Disturbing Trends of the Culture of Crazy

Disturbing Trend Two: "Super People"— Excellence is the New Average

1. Deresiewicz, W. (2014, July 21). Don't send your kid to the Ivy League. *New Republic*. Retrieved from http://www.newrepublic.com/article/118747/ivy-league-schools-are-overrated-send-your-kids-elsewhere

Disturbing Trend Three: Activity Overload

2. Student A. (personal communication, October 2, 2015).
3. Student B. (personal communication, October 2, 2015).
4. Jones, M. and Ginsburg, K.R. (2006). *Less stress, more success: A new approach to guiding your teen to college admissions and beyond*. CITY: American Academy of Pediatrics.
5. Weissbourd, R. (2011, May). The overpressured student. *ASCD*, 68 (8) 22-27. Retrieved from:http://www.ascd.org/publications/educational-leadership/may11/vol68/num08/The-Overpressured-Student.aspx

Disturbing Trend Four: Imposter Syndrome

6. Clance, P.R and Imes, S. A. (1978). The imposter phenomenon in high achieving women: Dynamics and therapeutic intervention. *Psychotherapy: Theory, Research & Practice*, Vol 15(3), 241-247. Retrieved from http://dx.doi.org/10.1037/h0086006
7. Dixon, G (Producer). (2015, May 14). After suicides MIT works to relieve student pressure. *All Things Considered*. National Public Radio. Retrieved from http://www.npr.org/sections/ed/2015/05/14/406727576/after-suicides-mit-works-to-relieve-student-pressure
8. Student C. (personal communication, October 2, 2015).

Disturbing Trend Five: Afraid to Fail

9. Scelfo, J. (2015, July 27). Suicide on campus and the pressure of perfection. *The New York Times*. Retrieved from http://www.nytimes.com. http://www.nytimes.com/2015/08/02/education/edlife/stress-social-media-and-suicide-on-campus.html?ribbon-ad-idx=4&rref=education/edlife&module=ArrowsNav&contentCollection=Education%20Life&action=swipe&region=FixedRight&pgtype=article&_r=0
10. Schultz, J. (2015, April 1). Lowering the pressure in order to prevent suicides at MIT. *Huffington Post*. Retrieved from http:/www.huffingtonpost.com/jerome-schultz/lowering-the-pressure-in-_b_6889466.html

Disturbing Trend Six: The Escalating Contagion of Achievement and Perfection

11. Parent A. (personal communication, May 8, 2015).
12. Parent B. (personal communication, June 6, 2015).
13. Scelfo, J. (2015, July 27). Suicide on campus and the pressure of perfection. *The New York Times*. Retrieved from http://www.nytimes.com. http://www.nytimes.com/2015/08/02/education/edlife/stress-social-media-and-suicide-on-campus.html?ribbon-ad-idx=4&rref=education/edlife&module=ArrowsNav&contentCollection=Education%20Life&action=swipe&region=FixedRight&pgtype=article&_r=0
14. Wojcicki, E. (2010). College education: Why many students should pass on Ivy league schools. *Edutopia*. Retrieved from http://www.edutopia.org/college-admissions-school-choice

Disturbing Trend Seven: "All or Nothing" Thinking

15. Student B. (personal communication, October 2, 2015).

Disturbing Trend Eight: Begone the Days of the Moral Compass?

16. Weissbourd, R. (2011, May). The overpressured student. *ASCD*, 68 (8) 22-27. Retrieved from:http://www.ascd.org/publications/educational-leadership/may11/vol68/num08/The-Overpressured-Student.aspx

Disturbing Trend Nine: Commoditization of Education

17. Brooks, D. (2014, September 18). Becoming a Real Person. *The New York Times*. Retrieved from http://www.nytimes.com/2014/09/09/opinion/david-brooks-becoming-a-real-person.html

18. Deresiewicz, W. (2014, July 21). Don't send your kid to the Ivy League. *New Republic*. Retrieved from http://www.newrepublic.com/article/118747/ivy-league-schools-are-overrated-send-your-kids-elsewhere

19. Deresiewicz, W. (2015, September). The neoliberal arts: How college sold its soul to the market. *Harper's Magazine*, 26.

Disturbing Trend Ten: Asking the Wrong Questions

20. Student D. (personal communication, September 6, 2015).
21. Student E. (personal communication, September 6, 2015).
22. Student F. (personal communication, August 15, 2015).

Chapter Four: The Culture of Crazy Takes a Physical and Mental Toll

The Handy Model of the Brain

1. Siegel, D. (2011). *Mindsight: The new science of personal transformation*. New York, NY: Bantam Books.

The Prefrontal Cortex

2. Siegel, D. (2013). *Brainstorm: The power and purpose of the teenage brain*. New York, NY: Penguin Group.

Stress and Your Brain

3. Hanson, R. (2013). *Hardwiring happiness: The new brain science of contentment, calm, and confidence*. New York, NY: Harmony Books.

4. Hanson, R., with Mendius, R. (2009). *Buddha's brain: The practical neuroscience of happiness, love and wisdom*. Oakland, CA: New Harbinger Publishing.

5. Hanson, R., with Mendius, R. (2009). *Buddha's brain: The practical neuroscience of happiness, love and wisdom*. Oakland, CA: New Harbinger Publishing.

Why All This Weird Brain Stuff Matters

6. Siegel, D. (2011). *Mindsight: The new science of personal transformation*. New York, NY: Bantam Books.

Sleep

7. Nudo, L. (October 2002). Sleep beats kids stress at any age. *Prevention*. Vol. 54 Issue 10, 52.

8. National Sleep Foundation (2006). 2006 Sleep in America poll. Retrieved from https://sleepfoundation.org/sites/default/files/2006_summary_of_findings.pdf

9. Richter, R. (2015, October 8). Among teens, sleep deprivation an epidemic. Stanford Medicine News Center. Retrieved from https://med.stanford.edu/news/all-news/2015/10/among-teens-sleep-deprivation-an-epidemic.html

10. UCLA Sleep disorders center. Retrieved from UCLA Sleep Disorders Center website http://sleepcenter.ucla.edu/

11. Ryan, F. (2014). Willpower for dummies. Good sleeping habits help support willpower. Wiley. http://www.dummies.com/how-to/content/good-sleeping-habits-help-support-willpower.html
12. Richter, R. (2015, October 8). Among teens, sleep deprivation an epidemic. Stanford Medicine News Center. Retrieved from https://med.stanford.edu/news/all-news/2015/10/among-teens-sleep-deprivation-an-epidemic.html

High Levels of Cortisol

13. Sleep patterns in children and teenagers could indicate risk for depression, researcher finds. (2009, August 13). *UT Southwestern medical center*. Retrieved from http://www.utsouthwestern.edu/newsroom/news-releases/year-2009/sleep-patterns-in-children-and-teenagers-could-indicate-risk-for-depression-researcher-finds.html

The Mental Toll

14. Noguchi, S. (2014, February 5). Teen health: Depression, anxiety and social phobias rising in kids, educators say. *San Jose Mercury News*. Retrieved from http://www.mercurynews.com/health/ci_25074044/teen-health-depression-anxiety-and-social-phobias-rising
15. Scelfo, J. (2015, July 27). Suicide on campus and the pressure of perfection. *The New York Times*. Retrieved from http://www.nytimes.com/2015/08/02/education/edlife/stress-social-media-and-suicide-on-campus.html?ribbon-ad-idx=4&rref=education/edlife&module=ArrowsNav&contentCollection=Education%20Life&action=swipe&region=FixedRight&pgtype=article&_r=0
16. American College Health Association. (2013, Spring). Reference Group Executive Summary. Received from http://www.acha-ncha.org/docs/ACHA-NCHA-II ReferenceGroup_ExecutiveSummary_Spring2013.pdf
17. Aragon, M.C., Eagan, K., Hurtado, S., Ramirez, J.J., Stolzenberg, E.B., & Suchard, M.R. (2014). The American freshman: National norms fall 2014. *Cooperative Institutional Research program at the Higher Education Research Institute at UCLA*. Retrieved from http://www.heri.ucla.edu/monographs/TheAmerican Freshman2014.pdf
18. Noguchi, S. (2014, February 5). Teen health: Depression, anxiety and social phobias rising in kids, educators say. *San Jose Mercury News*. Retrieved from http://www.mercurynews.com/health/ci_25074044/teen-health-depression-anxiety-and-social-phobias-rising
19. Noguchi, S. (2014, February 5). Teen health: Depression, anxiety and social phobias rising in kids, educators say. *San Jose Mercury News*. Retrieved from http://www.mercurynews.com/health/ci_25074044/teen-health-depression-anxiety-and-social-phobias-rising
20. Gallagher, R.P. (2014). National Survey of College Counseling Centers. International Association of Counseling Centers. Inc. Retrieved from http://www.collegecounseling.org/wp-content/uploads/NCCCS2014_v2.pdf
21. Gallagher, R.P. (2014). National Survey of College Counseling Centers. International Association of Counseling Centers. Inc. Retrieved from http://www.collegecounseling.org/wp-content/uploads/NCCCS2014_v2.pdf

Mental Health Counseling

22. Peale, C. (2014, April 7). Students flood college counseling offices. *USA Today*. Retrieved from http://www.usatoday.com. http://www.usatoday.com/story/news/nation/2014/04/07/college-students-flood-counseling-offices/7411333/

23. Thompson, R. (2014, December 14). Student deaths inspire new focus on mental health at Tulane. *The New Orleans Advocate*. Retrieved from http://www.theneworleansadvocate.com/news/11069357-123/student-deaths-inspire-new-focus

24. Golgowski, N. (2015, February 17). Ex-teacher of UPenn track star who took her own life pushes for law to combat student suicides. *New York Daily News*. Retrieved from http://www.nydailynews.com/news/national/law-combat-college-suicides-pushed-upenn-teen-article-1.2118880

25. Persky, J. (2014, March 7). Trouble in paradise: the state of mental health at Stanford. *The Stanford Daily*. Retrieved from http://www.stanforddaily.com/2014/03/07/trouble-in-paradise-the-state-of-mental-health-at-stanford/

26. Svrluga, S. (2015, April 15). Suicide at William and Mary, fourth student death this year, triggers concern. *The Washington Post*. https://www.washingtonpost.com/news/grade-point/wp/2015/04/15/suicide-at-william-mary-fourth-this-year-triggers-concern-about-mental-health/

27. Active Minds. *About. Our story*. Retrieved from http://www.activeminds.org/about/our-story

28. Wojcicki, E. (2010). College education: why many students should pass on Ivy league schools. *Edutopia*. Retrieved from http://www.edutopia.org/college-admissions-school-choice

29. Dixon, G (Producer). (2015, May 14). After suicides MIT works to relieve student pressure. *All Things Considered*. Retrieved from http://www.npr.org/sections/ed/2015/05/14/406727576/after-suicides-mit-works-to-relieve-student-pressu

30. Svrluga, S. (2015, April 15). Suicide at William and Mary, fourth student death this year, triggers concern. *The Washington Post*. Retrieved from https://www.washingtonpost.com/news/grade-point/wp/2015/04/15/suicide-at-william-mary-fourth-this-year-triggers-concern-about-mental-health/

31. Svrluga, S. (2015, April 15). Suicide at William and Mary, fourth student death this year, triggers concern. *The Washington Post*. Retrieved from https://www.washingtonpost.com/news/grade-point/wp/2015/04/15/suicide-at-william-mary-fourth-this-year-triggers-concern-about-mental-health/

32. Keefer, L. (2015, April 16). An Open Letter to the College of William and Mary. *The Flat Hat*. Retrieved from http://flathatnews.com/2015/04/16/an-alums-response-to-pauls-passing/

33. Alvardo, E. (2015, April 29). CM's top 10 most stressful colleges. *College Magazine*. Received from http://www.collegemagazine.com/cms-top-10-stressful-colleges/11/

Not Just Elite Campuses

34. Benazir, A. (2010, September 16). How to prevent your Ivy league child from be coming suicidal. *The Huffington Post*. Retrieved from http://www.huffingtonpost.com/dr-ali-binazir/how-to-prevent-your-ivy-l_b_694689.html

35. Centers for Disease Control and Prevention. (2015). *Injury prevention and control: Division of violence prevention*. Suicide Prevention; Youth suicide. Retrieved from http://www.cdc.gov/violenceprevention/suicide/youth_suicide.html

36. Centers for Disease Control and Prevention. (2012, June 8). Youth Risk Behavior Surveillance—United States, 2011. 61(SS04); 1-162. Retrieved from http://www.cdc.gov/mmwr/preview/mmwrhtml/ss6104a1.htm

37. Gallagher, R.P. (2014). National Survey of College Counseling Centers. International Association of Counseling Centers. Inc. Retrieved from http://www.collegecounseling.org/wp-content/uploads/NCCCS2014_v2.pdf

The Most Disturbing Fact of All

38. Jed Foundation. (2007). *The Jed foundation parent survey.* Received from http://www.jedfoundation.org/parents/programs/ transition-year-project

39. Gallagher, R.P. (2014). National Survey of College Counseling Centers. International Association of Counseling Centers. Inc. Retrieved from http://www.collegecounseling.org/wp-content/uploads/NCCCS2014_v2.pdf

The Stigma of Mental Health

40. Noguchi, S. (2014, February 5). Teen health: Depression, anxiety and social phobias rising in kids, educators say. *San Jose Mercury News*. Retrieved from http://www.mercurynews.com/health/ci_25074044/teen-health-depression-anxiety-and-social-phobias-rising

Why This State of Health Impacts the Future of Our Students

42. Gumbiner, L. (2015, May 1). Early decision, regular decision, mental health decision: Teen depression and the college admissions process. *Erica's Lighthouse*. Retrieved from http://www.erikaslighthouse.org/blog/early-decision-regular-decision-mental-health-decision-teen-depression-college-admissions-process/

43. Zunker, V. (2008). *Career, work and mental health: Integrating career and personal counseling*. Thousand Oaks, CA: SAGE Publications, Inc.

44. Walker, J.V. and Peterson, G.W. (2012) Career thoughts, indecision, and depression: Implications for mental health assessment in career counseling. *Journal of Career Assessment*, 20 (4), pp. 497-506.

45. Lenz, J.G., Peterson, G.W., Reardon, R.C., & Saunders, D.E. (2010). Connecting career and mental health counseling: Integrating theory and practice. Retrieved from http://counselingoutfitters.com/vistas/vistas10/Article_01.pdf

46. Saunders, D. E., Peterson, G. W., Sampson, J. P., & Reardon, R. C. (2000). Relation of depression and dysfunctional career thinking to career indecision. *Journal of Vocational Behavior*, 56, 288-298.

47. Keatinge, C., and Woo, S. (2008). *Diagnosis and treatment of mental disorders across the lifespan*. Hoboken, NJ: John Wiley and Sons Inc.

48. Walker, J.V. and Peterson, G.W. (2012). Career thoughts, indecision, and depression: Implications for mental health assessment in career counseling. *Journal of Career Assessment*, 20 (4), 497-506

Chapter Five: Questioning our Assumptions

1. Meadows, D.H. (2008). *Thinking in systems: A primer*. White River Function, VT: Chelsea Green Publishing Company.

The Iceberg
2. Senge, P. (1990). *The fifth discipline: The art and practice of the learning organization.* New York, NY: Doubleday.

Mental Models
3. Senge, P., Roberts, C., Ross, R.B., Smith, B.J., and Kleiner, A. (1994). *Fifth discipline fieldbook.* New York, NY: Doubleday.

The Ladder of Inference
4. Senge, P., Roberts, C., Ross, R.B., Smith, B.J., & Kleiner, A. (1994). *Fifth Discipline Fieldbook.* New York, NY: Doubleday.
5. Senge, P., Roberts, C., Ross, R.B., Smith, B.J., & Kleiner, A. (1994). *Fifth Discipline Fieldbook.* New York, NY: Doubleday.

The What, How, Why Exercise
6. Senge, P., Roberts, C., Ross, R.B., Smith, B.J., and Kleiner, A. (1994). *Fifth discipline fieldbook.* New York, NY: Doubleday.

Chapter Six: Revealing the Myths

Myth #1: Getting into College is Harder than Ever
1. Katzman, J. S., (2014, September 11). Relax. Getting into college has actually gotten easier. *The Washington Post.* Retrieved from https://www.washingtonpost.com/posteverything/wp/2014/09/11/relax-getting-into-college-has-actually-gotten-easier/
2. Clinedinst, M. (2014). State of college admission. Retrieved from NACAC http://www.nacacnet.org/research/PublicationsResources/Marketplace/research/Pages/StateofCollegeAdmission.aspx
3. Institute of Education Sciences. Fast Facts. National Center for Education Statistics. Retrieved from https://nces.ed.gov/fastfacts/display.asp?id=84

The Global Age
4. Belyavina, R., Bhandari, R. and Li, J. (2013). New frontiers: U.S. students pursuing degrees abroad. *Institute of International Education.* Retrieved from http://www.iie.org/Research-and-Publications/Publications-and-Reports/IIE-Bookstore/New-Frontiers

Community Colleges
5. *Fact sheet: About community colleges.* (2015) American Association of Community Colleges. Retrieved from http://www.aacc.nche.edu/AboutCC/Pages/default.aspx
6. *Average community college acceptance rate.* (n.d.). Community College Review. Retrieved from http://www.communitycollegereview.com/acceptance-rate-stats/national-data
7. Smith, A.A. (2015, March 26). Community college to bachelor's. *Inside Higher Ed.* Retrieved from https://www.insidehighered.com/news/2015/03/26/nearly-half-four-year-college-graduates-attended-two-year-college

8. *Fact Sheet.* (2014). American Association of Community Colleges. Retrieved from http://www.aacc.nche.edu/AboutCC/Documents/Facts14_Data_R3.pdf
9. *Fact Sheet.* (2014). American Association of Community Colleges. Retrieved from http://www.aacc.nche.edu/AboutCC/Documents/Facts14_Data_R3.pdf

Myth #2: Getting a College Degree Guarantees Your Success

10. Busteed, B. (2015, April 8). Is college worth it? That depends. *Gallup.* Retrieved from: http://www.gallup.com/opinion/gallup/182312/college-worth-depends.aspx
11. Busteed, B. (2015, April 8). Is college worth it? That depends. *Gallup.* Retrieved from: http://www.gallup.com/opinion/gallup/182312/college-worth-depends.aspx
12. Kafka, S. and Ray, J. (2014, May 6). Life in college matters for life after college. *Gallup.* Retrieved from: http://www.gallup.com/poll/168848/life-college-matters-life-college.aspx

Myth #3: You Have to Go to a Selective School to Be Successful

13. Kafka, S. and Ray, J. (2014, May 6). Life in college matters for life after college. *Gallup.* Retrieved from: http://www.gallup.com/poll/168848/life-college-matters-life-college.aspx
14. Hymowitz, C. (2006, September 18). Any college will do: Nation's top chief executives find path to the corner office usually starts at state university. *The Wall Street Journal.* Retrieved from http://www.wsj.com/articles/SB115853818747665842
15. Bailey, A.L. (2015, July 15). Why we do not higher law school graduates from the Ivy League schools. *The Huffington Post.* Retrieved from http://www.huffingtonpost.com/adam-leitman-bailey/why-we-do-not-hire-law-sc_1_b_7789022.html
16. Deresiewicz, W. (2014). *Excellent sheep: The miseducation of the American elite and the way to a meaningful life.* New York, NY: Free Press.
17. Bruni, F. (2015). *Where you go is not who you'll be: An antidote to the college admissions mania.* New York, NY: Hachette Book Group.
18. Calderon, V.J. and Sidhu, P. (2014, February 25). Business leaders say knowledge trumps college pedigree. *Gallup.* Retrieved from http://www.gallup.com/poll/167546/business-leaders-say-knowledge-trumps-college-pedigree.aspx
19. Calderon, V.J. and Sidhu, P. (2014, February 25). Business leaders say knowledge trumps college pedigree. *Gallup.* Retrieved from http://www.gallup.com/poll/167546/business-leaders-say-knowledge-trumps-college-pedigree.aspx

Myth #4: You Have to Be a Superhero to Get into College

20. 199 "Top Tier" Schools which Deemphasize the ACT/SAT in Admissions Decisions per *U.S. News & World Report Best Colleges Guide.* (2015, November 17). Fair Test. Retrieved from http://www.fairtest.org/sites/default/files/Optional-Schools-in-U.S.News-Top-Tiers.pdf
21. Rooney, C., with Schaeffer, B. (1998, September). Test scores do not equal merit: Enhancing equity and excellence in college admissions by deemphasizing SAT and ACT results. *Fair Test.* Retrieved from http://docslide.us/documents/optrept-standardized-test.html
22. Fair Test. (2015, April 29). New survey shows record numbers of colleges and universities dropped ACT/SAT exam score requirements in past year. *Fair Test.* Retrieved from http://www.fairtest.org/new-survey-shows-record-number-colleges-and-univer

23. Redding, A.B. (2013). Extreme pressure: The negative consequences of achievement culture for affluent students during the elite college admission process. *Journal of College Admission*, (221), 32-37.
24. Student B. (personal communication, October 2, 2015)
25. Abrams, T. (2013, May 13). Advice from a dean of admissions on selecting high school courses. *The New York Times*. Retrieved from http://thechoice.blogs.nytimes.com/2013/05/13/selecting-high-school-courses/
26. Redding, A.B. (2013). Extreme pressure: The negative consequences of achievement culture for affluent students during the elite college admission process. *Journal of College Admission*, (221), 32-37.
27. Fortenbury, Jon. (2011, December 22). Importance of extracurricular activities in high school. *USA Today*. Retrieved from http://college.usatoday.com/2011/12/22/college-admissions-importance-of-extracurricular-activities-in-high-school/

Myth #5: The Only Way to Get an Education is Through the Traditional U.S. Approach

28. Smith, A.A. (2015, March 26). Community college to bachelor's. *Inside Higher Ed*. Retrieved from https://www.insidehighered.com/news/2015/03/26/nearly-half-four-year-college-graduates-attended-two-year-college
29. Blackman, A. (2015, September 20). Why more U.S. students are going abroad for college. *The Wall Street Journal*. Retrieved from http://www.wsj.com/articles/why-more-u-s-students-are-going-abroad-for-college-1442800929
30. Blackman, A. (2015, September 20). Why more U.S. students are going abroad for college. *The Wall Street Journal*. Retrieved from http://www.wsj.com/articles/why-more-u-s-students-are-going-abroad-for-college-1442800929
31. Noack, R. (2014, October 29). 7 countries where Americans can study at universities in English for free, or almost free. *The Washington Post*. Retrieved from https://www.washingtonpost.com/news/worldviews/wp/2014/10/29/7-coun-tries-where-americans-can-study-at-universities-in-english-for-free-or-almost-Ufree/
32. Noack, R. (2014, October 29). 7 countries where Americans can study at universities in English for free, or almost free. *The Washington Post*. Retrieved from https://www.washingtonpost.com/news/worldviews/wp/2014/10/29/7-coun-tries-where-americans-can-study-at-universities-in-english-for-free-or-almost-Ufree/
33. Nelson, S. (2015, June 28). For Americas seeking affordable degrees, German schools beckon. National Public Radio. Retrieved from http://www.npr.org/sec-tions/parallels/2015/06/28/418262031/for-americans-seeking-affordable-de-grees-german-schools-beckon
34. Nelson, S. (2015, August 27). Americans looking for affordable degrees head to Germany. National Public Radio. Retrieved from http://www.npr.org/2015/08/27/435113613/americans-looking-for-affordable-degrees-head-to-germany
35. Snider, S. (2014, October 28). Calculate the cost of earning an overseas degree. *US News & World Report*. Retrieved from http://www.usnews.com/education/best-global-universities/articles/2014/10/28/calculate-the-cost-of-earning-an-overseas-degree

Online Disruption

36. Schnaars, C. and Toppo, G. (2012, August 7). Online education degrees sky rocket. *USA Today*. Retrieved from http://usatoday30.usatoday.com/news/education/story/2012-08-07/online-teaching-degrees/56849026/1

37. Schnaars, C. and Toppo, G. (2012, August 7). Online education degrees sky rocket. *USA Today*. Retrieved from http://usatoday30.usatoday.com/news/education/story/2012-08-07/online-teaching-degrees/56849026/1

MOOCs

38. Johnson, J. (2012, September 24). What in the world is a MOOC? *The Washington Post*. Retrieved from http://www.washingtonpost.com/blogs/campus-overload/post/what-in-the-world-is-a-mooc/2012/09/24/50751600-0662-11e2-858a-5311df86ab04_blog.html

39. Daly, J. (2013, January 2). The MOOCs are here: Are you excited or scared? *Ed Tech*. Retrieved from http://www.edtechmagazine.com/higher/article/2013/01/moocs-are-here-are-you-excited-or-scared-infographic

40. Haynie, D. (2013, May 14). MOOCs stir up controversy. *US News*. Retrieved from http://www.usnews.com/education/online-education/articles/2013/05/14/explore-the-mooc-controversy

Unschooling and the DIY Education Movement

41. Stephens, D. (2013). *Hacking your education: Ditch the lectures, save tens of thousands, and learn more than your peers ever will.* New York, NY: Perigee.

42. About the fellowship. (2015). The Thiel Foundation. Retrieved from http://thielfellowship.org/about/

43. Nakatsu, T. Emerging options for students navigating life. *The Huffington Post*. [Podcast]. Retrieved from http://www.huffingtonpost.com/gendiy/getting-smart-podcast--em_b_8393576.html

44. Schiller, B. (2013, August 15). 8 new jobs people will have in 2025. *Fast Company*. Retrieved from http://www.fastcoexist.com/3015652/futurist-forum/8-new-jobs-people-will-have-in-2025

Story Busting: Reimagining Possibilities

45. Zander, R.S. and Zander, B. (2000). *The Art of possibility: Transforming professional and personal life.* New York, NY: Penguin.

46. Senge, P., Roberts, C., Ross, R.B., Smith, B.J., and Kleiner, A. (1994). *Fifth discipline fieldbook.* New York, NY: Doubleday.

You Are the Answer You've Been Waiting For

47. Anderson, V. and Johnson, L. (1997). *Systems thinking basics: From concepts to causal loops.* Waltham, MA: Pegasus Communications Inc.

48. Meadows, D.H. (2008). *Thinking in systems: A primer.* White River Function, VT: Chelsea Green Publishing Company.

Chapter Seven: Designing You—The U Map

The Missing Piece
1. Silverstein, S. (1976). *The missing piece*. New York, NY: Harper Collins Publishers.
2. Boldt, L. (2004). *How to Find the Work You Love*. New York, NY: Penguin Group.

Designing Your Future: From University to Youniversity
3. "University." (2014). *Webster Dictionary*. Retrieved from http://www.webster-dictionary.net/definition/university

Theory U
4. Scharmer, C.O. (2009). *Theory U: Leading from the future as it emerges*. San Francisco, CA: Berrett-Koehler Publishers

Design Thinking
5. Brown, T. (2009). *Change by design: How design thinking transforms organizations and inspires innovation*. New York, NY: HarperCollins.
6. Brown, T. (2009). *Change by design: How design thinking transforms organizations and inspires innovation*. New York, NY: HarperCollins.
7. About IDEO. Our approach: Design thinking. (2015). IDEO. Retrieved from the IDEO website https://www.ideo.com/about/

Divergent and Convergent Thinking
8. Brown, T. (2009). *Change by design: How design thinking transforms organizations and inspires innovation*. New York, NY: HarperCollins.

What I am Designing For?: The Good Life
9. Adapted from Seligman, M. (2011). *Flourish: A visionary new understanding of happiness and well being*. New York, NY: Atria.
10. Maslow, A.H. (1943). A theory of human motivation. *Psychological Review*, 50, 370-396. Retrieved from http://psychclassics.yorku.ca/Maslow/motivation.htm
11. Maslow, A. (1987). *Motivation and personality*. Harlow, United Kingdom: Longman.
12. Rogers, C. (1961). *On becoming a person: A distinguished therapist's guide to personal growth and creativity*. New York, NY: Houghton Mifflin.

Chapter Eight: U Map Step One—Get Quiet

1. Carr, K. (2011) *Crazy sexy diet*. Guilford, CT: Skirt! Books.

Chapter Nine: U Map Step Two—Discover

The Story of You

1. Donnellan, L. (2004). *Passion into practice: The path to remarkable work*. Brooklyn, NY: Passion into Practice Inc.

Nugget Mining #3: Birthright Gifts

2. Parker, P. J. (2000). *Let your life speak: Listening for the voice of vocation*. San Francisco, CA: John Wiley & Sons, Inc.
3. Redford, R. (Director) Eberts, J., Nozik, M. and Redford, R. (Producers). (2000). *The legend of Bagger Vance*. United States: Dreamworks Studio.

Nugget Mining #4: Strengths and Edges

4. What is the difference between a talent and a strength? *Gallup*. Retrieved from http://strengths.gallup.com/help/general/125543/difference-talent-strength.aspx

Nugget Mining #5: Flow

5. Csikszentmihalyi, M. (1990). *Flow: The Psychology of optimal experience*. New York, NY: Harper and Row.
6. Csikszentmihalyi, M. (1990). *Flow: The psychology of optimal experience*. New York, NY: Harper and Row.
7. Sobel, Dava. (1995, January). Mihaly Csikszentmihalyi—Polymath and professor of education at the University of Chicago. *Omni*. 17(4).
8. Sobel, Dava. (1995, January). Mihaly Csikszentmihalyi—Polymath and professor of education at the University of Chicago. *Omni*. 17(4).

Nugget Mining #6: Motivations

9. Forni, P.M. (2011). *The thinking life: How to thrive in the age of distraction*. New York, NY: St. Martin's Press.

Chapter Eleven: U Map Step Four— Synthesize

Identify Your Multiple Selves

1. Bellman, G.M. (1996). *Your signature path: Gaining new perspectives on life and work*. San Francisco, CA: Berrett-Koehler Publishers.

Are you a Multipotentialite or a Specialist?

2. Wapnick, E. (2015, October). Why some of us don't have one true calling. [TED]. Retrieved from https://www.ted.com/talks/emilie_wapnick_why_some_of_us_dont_have_one_true_calling/transcript?language=en
3. Lobenstine, M. (2006). *The renaissance soul: How to make your passions your life*. New York, NY: Random House.
4. Sher, B. (2006). *Refuse to choose: Use all of your interests, passions, and hobbies to create the life and career of your dreams*. New York, NY: Rodale.

5. Lobenstine, M. (2006). *The renaissance soul: How to make your passions your life*. New York, NY: Random House.

Toward Integration: Life on the Möbius Strip
6. Teacher as transformer. (2012, April 14). *Mobius strip meditation by Parker Palmer*. Retrieved from http://ivonprefontaine.com/2012/04/14/mobius-strip-meditation-by-parker-palmer
7. Teacher as transformer. (2012, April 14). *Mobius strip meditation by Parker Palmer*. Retrieved from http://ivonprefontaine.com/2012/04/14/mobius-strip-meditation-by-parker-palmer
8. Teacher as transformer. (2012, April 14). *Mobius strip meditation by Parker Palmer*. Retrieved from http://ivonprefontaine.com/2012/04/14/mobius-strip-meditation-by-parker-palmer

Your Brain Needs Integration, Too!: The Left and Right Sides of the Brain
9. Siegel, D. (2011). *Mindsight: The new science of personal transformation*. New York, NY: Bantam Books.

Chapter Twelve: U Map Step Five—Clarify

Your Contributions
1. Zander, R.S., & Zander, B. (2000). *The Art of possibility: Transforming professional and personal life*. New York, NY: Penguin.

Your Values
2. Kimsey-House, H., Kimsey-House, L., Sandahl, P. and Whitworth, L. (2011). *Co-Active coaching*. Boston, MA: Nicholas Brealey Publishing.

The Cover Story of You
3. Clark, T., with Osterwalder, A. and Pigneur, Y. (2012). *Business model you: A one-page method for reinventing your career*. Hoboken, NJ: John Wiley & Sons, Inc.

Mine/Theirs: Values in Action
4. Lobenstine, M. (2006). *The renaissance soul: How to make your passions your life*. New York, NY: Random House.

What is True Power?
5. Shriver, M. (2007, October 9). Maria Shriver on leadership. *Newsweek*. Retrieved from http://www.newsweek.com/maria-shriver-leadership-103411

Chapter Thirteen: U Map Step Six—Imagine

Your Brand New Life

1. Adapted from Clark, T., with Osterwalder, A. and Pigneur, Y. (2012). *Business model you: A one-page method for reinventing your career.* Hoboken, NJ: John Wiley & Sons, Inc.

The Genie Do/Be/Have List

2. Stanny, B. (2014). *Sacred success: A course in financial miracles.* Dallas, TX: BenBella Books, Inc.

Intentions and Goals

3. Gawain, S. (2002). *Creative visualization: Use the power of your imagination to create what you want in life.* Novato, California: Nataraj Publishing.

Prioritizing Your Intentions and Goals

4. Lobenstine, M. (2006). *The renaissance soul: How to make your passions your life.* New York, NY: Random House.

Chapter Fourteen: Opening the Door to New Possibilities: U Map Step Seven—Crossing the Threshold

Why College?

1. Brooks, D. (2014, September 18). Becoming a real person. *The New York Times.* Retrieved from http://www.nytimes.com/2014/09/09/opinion/david-brooks-becoming-a-real-person.html
2. Deresiewicz, W. (2014, July 21). Don't send your kid to the Ivy League. *New Republic.* Retrieved from http://www.newrepublic.com/article/118747/ivy-league-schools-are-overrated-send-your-kids-elsewhere
3. Kastner, L. and Wyatt, J. (2002). *The launching years: Strategies for parenting from senior year to college life.* New York, NY: Three Rivers Press.

Constraints

4. Joni, S.N. (2010, January 14). Why we all need more design thinking. *Forbes.* Retrieved from http://www.forbes.com/2010/01/14/tim-brown-ideo-leadership-managing-design.html
5. Brown, T. (2009). *Change by design: How design thinking transforms organizations and inspires innovation.* New York, NY: HarperCollins.
6. Kastner, L. and Wyatt, J. (2002). *The launching years: Strategies for parenting from senior year to college life.* New York, NY: Three Rivers Press.

Where Will You Flourish?

7. Seligman, M. (2011). *Flourish: A visionary new understanding of happiness and well being.* New York, NY: Atria

Break Up with the "One"

8. Katzman, J. (2014, September 23). Getting into college is easier than you think. *The Huffington Post*. Retrieved from http://www.huffingtonpost.com/john-katzman/getting-into-college-is-e_b_5861918.html

Chapter Fifteen: U Map Step Eight — Adventure

Take Action

1. Adapted from Clark, T., with Osterwalder, A. and Pigneur, Y. (2012). *Business model you: A one-page method for reinventing your career*. Hoboken, NJ: John Wiley & Sons, Inc.

First Key: Dare

2. Brown. B. (2015). *Daring greatly: How the courage to be vulnerable transforms the way we live, love, parent, and lead*. New York, NY: Avery.
3. Gilbert, E. (2013, November 23). This quote is not true! [Web log post] Face book. Retrieved from http://www.elizabethgilbert.com/this-quote-is-not-true-listen-up-you-guys-its-time-to-set-the-record-stra/
4. Mohr, T. (2014). *Playing big: Find your voice, your mission, your method*. New York, NY: Penguin Books.
5. Mohr, T. (2012, August 9). My favorite teaching about fear. [Web log post]. Tara Sophia Mohr. Retrieved from http://www.taramohr.com/2012/08/yirah/

Still Have Too Much Fear to Chase Your Dreams?

6. Ware, B. (2009, November 19). Regrets of the dying. [Web log post]. Bronnie Ware. Retrieved from http://bronnieware.com/regrets-of-the-dying/

Second Key: Grow

7. Dweck, C. (2008). *Mindset: The new psychology of success*. New York, NY: Random House.
8. Dweck, C. (2008). *Mindset: The new psychology of success*. New York, NY: Random House.
9. Dweck, C. (2008). *Mindset: The new psychology of success*. New York, NY: Random House.

Third Key: Grit

10. Duckworth, A.L. (2013, April). "The key to success? Grit." [TED] Retrieved from http://www.ted.com/talks/angela_lee_duckworth_the_key_to_success_grit?language=en
11. Duckworth, A.L. (2013, April). "The key to success? Grit." [TED] Retrieved from http://www.ted.com/talks/angela_lee_duckworth_the_key_to_success_grit?language=en

Hack Mindset
12. Madsen, S. (2015, March 3). The "hack" mindset for school-wide change. Getting Smart. Retrieved from http://gettingsmart.com/2015/03/hack-mindset-school-wide-change/

The Changing Face of Purpose

13. Clark, T., with Osterwalder, A. and Pigneur, Y. (2012). *Business model you: A one-page method for reinventing your career.* Hoboken, NJ: John Wiley & Sons, Inc.

Your Purpose Grid
14. Adapted from Clark, T., with Osterwalder, A. and Pigneur, Y. (2012). *Business model you: A one-page method for reinventing your career.* Hoboken, NJ: John Wiley & Sons, Inc.

From Grid to Statement
15. Adapted from Clark, T., with Osterwalder, A. and Pigneur, Y. (2012). *Business model you: A one-page method for reinventing your career.* Hoboken, NJ: John Wiley & Sons, Inc.

Chapter Sixteen: U Map Step Nine—Evolve Toward Purpose

Live the Question and Stay Open
1. Alon, U. (2013, June). "Why truly innovative science demands a leap into the un known." [TED]. Retrieved from https://www.ted.com/talks/uri_alon_why_truly_innovative_science_demands_a_leap_into_the_unknown?language=en

Emergent Strategy
2. Mintzberg, H., Quinn, J.B., and Ghoshal, S. (1998). *The strategy process.* New York, NY: Prentice Hall
3. Adapted from Holmann, P. (2010). *Engaging emergence: Turning upheaval into opportunity.* San Francisco, CA: Berrett-Koehler Publishers.
4. Adapted from Holmann, P. (2010). *Engaging emergence: Turning upheaval into opportunity.* San Francisco, CA: Berrett-Koehler Publishers.

Conclusion

1. Adapted from Holmann, P. (2010). *Engaging emergence: Turning upheaval into opportunity.* San Francisco, CA: Berrett-Koehler Publishers.
2. Gibran, K. (1923). *The prophet.* New York, NY: Alfred A. Knopf.

Selected Resources

There are many wonderful resources on the topics addressed in this book. While by no means comprehensive in scope, this list highlights some of my personal favorites.

Finding Your Passion and Purpose

Beck, M. (2001). *Finding your own north star: Claiming the life you were meant to live*. New York, NY: Three Rivers Press.

Beck, M. (2008). *Steering by starlight: The science and magic of finding your destiny*. New York, NY: Rodale.

Boldt, L. (2004). *How to find the work you love*. New York, NY: Penguin Group.

Bellman, G.M. (1996). *Your signature path: Gaining new perspectives on life and work*. San Francisco, CA: Berrett-Koehler Publishers.

Clark, T., with Osterwalder, A. and Pigneur, Y. (2012). *Business model you: A one-page method for reinventing your career*. Hoboken, NJ: John Wiley & Sons, Inc.

Donnellan, L. (2004). *Passion into practice: The path to remarkable work*. Brooklyn, NY: Passion into Practice Inc.

Gawain, S. (2002). *Creative visualization: Use the power of your imagination to create what you want in life*. Novato, California: Nataraj Publishing.

Hurst, A. (2014). *The purpose economy: How your desire for impact, personal growth, and community is changing the world*. Boise, ID: Elevate.

Mohr, T. (2014). *Playing big: Find your voice, your mission, your method*. New York, NY: Penguin Books.

Palmer, P. J. (2000). *Let your life speak: Listening for the voice of vocation*. San Francisco, CA: John Wiley & Sons, Inc.

Robinson, K. (2009). *The element: How finding your passion changes everything*. New York, NY: Viking.

Robinson, K. (2013). *Finding your element: How to discover your talents and passions and transform your life*. New York, NY: Viking.

Rogers, C. (1961). *On becoming a person: A distinguished therapist's guide to personal growth and creativity*. New York, NY: Houghton Mifflin.

Slim, P. (2013). *Body of work: Finding the thread that ties your story together*. New York, NY: Penguin Group

Whittaker, T. (2009). *Live your bliss: Practices that produce happiness and prosperity*. Novato, CA: New World Library.

Zander, R.S. and Zander, B. (2000). *The art of possibility: Transforming professional and personal life*. New York, NY: Penguin.

Inner Critic

Carson, R. (2003). *Taming your gremlin: A surprisingly simple method for getting out of your own way*. San Francisco, CA: HarperCollins.

Stone, H. and Stone, S. (1993). *Embracing your inner critic: Turning self criticism into a creative asset*. San Francisco, CA: HarperCollins.

Exploring Your Many Interests

Sher, B. (2006). *Refuse to choose: Use all of your interests, passions, and hobbies to create the life and career of your dreams*. New York, NY: Rodale.

Lobenstine, M. (2006). *The renaissance soul: How to make your passions your life*. New York, NY: Random House.

Brain Science

Pink, D. (2006). *A whole new mind: Why right-brainers will rule the future*. New York, NY: Riverhead Books.

Hanson, R. (2013). *Hardwiring happiness: The new brain science of contentment, calm, and confidence*. New York, NY: Harmony Books.

Hanson, R., with Mendius, R. (2009). *Buddha's brain: The practical neuroscience of happiness, love and wisdom*. Oakland, CA: New Harbinger Publishing.

Siegel, D. (2013). *Brainstorm: The power and purpose of the teenage brain*. New York, NY: Penguin Group.

Siegel, D. (2011). *Mindsight: The new science of personal transformation*. New York, NY: Bantam Books.

Research

Brown. B. (2015). *Daring greatly: How the courage to be vulnerable transforms the way we live, love, parent, and lead*. New York, NY: Avery.

Dweck, C. (2008). *Mindset: The new psychology of success*. New York, NY: Random House.

Csikszentmihalyi, M. (1990). *Flow: The psychology of optimal experience*. New York, NY: Harper and Row.

Pink, D. (2009). *Drive: The surprising truth about what motivates us*. New York, NY: Riverhead Books.

Seligman, M. (2011). *Flourish: A visionary new understanding of happiness and well being*. New York, NY: Atria

Mental Health

Active Minds. Learn more at http://www.activeminds.org/about/our-story

Jed Foundation. Learn more at http://www.jedfoundation.org

Project LETS, Inc. Learn more at http://letserasethestigma.com

The Jed and Clinton Health Matters Campus Program. Learn more at http://www.thecampusprogram.org

U Lifeline. Learn more at http://www.ulifeline.org

Half of Us. Learn more at http://www.halfofus.com

Love is Louder. Learn more at http://www.loveislouder.com

Project Semicolon. Learn more at http://www.projectsemicolon.org

Transition Year. Learn more at http://www.transitionyear.org

Education and College

Bruni, F. (2015). *Where you go is not who you'll be: An antidote to the college admissions mania*. New York, NY: Hachette Book Group.

Deresiewicz, W. (2014). *Excellent sheep: The miseducation of the American elite & the way to a meaningful life*. New York, NY: Free Press.

Robinson, K. (2015). *Creative schools: The grassroots revolution that's transforming education*. New York, NY: Viking.

Stephens, D. (2013). *Hacking your education: Ditch the lectures, save tens of thousands, and learn more than your peers ever will*. New York, NY: Perigee.

Tough, P. (2013). *How children succeed: Grit, curiosity, and the hidden power of character*. Wilmington, MA: Mariner Books.

Wagner, T. (2015). *Creating innovators: The making of young people who will change the world*. New York, NY: Scribner.

Wagner, T. and Dintersmith, T. (2015). *Most likely to succeed: Preparing our kids for the innovation era*. New York, NY: Scribner.

College Guides

Doe, M. and Hernandez, M. (2005). *Don't worry, you'll get in: 100 winning tips for stress-free college admissions*. New York, NY: Marlowe & Company.

Matthews, J. (2003). *Harvard schmarvard: Getting beyond the Ivy League to the college that is best for you*. New York, NY: Three Rivers Press.

Pope, L. (2007). *Looking beyond the Ivy League: Finding the college that's right for you*. New York, NY: Penguin.

Pope, L. and Oswald, H. (2012). *Colleges that change lives: 40 schools that will change the way you think about college*. New York, NY: Penguin.

Shaevitz, M.H. (2012). *Admission possible: The "dare to be yourself" guide for getting into the best colleges for you*. Naperville, IL: Sourcebooks.

Sweetland, J. and Glastris, P. (2015). *The other college guide: A road map to the right school for you*. New York, NY: The New Press.

White, Kristin. (2015). *It's the student, not the college: The secrets of succeeding at any school without going broke or crazy*. New York, NY: The Experiment.

Doing It Differently

Generation Do-It-Yourself (#GenDIY). Learn more at http://www.gettingsmart.com

Thiel Fellowship. Learn more at http://www.thielfellowship.org

Uncollege. Learn more at http://www.uncollege.org

TED Talks

Alon, U. (2013, June). Uri Alon: Why truly innovative science demands a leap into the unknown. [Video file]. Retrieved from https://www.ted.com/talks/uri_alon_why_truly_innovative_science_demands_a_leap_into_the_unknown

Brown, B. (2010, June). Brene Brown: The power of vulnerability. [Video file]. Retrieved from https://www.ted.com/talks/brene_brown_on_vulnerability

Duckworth, A. (2013, April). Angela Duckworth: The key to success? Grit. Retrieved from https://www.ted.com/talks/angela_lee_duckworth_the_key_to_success_grit

Dweck, C. (2014, December). Carl Dweck: The power of believing that you can improve. Retrieved from https://www.ted.com/speakers/carol_dweck

Pink, D. (2009, July). Daniel Pink: The puzzle of motivation. [Video file]. Retrieved from https://www.ted.com/talks/dan_pink_on_motivation

Robinson, K. (2007, January 6). Sir Jen Robinson: Do schools kill creativity? [Video file]. Retrieved from https://www.ted.com/talks/ken_robinson_says_schools_kill_creativity

Wapnick, E. (2015, April). Emilie Wapnick: Why some of us don't have one true calling. [Video file]. Retrieved from https://www.ted.com/talks/emilie_wapnick_why_some_of_us_don_t_have_one_true_calling/transcript?language=en

For Parents

Doe, M. (2004). *Nurturing your teenager's soul: A practical approach to raising a kind, honorable, compassionate teen.* New York, NY: Perigee.

Faber, A. and Mazlish, E. (2012). *How to talk so kids will listen & listen so kids will talk.* New York, NY: Scribner.

Kastner, L. and Wyatt, J. (2002). *The launching years: Strategies for parenting from senior year to college life.* New York, NY: Three Rivers Press.

Design Thinking

Kelley, T. and Kelley, D. (2013). *Creative confidence: Unleashing the creative potential within us all.* New York, NY: Crown Business.

Brown, T. (2009). *Change by design: How design thinking transforms organizations and inspires innovation.* New York, NY: HarperCollins.

Emergence

Holmann, P. (2010). *Engaging emergence: Turning upheaval into opportunity.* San Francisco, CA: Berrett-Koehler Publishers.

Systems Thinking

Senge, P. (1990). *The fifth discipline: The art and practice of the learning organization.* New York, NY: Doubleday.

Senge, P., Roberts, C., Ross, R.B., Smith, B.J., and Kleiner, A. (1994). *Fifth discipline fieldbook.* New York, NY: Doubleday.

Theory U

Scharmer, C.O. (2009). *Theory U: Leading from the future as it emerges.* San Francisco, CA: Berrett-Koehler Publishers

ABOUT THE AUTHOR

Lisa Fisher is a multi-award winning educator who has worked nationally and internationally as a teacher, college counselor and educational consultant for more than 20 years. Lisa's innovative approaches to helping students find and pursue their dreams have touched the lives of thousands of principals, teachers, counselors and students. She lives in the Pacific Northwest with her husband, Rand Harper.

elevate
publishing

A strategic publisher empowering authors to strengthen their brand.

Visit Elevate Publishing for our latest offerings.
www.elevatepub.com

NO TREES WERE HARMED
IN THE MAKING OF THIS BOOK

OK, so a few
did need to make the ultimate sacrifice.

In order to steward our environment,
we are partnering with *Plant With Purpose*, to plant
a tree for every tree that paid the price for the printing of
this book.

⟹ PLANT W TH PURPOSE

www.plantwithpurpose.org

go to www.elevatepub.com/about to learn more